ON THE WAY TO SATORI

A Woman's Experience of Enlightenment

Gerta Ital was the first western woman in the early 1960s to be admitted as a student to a Japanese Zen monastery.

Originally an acclaimed actress in Germany, Gerta Ital became a pupil of the German Zen Master Eugen Herrigel in 1953. In 1962, she travelled to Japan where she spent ten years studying Zen. She wrote two books about her experiences in Japan. *The Master Monks and I* was the first volume, and *On the Way to Satori* is the sequel. Gerta Ital died in 1988.

ON THE WAY TO SATORI

A Woman's Experience of Enlightenment

GERTA ITAL

Translated from the German by
Timothy M Green

ELEMENT BOOKS

First published in 1988 by Scherz Verlag, Germany.
This edition first published in Great Britain in 1990 by
Element Books Limited
Longmead, Shaftesbury, Dorset

Cover design by Max Fairbrother
Cover illustration by Werner Bischof – Magnum Photos
Designed by Roger Lightfoot

Phototypeset by Input Typesetting Ltd, London

Printed and bound in Great Britain by
Dotesios Ltd, Trowbridge, Wiltshire

British Library Cataloguing in Publication Data
Ital, Gerta
On the way to Satori.
1. Japan, Zen Buddist life- personal observations
I. Title
294.3444

ISBN 1–85230–155–4

Contents

1

How This Book Came to be Written

I have always had a strong aversion to talking or writing about the more intimate spiritual experiences which I have had on my long journey back to God. In 1967, however, a book and an unexpected visit forced me to begin to ask myself whether this attitude was really entirely justified.

My own book about my sojourn in a Zen Buddhist monastery in Japan, *The Master, the Monks and I*, had been published the year before, and up until then I hadn't had the slightest intention of adding so much as a single word to what I had written. This book is a description of what it is like to live in a genuine Zen monastery as the disciple of one of the greatest living Zen Masters. It is the story of an inner battle with a *kōan* given to me by my Master, a battle which was not to end until, in a shattering breakthrough, the 'One' finally revealed itself within me as the one and only reality. It is a personal, firsthand account of a unique process of spiritual transformation, and there is no way I could add anything to it to make it more meaningful, even if I wanted to.

My experience of enlightenment in Zen was a finale, the overwhelming climax of a life spent searching for and wrestling with God. In an earthly body, at least, I don't think it is possible to go beyond what I experienced there. In *The Master, the Monks and I*, I only described the events which were essential to understanding what I had experienced on the path of Zen, avoiding the more personal transcendental experiences which had taken place beforehand. I did provide an objective account of the first, all-important intervention of Heaven in my life – for it was this which set everything in motion – and of all the great trials with which I was tested, but I avoided any detailed mention of the unique mystical experiences which accompanied these events. (I know that the word 'mystical' is often associated with illusion and delusion, and I should like to stress that I am not using it in this sense. When I say that something which I experienced was mystical I mean that it was of an order of reality which was much more 'real' and tangible than our so-called daily life.)

The book which made me begin to wonder whether my decision to remain silent on these subjects was really justified was a collection of memoirs by the famous Swiss psychologist C. G. Jung, *Memories, Dreams, Reflections.* It wasn't the actual content of the book which impressed me – his description of his life, his dreams and his supernatural and occult experiences didn't have the slightest similarity to my own path – it was the courage with which he described a whole series of rather mediocre phenomena originating from his own unconscious mind, phenomena which are only made interesting by the fact that it is Jung who experienced them. The only part of the book which is really noteworthy is the passage in which he describes a series of profound visions which he had in the course of a severe illness; these really do appear to have been unique experiences of transcendence, and I shall return to them later in another context.

As a young doctor working in the psychiatric ward of the University Hospital in Zurich Jung was confronted, for the first time in his life, with the shatteringly incomprehensible phenomenon of schizophrenia, and it was in order to be able to understand and treat this terrible and mystifying mental illness that he started to delve into the deeper regions of his own mind. He devoted the rest of his life to the courageous attempt to dissolve the barriers between the conscious and the unconscious, using himself as a guinea-pig. His primary motive for this work was the fact that he desperately wanted to find better ways of understanding and thus helping his patients, but it is also very clear that the journey into the deeper regions of the mind was something by which he was utterly fascinated, and he probably would have carried out his investigations even if he hadn't had any patients who could have benefited from his work.

Despite all his efforts, however, the esoteric answers which he received to his questions were limited (with the exception of the visions mentioned above), and he himself doubted them for many years. None the less, he courageously chose to share everything he had seen with the public, no matter whether it was banal or profound, in order to give the world a complete and true account of the path which he had travelled in his attempts to discover new methods of psychological treatment. It was this which made me ask myself whether I could justify my own silence.

As I have already pointed out, my own way was very different from Jung's. I never tried to delve into the depths of my own unconscious. Everything which happened to me after heeding the first ringing call which I received from the unknown was completely unplanned and unexpected. Heaven, and not I, was the active party in my case. The events which took place were always unique, and so personal and specific that I was forced to accept that they really were intended for me alone. The effects of these events were deeply shattering, changing not only my superficial attitude to my life but also my life itself, transforming it by destroying its external form and forcing me to embark upon an inner journey towards the goal which existence had chosen for me.

I was familiar with most of the experiences of the famous mystics from the accounts of their lives, and everything which I had read there was radically different from that which I myself had experienced. There was simply no comparison. Could I, should I tell my story, had the time come? This was a question which I was unable to answer. All I could do was hope that the answer to the question would come of its own accord in the Zen monastery in Japan, as I was planning to return there to be with my Rōshi, or Master, again in the spring of 1967. As it turned out, however, there wasn't any need to meditate over the pros and cons of the matter in Japan. The unexpected visit which I mentioned at the beginning of the chapter decided the matter for me. It was so timely that I was forced to accept it as a clear message from Existence.

It all began one morning with a telephone call. The man on the other end of the line told me his name, which sounded Scandinavian, and asked me if I would permit him to come and pay a visit on me. He spoke excellent German, with a slight touch of a foreign accent. Hearing my initial hesitation he went on to say that a German relative of his had sent him a copy of my book some time before, and that it had moved him 'very

very deeply'. He had flown all the way from the north of Sweden especially to see me. Hearing this I assented at once, and he arrived later that afternoon. He was a handsome gentleman in his early fifties, tall and slim – so much so that he almost looked haggard – and very elegantly dressed.

Mr van M. sat down in my living room and told me about the tragic event which had made my book so important for him: a year before both his wife and his only son had been killed in a swimming accident.

'It happened during the Whitsun holidays,' he began. 'My wife and my son went to the beach every morning to go swimming. My chauffeur always drove them, as I had work to attend to in my factory. On the day it happened the chauffeur waited for them in the car, as usual. Harald – he was just fourteen – and my wife were both in the water. From where he was sitting the chauffeur saw Harald lift up his arm, as if he was waving, and then he suddenly disappeared under the surface of the water. At first he thought that Harald had been waving to my wife, who had been swimming towards him, but then she disappeared as well.

'He jumped out of the car and raced down the beach, throwing off his heavy uniform as he ran, but it was too late. They had both been drowned and drawn out to sea by the current before he was able to reach them, and their bodies weren't found until many hours later.

'The autopsy revealed that Harald had had an attack of angina pectoris in the cold water, and he was in such panic that he pulled my wife down with him. She was a very delicate woman.'

Mr van M. told me that he had met his wife on a business trip to India eighteen years before. They had got married a year later, and although they lived in the West they had returned to India for a few weeks every two years in order to prevent his wife from feeling too homesick.

'We were very much in love, and very very happy. My wife was brought up in the Hindu faith – she was extremely religious and an ardent admirer of the great teacher and saint Ramakrishna. I never interfered in any way, she had her own prayer room . . . ' His voice trailed off for a moment. After a brief pause, he asked if it would be all right if he smoked a cigarette. I assented, and after a few deep pulls on the cigarette he started speaking again.

'My wife's only sorrow was that I was never in the least bit religious myself. I was brought up as a Protestant. I played along with it to a certain extent, in order to avoid hurting my parents' feelings. But after being confirmed I decided that I had done enough to please them, and I never set foot in a church again. I found everything that the priests said about God utterly ludicrous. And I wasn't alone in this – all of my contemporaries felt the same way. I tried to make the best of my life, as honestly and decently as I could. It wasn't difficult for me, as I was happy, and I lacked for nothing.' He made frequent little pauses, as if he were carrying a deep, inner exhaustion within him. I waited patiently, not wanting to interrupt his pauses any more than his story.

'The double catastrophe struck me like . . . I can't find any words for it. In the first days after it happened I was totally numbed by the blow. I didn't have any idea what was going on. I wandered around like a sleepwalker, doing everything that had to be done automatically, without thinking about it or being aware of it. It was as if there were a machine inside of me which had taken over.

'Then, when I finally woke up out of this daze, I broke down completely and decided that I was going to follow my beloved ones into the grave. My continued existence had become completely meaningless to me. I took an overdose of sleeping pills.

'It is because of what happened next that I have come to see you. Some time later, I don't know exactly when, I regained consciousness again in the hospital. But I thought I was dead, because of something that had happened as I regained consciousness. In the moment that I felt my consciousness returning – it was much clearer than usual in that moment, overwhelmingly clear in fact – I saw my wife standing there, right next to me. She was as beautiful as she had been when we first met and fell in love. She smiled at me and said, "We are happy".

'I lost consciousness again twice after that, and the same experience was repeated every time my consciousness returned. My wife stood there next to me, radiantly beautiful, and repeated the same sentence, "We are happy".

'Later the doctors told me that they had battled for two days to save my life. But that is irrelevant. What is really important is something which I find completely inexplicable: after my return from the dead, so to speak, all my despair at the tragedy which had struck me was gone, even though it had only been a few short weeks since the loss had taken place. This threw me into utter confusion, all over again. I searched everywhere trying to find my pain. But there was nothing I could do, I simply had to accept the fact of the matter: for some inexplicable reason I had been completely freed of all my torments. And not only that, I had also been freed of myself. Nothing seemed excessively important any more, nothing really mattered, even though I went about my business and did my duty as I had always done.

'Then I read your book. As I said on the phone, it moved me very very deeply. I immediately decided to practise the meditation exercises you describe in the book, following your instructions to the letter. I wanted to find myself, or perhaps I should say, my true Self. I wanted to stop feeling like a stranger living within the boundaries of my own skin.

'My wife had already taught me how to sit in the lotus position, so that didn't cause me any trouble. I sat in meditation for an hour before going to work in the factory every morning and for another two hours in the evening, sometimes for half the night.

'In your book you mentioned an experience in which you were visited by a Master who was not of this world, and you said that this experience changed your entire life. After about seven months of constant practice and meditation I had a similar experience.'

I stared at him in astonishment and disbelief.

'Unfortunately, you didn't provide any concrete details regarding this experience in your book,' he continued quietly, 'and I would be very grateful if you could tell me if it was similar to mine or not. Since then I have read a book by the English writer Paul Brunton, in which he describes a number of mystical experiences which showed him the way, but the beings which appeared to him were living Indian Masters, and from his detailed descriptions it is clear to me that his experiences were different from my own.

'On the evening in question I had meditated for an unusually long time, and it was past two when I finally went to bed. I fell asleep immediately. A while later I woke up suddenly with the frightening feeling that there was something inexplicably alien in my bedroom, and I sat up in bed. I was wide awake, and my initial feeling of shock soon gave way to one of indescribable bliss.

'Standing before me at the foot of my bed was a being which was so wonderful, so suffused with inner radiance that I can only describe it as divine. I was unable to say a single word. The being gazed at me piercingly. I don't know how long the manifestation lasted. It was suddenly gone, just as suddenly as it had appeared.

'If I had been a practising Christian I would probably have reacted in the same way as Pope Pius XII, who got up one morning and told his attendant nun that the Lord had appeared to him. But I am not a Christian, and I have no idea who or what it was. All I can say is that this experience transformed my life, totally and utterly.

'I hope that you don't find it presumptuous of me when I ask you to tell me whether your experiences were similar to mine or not? Please believe me, I am not asking out of mere curiosity. I am desperately in search of the truth.'

There was no way that I could maintain my reticence in the face of this man and his story. I sensed that he had been 'sent' to me in order to obtain the certainty which he so badly needed, and so I broke my silence and told him the story of my own experiences.

He remained silent for a long time after I had finished. 'How could you keep such wonderful things secret?' he said finally. 'How can you justify your silence? Not every desperate seeker after truth is able to get into an aeroplane and come and visit you. In this short hour you have given me a great treasure and made me very happy. Why are you not willing to share this with everyone?'

'Because there is a great danger that such an account would be misunderstood,' I replied. 'I am particularly concerned about the huge numbers of daydreamers and pseudo-mystics whose ignorance has been the source of so much confusion all through the ages. Only strong people who take their earthly duties just as seriously as their spiritual pilgrimage are capable of embarking on the path of realisation.'

'That is true,' he replied, 'and I hope that I will prove to be one of those who have that strength. But at the same time I am also certain that that which transformed me could also transform others. Forget about those other people. Do you want to refuse the help and happiness and comfort and faith you could give to so many people, just for the sake of a few daydreamers?

'I know that you are not a Catholic, you said so in your book. And precisely because you are not a Catholic I should like to remind you that the mystical experiences of Pope Pius

XII were published everywhere, just a few years ago. He obviously had no objections to their publication, even though he didn't really give his permission. From what I have read it was more of an indiscretion than anything else. Our newspapers were full of reports about his vision of the sun and the manifestation of Christ by which it was followed.'

'I remember it well,' I said. 'But then,' I added, laughing, 'you are forgetting the role of the Church notables in that indiscretion!'

'I am not forgetting it at all. That is precisely what I am driving at. They revealed these things of their own accord, things which would have been regarded as very, shall we say, unusual, before then, at least within the Catholic Church. I know that it wouldn't be right to press you, but please consider breaking your silence, for the sake of others like me.'

There was no way I could hide the fact that the astonishing timeliness of our discussion had moved me deeply. I told Mr van M. that I had been ruminating over just this very problem for the last few weeks.

'I must admit that your visit is a very strong positive indication,' I continued. 'I must examine myself and my motives further.'

'Please be so good as to answer one more question,' he asked then, looking visibly satisfied at my response. 'Was my experience something like what you described as a "satori" in your book?'

'No,' I replied. 'The satori of Zen Buddhism is something completely different. In the experience of satori everything which we could call "the other" simply dissolves and ceases to exist. There is no question of a meeting or an encounter in satori, it is simply not possible.'

'But what is the purpose of such experiences then?' asked Mr van M., his voice hard. 'It all seems so meaningless.'

'Was your experience meaningless for you?' I replied. He started to smile, and I continued: 'The only possible meaning of such an experience is to show the seeker that he is on the right path, that his efforts have been recognised and that he is expected to continue in his spiritual work.'

'Do you mean that it was a kind of initiation?'

'Yes, if you like to think of it that way. But don't forget that all terminology is a human invention. Zen categorically rejects all definitions and descriptions.'

'Does that mean that all that remains is the "Void"?'

'One must pass through "nothingness", or the "Void", in order to achieve contact or union with the Original Source. But remember, one must return from this union, one must come back, and the experience only lasts a few seconds. And then, according to Zen, trees are once again trees and mountains are once again mountains. So why shouldn't Masters be Masters again, and Gods Gods?

'There is no doubt at all that everything which is really exists. The important point is that the person who has attained enlightenment is no longer dependent on anything, no matter whether it exists or not.'

'Good,' replied Mr van M., nodding, 'I shall have to meditate on this and digest it. I think that my inner being is ready for it. But I do have one more question – if you are willing to answer it, if you are allowed to answer it: who was this being whose mere appearance was enough to transform this Saul into a Paul?' He pointed to himself as he spoke. 'You have had such profound, transcendental experiences, you must know who it was.'

'No,' I replied firmly, 'I don't know who it was. And it is not something which one should try to find out . . . '

'That is the voice of Zen in you,' he interrupted in agitation, 'but the wonderful experiences which you have just described to me took place many years before you came into contact with Zen. I am sure that at least back then when it happened you must have tried to find out who had come out of the divine world to visit you.'

'I know that it may seem strange and unnatural to you, Mr van M., but I didn't. It is a phenomenon which surprises me just as much as it does you, and when I started living in the spirit of Zen I often asked myself why it was that I had never had any inclination to investigate the question back then, or even to think about it. The only possible explanation is that I was already carrying the spirit of Zen within me, right from the start, even though I wasn't consciously aware of it at first. For instance, I often admired other people, but that was all. My passionate love and surrender was always reserved for the One, the Eternal, God, call it what you will. That was all I was ever interested in, and it was the object of all my ardour. But even back then it was an ardour without sentimentality or mushy emotionalism.

'The experiences which I was granted filled me with joy and gratitude which are still an inseparable part of my being today, and I shall carry them within me until my very last breath. But I received everything which was given to me without overestimating it, and without overestimating myself either. I simply went on living, and I think that that was the spirit of Zen which I carried within me, even though I wasn't aware of what it was then.'

'It's all very well for you,' said Mr van M. sadly, shaking his head as though he were reluctant to accept what I was saying.

'I was simply answering your question. And remember, it was me that you asked . . . ' I replied. At that we both started laughing, and the tension of the moment evaporated.

'What I am trying to say is this,' I continued, feeling relieved. 'It seems that your determined and earnest search for truth has been rewarded. Some portion of the light from the realm of the eternal and divine has seen fit to contact you and to tell you, without using words of course, that you are on the right path, and that you will find if you continue seeking. It would be wrong to try to personify this portion of the divine light just because your mind wishes to find a label for it. After all, the only reason it took on a form at all was to make it possible for you to see it. In Zen terms . . .'

'No, please stop!' Mr van M. lifted up his hands defensively. 'Please, don't give me explanations! Just tell me what I should do next, with Zen or without it.'

'The only thing which I can suggest is that you should meditate upon the being of light which appeared to you. Become one with it. If you do that you will not only dissolve all your doubts, you will also be carrying out its wordlessly expressed request. No human being can do more than that.'

A short time after my talk with Mr van M. I became ill, and I was forced to postpone my departure to Japan for two weeks. I wasn't the least bit upset about this, however. On the contrary, I regarded it as an act of Providence, as it made it possible for me to relax for a while. I simply had no other choice.

It was very pleasant to be able to lie in bed quietly without having to rush around doing this or that. It gave me time to think about the decision which I was now going to have to make. Should I write about the experiences which I had described to Mr van M. or not? After much deliberation I came to the conclusion that there was only one real objection: If the idea of sharing my possibly unique transcendental experiences with others were associated with even the faintest shadow of a desire that I should be regarded as someone special, then it would have to remain a secret, at least until my death. One positive sign was the fact that I had already remained silent for thirty years – I had never told anyone anything about these things before.

Mr van M.'s story had stirred up something within me, something which I had kept hidden within the privacy of my heart for almost an entire lifetime. After weighing everything as carefully as I could and examining the question from all sides I finally made two decisions: First, I would examine myself mercilessly in order to be certain of the purity of my motives; and second, I would leave the final decision up to God. Without a sign from Him, one way or the other, I would do nothing.

A few days later, with this resolution in my heart, I boarded the plane for Japan.

2

My Childhood, and My Parents' Death

It wasn't until later on in life that I realised how lucky I had been to have been brought up in a family which, although it was fundamentally religious in outlook, was nonetheless wholly undogmatic. My mother was a Catholic and my father a Protestant, and as there was every reason to believe that there would be no more relatives on my mother's side of the family by the time I was grown up it was decided to baptise me as a Protestant. My parents never had any differences in religious matters, and I grew up in an atmosphere in which tolerance was something to be taken for granted, so much so that I didn't even know what it was. At the time I had no idea that this was to prove the firm foundation which would later enable me to absorb the teachings of the great religions of the world without any prejudices, even if I was only to understand these teachings on a purely intellectual level at first.

When I was six years old my father started giving me piano lessons. When I was twelve we moved to the west of Berlin, where we lived in a house in the Schlüterstraße on the corner of the Kurfürstendamm. It was a gloriously beautiful and elegant neighbourhood then, more so than one can even imagine nowadays, and it was to remain our home for the rest of my parents' lives.

The curriculum of the school I attended was very demanding, and in addition to this I also devoted a great deal of my time to the study of music. I had to work very hard, and I was frequently overtired, so much so that I developed anaemia and chronic splitting headaches. Even so, it was a very happy time for me, and I wouldn't have missed it for the world.

Around the corner from our house on the Kurfürstendamm was the conservatory of the great concert pianist and virtuoso chamber musician Marta Remmert, who was very famous at the time. She was already an old lady when I first met her, but even then, when she sat down at her concert piano and started to play it always took my breath away. She had been Franz Liszt's last student. Her conservatory was small, but very exclusive. In addition to our piano lessons we also received instruction in musical theory and sight-reading, and once a month we presented an evening of chamber music, in which a few 'genuine' chamber musicians from the *Lindenoper* also took part. We had to practise very hard to prepare for these evenings, for the presence of these superlative artists from the *Lindenoper* in our midst meant that we had to play our parts perfectly, without the slightest hint of a mistake.

In an article which he wrote in the course of his courageous debate with the Nazi regime on the subject of Paul Hindemith, Wilhelm Furtwängler once wrote that he expected any critic who took it upon himself to judge great music to be able to write a four-part harmony, at the very least. This is something which all of us at Marta Remmert's conservatory were capable of doing. And whenever I got into difficulties with things like this my father, who was a conductor by profession, was always there to help me.

My father was the very incarnation of integrity and honesty. This was something which deeply impressed everyone who came into contact with him, no matter whether they were close friends or just business associates. He radiated an aura of kindness and goodwill, showering his love on everyone around him. I know that this may sound exaggerated, but it is not, that is really the way he was. At the same time, however, there was nothing weak or soft about him; he opposed any and every injustice fearlessly and with impressive energy, and the musicians in his orchestra were all too well aware of his exemplary professional discipline.

Nothing could ever cause the kindness and generosity of his heart to falter. He was always the same, even during a period when his musical career suffered some very serious setbacks. Later on, when the conductors of all the orchestras in Germany banded together in the 1920s to found the *Kapellmeisterverband für Groß-Deutschland*,[1] Louis Ital was honoured by all of his colleagues, great and small, by being elected to be the first president of the association, a position which he retained until his death.

The love which I felt for my parents and the unswerving trust which held our little family together were the foundations of my childhood. Even though I was an only child I was never spoiled or mollycoddled. I was expected to be honest, upright and hardworking, and my parents also set great store by politeness and good manners. Violations of these principles were always punished immediately. My mother had a quick temper, and she had no aversion to the occasional spanking, character traits which sometimes made her seem unjust, although she didn't mean it that way. Even so, I was none the worse for it, and it certainly didn't give me any 'complexes'.

Although my father had a good, comfortable income we weren't what one could call wealthy, and there was no reason to expect that we ever would be. Realising this, he and my mother took great pains to make sure that I got the best education possible, from the best teachers available. My father's dream was that I should become a teacher myself. I suspect that every musician hopes and prays that he will be able to help his children to escape from the purgatory of constant insecurity which is the artist's lot, and to settle down in a solid profession with a guaranteed salary.

Needless to say, things didn't turn out that way. My dream, the only thing I wanted, more than anything else, was to become an actress. I confided in my mother, as I knew that she would understand me. She had been a singer herself, and even before she had met my father (he was a little younger than her) she had travelled all over the world to give performances. She had given up her career when I started school.

Before we even considered telling my father about my decision, my mother insisted that all of the most famous actors and actresses of the day (and in those days these people were *real* artists, not mere performers!) should first pass judgement on my talent. Simply finding out whether I had talent or not wasn't enough for her, either; she also wanted to know whether my talent was 'unusual', for only an 'unusual' talent would suffice; only then, she had said, would both she and my father be willing to give me their support in fulfilling my dream of becoming a professional actress. And so I auditioned, not only with one master of the theatre, but with all the greats of the Berlin stage. My mother was adamant that all of them, without a single exception, should confirm that my talent was worthy of development before we proceeded any further. And all of them did.

I received the most thorough training which one can possibly imagine. Before I could even begin to think about learning acting and character I had to devote nine months to speech and voice training. Every single syllable, every vowel and every consonant had to be just right. It was a gruelling training. I had to practise each sound right across two full octaves, all the way from the softest whisper to the most overpowering shriek, until the art of speaking had become second nature to me. This was then followed by a marvellous course in character acting taught by Eduard von Winterstein.

Once the decision had been made, my parents did everything possible to help me to prepare for my chosen profession. I continued with my piano lessons, in addition to all my other work, and I also went to theatre almost every night, to really wonderful productions at Reinhardt's *Deutsches Theater* or in the *Kammerspiele.* These years of training and learning were a magical, unforgettable time for me, and they were followed by fulfilling years on the stage, during which I was allowed the luxury of living out my abilities to the full.

I poured all of the energy which I was later to turn inwards into my art, into every part which I played. And the audience felt it. The reviewers often used to write that the entire house had been spellbound by my performance. My art was the only thing which existed for me. Acting was my religion and the stage was my temple.

However, it wasn't long before Heaven started to take an active hand in the planning of my life. The first 'intervention' on Heaven's part, which I have already mentioned in passing in my first book, struck me like a bolt of lightning out of the blue. I shall never forget it. I was employed by the State Theatre Company at the time, playing the role of the much-courted Countess in Eichendorff's *Suitors* at the Gendarmenmarkt Theatre.

One evening, after the performance at the theatre was over, a friend of mine called and invited me round to a late dinner. There were only a few people present. At the dinner table my host informed me that he was giving the party in order to give a friend of his from Dresden, a man I already knew quite well, an opportunity to conduct an esoteric experiment.

'What kind of experiment?' I asked. He went on to explain that this man had, by coincidence, recently discovered that he had 'magnetic' talents. He claimed that his friend could put people into a deep trance simply by stroking their foreheads. 'He also has healing powers,' continued my host, 'and he is a truly phenomenal medium. Wait and see.'

I was speechless. It was the first time I had ever come into contact with this kind of thing. My host was a well-known industrial magnate, his friend from Dresden was an important financial expert, and most of the others present had similarly serious, weighty professions. I and Ernst Legal, the director of the National Theatre, were the only outsiders present.

The more my host told me about the strange doings of his friend, whom I had always known as a very sober character, the more determined I became that I would avoid the company of these people in future. I was convinced that they had all gone out of their minds. It was a pity, of course, and I felt sorry for them, but I didn't wish to have anything to do with people like that.

To top everything else I found myself afflicted by a terrible, inexplicable drowsiness. It overcame me as soon as my host started telling me about his friend's clairvoyant abilities, and I really had to struggle to keep my eyes open at all. This was very unusual for me, as I was usually very much of a night owl.

In the drawing room everything had been prepared for the planned seance: on the oval table lay a large piece of shiny white cardboard, on which the letters of the alphabet had been inscribed in a broad circle. A small water glass stood in a smaller circle at the centre. When everyone had entered the room our friend from Dresden gave us a brief introduction.

'Now, the first person who will speak to us will be my dead friend Arthur,' he explained, 'and after I have exchanged a few words with him any of you who wishes to contact some beloved one who has passed away can say their name and Arthur will put us in contact with them.'

The others all took their places at the table, but I withdrew to the other side of the room and watched from a distance. I was so incensed at all this nonsense that I only had one thought in my mind: to find some way of escaping as soon as possible, without being too impolite.

The man from Dresden and our host sat on opposite sides of the table, and each of them placed two fingers on the glass, whose movements 'Arthur' was supposed to direct. Two other gentlemen with notepads sat next to them, one on the left and one on the right, ready to write everything down so that none of the golden words which were to issue from the ether of the beyond should be lost. The seance was ready to begin.

'That's odd,' said our clairvoyant friend after a few moments, a puzzled expression on his face, 'that isn't Arthur. Let's try again.' After a short pause he spoke again, sounding even more disconcerted this time. 'What on earth is going on? I've never experienced anything like this before. It's still not Arthur, it's someone else.' He removed his hand from the glass.

'Why don't we let whoever it is tell us who they are,' said our host, 'perhaps Arthur couldn't come today.' They started again, for the third time, saying the letters out loud as the glass moved.

'Carlital?' Nobody could make head or tail of the name, until one of the gentlemen with the notepads spoke up.

'You have to divide the word in two,' he said. 'Then it's Carl Ital.' They asked the glass if this was the right interpretation.

'Yes. I call Gerta.'

I leapt up from my chair, thunderstruck. Everyone turned around and stared at me.

'Do you know someone called Carl Ital?'

'Yes,' I stammered, feeling as though I was about to faint, 'my uncle.' The glass started to move again.

'Gerta, there are hard times ahead for you. But you are going to manage, never fear. Rejoice. I have come to tell you that the aid from the East which is yours is mighty indeed. I repeat. Rejoice, for the aid from the East which is yours is mighty indeed. Farewell.'

'Can we call you to us again?' asked the clairvoyant from Dresden.

'No,' came the reply, 'I shall not come again. I am very far away from your plane.'

'Do you have anything else to say?'

'No. We must stop now. It is too tiring for Gerta.'

And so the seance came to an end. Everyone was speechless

with astonishment. After a while, as though through a thick fog, I heard our clairvoyant's astonished voice.

'He must be incredibly powerful if he's capable of keeping all of my friends back,' he said. 'And he wanted to stop, just like that. I've never ever known one of them say that they wanted to stop before.'

Uncle Carl had been one of my father's younger brothers, and he had died suddenly at the age of forty, just a few years before. Nowadays one would probably say that it had been a heart attack. I had loved him very much.

He had lived in a house of his own in Bad Soden in the Taunus district, driving to work in his office in the Hoechst paint and dye works every day. It had been a very responsible, down-to-earth job. When I got home from the dinner party I suddenly remembered that I still had a letter from him, which he had written to me at the time of my confirmation. Even then I had felt that there was something special about this letter, without knowing why, and I had kept it carefully ever since. It took me quite a while to find it again, and when I finally sat down to read it I was astonished. It wasn't the sort of letter that a grownup writes to a little girl; Uncle Carl had written to me as if I had been an adult.

A few years later, after I had experienced a great deal on the spiritual path, I took the letter out and read it again. This time my astonishment was even greater, for it was now perfectly clear to me that he had been a man of knowledge. The letter contained his own profound vision, worded in such a way that I would only be able to understand it when I was ready for it.

How lonely he must have been with his great realisation! Did he know that his words would reach me one day, and that I would be able to understand them? His blessed memory has a very special place in my heart, and I am deeply, deeply grateful to him for returning from his distant world to speak to me when the time came for my awakening.

For those readers who are unfamiliar with my first book I should now like to provide a brief summary of the developments which followed this event, for without them it would be difficult to understand the path which I had to travel or the experiences which I had on that path, which are the central theme of this book. In order to do this I must, unfortunately, quote from my own book.[2] I hope the reader will forgive me for this – I promise to do my best to keep these quotes to an absolute minimum.

It was Uncle Carl's message from the beyond which made me set out on my spiritual journey. Before this, as I have already indicated, my only interest in life had been my art. 'Rejoice,' he had said, 'for the aid from the East which is yours is mighty indeed.'

'Aid from the East'? I didn't have the foggiest notion what these words could possibly mean. But I set to work at once, reading all the available literature about India and all the translations of important Indian works I could lay my hands on.

The doctrine of the law of karma struck my consciousness like a bolt of lightning, and it simply dissolved all of the seemingly insoluble questions that had been tormenting me. In fact, from the very moment of this realization onwards I had no more questions to ask, at least as far as the 'great questions' were concerned, the questions which have plagued mankind ever since we became aware of our own existence – about life and death and the incomprehensibility of 'blind fate'.

Like all the world religions, Christianity has laid down rules governing moral behaviour. However, our scriptures give us no practical guidance, they do not tell us how we can manage to comply with the requirements of the Sermon on the Mount and at the same time hold our own in our daily lives. The yogic teachings of India provided me with the key I had been looking for, a practical method of attaining this goal, and I lost no time in making use of it. I started living by the rules of Yoga, beginning with the control of thoughts.

It's very easy to read a phrase like 'the control of thoughts' without paying much attention to what it really means. Controlling one's thoughts is something which is easier said than done, however. This is work upon one's own self, and if it is to be successful it must be extremely rigorous. Half-hearted attempts are a complete waste of time. In a sense one must become the watchdog of one's own consciousness, giving tongue as soon as any unawareness attempts to raise its head.

After a year's constant practice of the control of thoughts I truly believed that I had already managed to transform my inner being completely. What I didn't realise, in my euphoria, was that all I had really done was to clear away the very coarsest rubbish from the top of the heap, so to speak. Nonetheless, I was certain that this inner triumph would soon be followed by others, and I swore a vow, before myself and God, that I would from now on follow the path of *Raja Yoga*, which is the hardest path of all, demanding the greatest sacrifices of the seeker.

In addition to constant work upon oneself, Raja Yoga also demands a strict and ascetic discipline in one's daily life, forbidding alcohol, non-vegetarian food, smoking and sexual intercourse. After a few years, once the seeker has advanced in his practice of the exercises and has steeled his inner resources, he does not need to be quite so cautious. At the outset of the journey, however, these sacrifices are an absolute precondition, for the *yogi* (and this applies to any being striving for enlightenment) must abandon all attachment. He must be master over himself and his desires. He who cannot abandon his cigarettes or cigars is their slave, and this is not a path for slaves.

Another precondition for any practice of Yoga is the strict adherence to the moral principles demanded by all religions, combined with absolute honesty and sincerity. Unless you build your practice upon these foundations all of your efforts will be a fruitless waste of time.

The first step was to learn the correct position or *asana* for sitting in meditation. Once I had progressed so far that I was able to sit in the lotus position for a while without it being too painful I moved on to the next step in Raja Yoga, which is the practice of *pranayama*, or yogic breathing. Detailed descriptions of the basic *pranayama* exercises can be found in my first book. Here I would only like to add that this inner path upon which I had embarked was and remained my own private secret. I continued with my work as an actress with the same devotion and joy as before, and only a very few of my friends even suspected that I was living a kind of double life.

I have always been profoundly grateful to Heaven that I was able to embark upon my spiritual path very early on and with such great intensity, as this made it much easier for me to bear the first great catastrophe which was to strike me, the death of my beloved mother.

Her doctors had suggested that she allow them to carry out a minor operation, as they had a suspicion (which turned out to be wholly unfounded) that something was wrong. She agreed, and to our great relief – we had all been very worried – she recovered from the operation astonishingly quickly. My father and I usually went to visit her in hospital in the afternoons, but on the day before she was due to be discharged it wasn't possible, as we were much too busy getting everything ready for her return, and we both had performances to give in the evening. She passed away suddenly while we were at the theatre.

It was late when we got back home, and so we didn't get the

news until the next morning. The telephone rang, and I answered it . . .

How does one survive shocks like that? I really don't know, but survive one does. Both my father and I were deeply scarred by our tragic loss. I find talking or writing about this event very difficult, but even so I would like to give a brief description of her passing. It was a beautiful death, a death which was worthy of the inner radiance and love of my mother's gentle soul. The nurse who was taking care of her happened to be in the room when it happened, and she told us what had happened.

My mother had always been a very talented talker, with the magical, spellbinding gift of the true storyteller. As the nurse had come into her room to get everything ready for the night she had been in the middle of telling the lady sharing the room with her, who happened to be an old aquaintance, the story of how she and my father had met and fallen in love in Strasbourg, and how strong their love for one another had been, right from the start.

And then, the nurse said, my mother had suddenly broken off and collapsed in the middle of a sentence. The nurse rushed to her bed and tried to revive her, but there was nothing to be done. She had had an embolism. Her heart had stopped beating right in the middle of her reminiscences about her one great love.

I had already experienced a fair amount on the spiritual 'path' at this point, but I did not yet know how to turn the terrible pain of separation and loss into a positive acceptance of fate. I was still too immature and inexperienced. But perhaps it was precisely this inability which made it possible for me to pour my entire heart into my daily hours of prayer and meditation for my mother's soul, in which I fervently beseeched all the powers of Heaven to help her and care for her. Of course, there is no way of telling whether it was something which she 'needed' or not, but I am certain that she felt that I was there for her, she *must* have felt it. And at the same time these passionate, unceasing prayers to God also helped me on my own path, enabling my spirit to rise up and go beyond its own limitations.

About two years after my mother's passing I had another very strange esoteric experience involving our friend from Dresden. I shall describe it exactly as it happened.

One of my best friends at the time was Dr Johannes Maria Verweyen, who was Professor of Philosophy at the University of Bonn. In addition to this academic post he was also Secretary General of the Theosophical Adyar Society, a position previously held by Rudolf Steiner. His work for Adyar made it necessary for him to come to Berlin quite often, and he never failed to come by and see me when he was there. On one of these visits I happened to tell him about my deceased uncle and the seance, and he said that he would very much like to get to know the man who had conducted the seance and, if possible, to be present at one of his sessions. I had kept in touch with him since that fateful evening – our relations had become quite friendly – and so it wasn't difficult for me to arrange a meeting. He invited Dr Verweyen and me to come and visit him in his villa in Dresden. It was a while before all three of us could manage to take a few days off at the same time, but we finally managed it, and on the appointed date Dr Verweyen and I set off from Bonn and Berlin to make our rendezvous at the banker's beautiful house, which was just as comfortable as it was tasteful.

We had expected another spiritualist seance, attended by a large group of people, but to my surprise our host didn't seem to have anything like this in mind. When we arrived he introduced us to his 'medium', who was a charming middle-aged lady. She was his wife's sister, and he had asked her to come to Dresden especially to meet us.

The whole affair was thus very private and intimate. The only other person present was a close friend of our host's, a famous and (in musical circles) greatly feared music critic.

Our host's wife had gone away to stay with relatives for the duration of our meeting, as she was afraid of 'that sort of thing', and so there were only five of us in all: our friend the banker and his medium, as the star performers, and the critic, Dr Verweyen and I as audience and potential participants.

The speed with which Mrs S. reacted was truly astonishing. Her brother-in-law simply stroked her forehead once, very gently, and she immediately sank into a deep trance.

The session started off with the type of experiment one often reads about in books on parapsychology and extrasensory perception. I found this rather boring myself, but our friend the music critic was fascinated by it.

We agreed that one of us would select a sentence at random from one of the books in the library next door, and that Mrs S. would then have to find the sentence for us. The music critic went and pulled out a volume of *Meyers Lexicon*, chose an entry, and wrote the word which Mrs S. was to find on a slip of paper, which he cautiously refused to show to us until later.

Then we all returned to the drawing room and sat down, and our host asked Mrs S. to go into the library and find the sentence the critic had selected. (I should mention here that there really were a very great many books in the library. All of the walls were lined with bookcases, all the way up to the ceiling.) She stood up, still in her trance, and walked into the library. I must admit that it took quite a while, but finally she stopped in front of the right volume. She pulled the book from the shelf and turned the pages with her eyes closed, running her index finger along the lines of text. Then her finger stopped moving.

'This is it,' she said in a soft voice. The music critic rushed over to her, waving his slip of paper excitedly. Her finger had come to rest on the word *Leitmotiv*, and exactly the same word was written on the piece of paper.

It was an amazing achievement, even when one considers that telepathy may have been involved. After all, we all knew that the book was a volume of *Meyers*, and even though the critic swore that he had been directing the Freischütz Overture in his mind the whole time in order to keep himself from thinking of the word in question I still don't think that the possibility that Mrs S. may have read his mind can be eliminated completely.

Our host then decided to carry out another experiment. After putting his sister-in-law into a deep trance once again he gave her the following command: 'You will now go to your flat in Kassel. Look around in the flat, and then come back and tell us exactly what Benno and Friedel were doing.' (Benno and Friedel were her husband and her adult daughter.)

Now it was getting more interesting – after all, we were in Dresden, which is more than 150 miles away from Kassel, as the crow flies.

After a while he brought her back and asked her to tell us where she had been and what she had seen there. She spoke in a halting voice, and she herself seemed to be very astonished at what she had seen.

'I was at home in my flat, yes, and I went through all the rooms there. Everything was all right. Benno was working at his desk in his study and Friedel was in her room . . . ' She was suddenly very wide awake. 'But why is my daughter packing her suitcases?' she said, looking confused, 'I don't understand it. There is no reason for her to go anywhere. What can it mean?'

'Let's check and see,' said our host, picking up the telephone. He dialled the operator and booked a call to Kassel. The suspense was tremendous.

'Benno, old chap,' he said at last, when he finally had his brother-in-law on the line, 'you must be sitting at your desk. You answered the phone so quickly.' Benno confirmed that he had been sitting there the whole evening going through his papers.

'And how's Friedel, what's she up to? You know how mothers are, always worried.' There was a short pause. And then:

'What? She's going away to Erfurt? Tomorrow morning? But why?' He cast a triumphant glance in our direction as he listened to Benno's explanation. When he had hung up he explained what had happened. The mother of one of Friedel's cousins had fallen ill suddenly, and since the cousin couldn't get away from her job during the day she had sent Friedel a telegram, begging her to come to Erfurt as soon as possible to help her.

This time we really were impressed. There was no doubt about it that Mrs S. had left her physical body and that she had visited a far-away city, returning with irrefutable proof that she had really been in her flat there and had seen what was happening.

While the agitated discussion about this remarkable feat was still in progress I was suddenly overcome by an overwhelmingly powerful desire to carry out an experiment myself, a desire which was almost primal in its intensity. I motioned to our host, indicating that he should follow me into the room next door, where I begged him to ask his sister-in-law to try to contact my deceased mother. I wanted her to ask her how she was feeling, and I wanted to know if she was happy and if she had anything to say to me. We had just seen that Mrs S. was able to leave her body and move around on the earthly plane. I reasoned that she might also be able to come into contact with beings outside this plane in the same way.

My friend was electrified at the prospect of carrying out such an exciting experiment. After allowing his sister-in-law to rest a little he put her into a deep trance again.

Then, with great intensity, he asked her to leave her body and to try to contact my mother. Dr Verweyen and the music critic looked at one another in surprise, as if they were both wondering whether something unusual was about to take place. I myself was in a very strange state of extreme excitement. 'You sat in your chair without changing your position once until the entire experiment was finished,' Dr Verweyen told me later, 'with your eyes tightly closed and your fists clenched. You were shivering all over.'

When our friend felt that the time had come to awaken his medium again he brought her back by stroking her forehead gently and carefully. When she had returned to her senses he asked her to tell us what she had experienced.

Mrs S. began to speak. She was still in a semi-trance state. She made frequent pauses, and her voice was almost inaudible.

'I flew . . . I flew. The earth was beneath me . . . I flew, and there were many, many others, all travelling like me, but then they continued on their way in other directions and I went on alone. Suddenly I saw a luminous sphere, it seemed as if it was very far away, and I wanted to go to it . . . but then I couldn't go any further . . . ' She paused for a while, and when she started speaking again her voice was even softer, as if she were still feeling the effects of some shock she had just received. 'And then . . . I had to come back.'

We were all speechless, and even after a fair amount of time had passed none of us felt any desire to say anything or discuss what had happened. We went up to our rooms and tried to go to sleep.

The next evening we all gathered together again in the drawing room.

'This time it will work,' announced our host in a confident voice. 'It didn't work yesterday because my command wasn't strong enough, and because Hedwig [his sister-in-law] had already over-exerted herself. But today we shall only perform this one experiment.'

This time he made his command much more forceful. As soon as his sister-in-law had fallen into a deep trance he gave her the same instructions as he had the evening before, but then he added, 'I order you to cross the barrier. You *must* make contact with Gerta Ital's mother. This is very very important.'

We sat there in silence and waited for what seemed like an eternity. My nerves were as taut as bowstrings. No one else so much as moved. Finally, our friend got up and walked over to Mrs S., who was slumped in her armchair as if she were dead, and he began to bring her back by stroking her head and forehead softly and gently. I suspect that I was not the only one who was shivering this time. It took a long time before her breathing became visible again, and even then it was almost imperceptible. He let her sit there in silence until her breath had returned to normal before telling her to recount what she had experienced.

There was a long pause before she started to speak. She kept her eyes closed, and when it finally came her voice was very monotonous and hesitant, almost as though she were speaking to herself. She sounded completely exhausted.

'I flew again . . . and it was the same as before. At first there were many others flying with me. But the further I flew the more alone I was, the fewer others were there around me, and suddenly I was completely alone again. I flew . . . and then I saw the glowing sphere again, far away in the distance. But again, I could go no further. Something indescribable, powerful, kept me back. But . . . I felt such an urgent need to break through the barrier that I finally managed to break the spell and to fly on. It was a golden sphere, I was getting closer to it . . . I heard music . . . I came closer and closer to the wonderful light . . . I wanted to go inside . . . I couldn't, it wasn't possible. I tried again, with all my strength, and then . . . a terrible voice, like thunder, coming out of the sphere, said "Go back!" and I fell, and I fell . . . '

For a while we all sat there, without moving, paralysed by the shock of what we had heard. Mrs S. laid her head back in the armchair and fell into an exhausted sleep. As soon as the rest of us had recovered enough to be able to stand up again we lifted her up gently and carried her over to the couch.

The next day Dr Verweyen, the critic and I took our leave of Mrs S. and the banker and departed in our different directions. I think that the failure of our experiment, and especially the astoundingly unusual way in which this failure had manifested itself, had been much more impressive for all of us than any success could ever have been.

Dr Verweyen's great interest in parapsychological experiments continued unabated. I often took part in these experiments as an observer, but I never again experienced anything like this session in Dresden. It was unique.

For my own part I had decided that enough was enough, and that I would not take an active part in any more such experiments myself.

And so, after my first 'call' from the beyond, delivered through the agency of my deceased Uncle Carl, I set to work on my spiritual development, with great devotion, joy and energy, praying ceaselessly to God for help on my path. Five years later something happened which gave me the blissful certainty that my prayers had been answered. In my first book I wrote the following words about this experience:

> I have no intention of describing this experience, as it is one of those spiritual secrets which one is not permitted to divulge, but this much I can say: In the course of that night I was initiated by a spiritual Master from another, non-earthly plane of existence, and I was granted the experience of mystic union with him. This is a very ancient mystical tradition, and it is a bond which can never again be broken.

Three years have passed since then, and it has now become possible for me to tell the story of what happened in that night, and of the events which followed. Such profound changes have taken place in my inner world during these three years that I have now been given the freedom to speak about my experiences at will.

It is a strange and wonderful fact that this event, just like the first 'call' which I had received from the beyond, took place just before a shattering catastrophe was to test all of my inner and outer resources to the utmost.

Four years after my mother had passed away my father unexpectedly collapsed and died. I shall keep my account short this time, for there are some things which overtax the human ability to bear suffering, even many years after they have actually taken place. Even so, and despite the pain it caused me, I have always thanked Heaven that I was lucky enough to be there with him when it happened. His death, and the manner of his death, were Heaven's will, and that is why I have decided to write about it here, for even though it was terrible it was not without mercy.

On that fateful day my father and I took supper together, and then he lay down on the couch, saying that he wanted to rest a while before going to the theatre for his performance. I was sorry to have to wake him when the time came for him to go, for he was very fast asleep. Unusually so, in fact – it took a long time to wake him, and when he finally opened his eyes and sat up he said that he wasn't feeling very good, and that the food we had eaten had probably disagreed with him.

The moment he opened his eyes I had a terrible feeling of foreboding. I tried to get him to lie down again, saying that I would go to the theatre and tell the first violinist that he would have to conduct the orchestra, but it was no good, of course. Nothing in the world could ever have made my father miss a performance, it was something which was simply unthinkable for him.

'Then I shall come with you,' I said firmly, a cold fear gripping my heart.

That awful, silent drive to the theatre! I couldn't have felt more miserable and terror-struck if I had been driving to my own execution. And what about my father himself? I am sure that he too had some sense of foreboding, some feeling that something terrible and unavoidable was about to take place, but he went out to confront it with the same quiet courage with which he had borne all the other trials and tribulations of his difficult life.

Astonishingly, there were some empty seats in the first row – God must have willed it so – and I was thus able to sit directly in front of the conductor's platform.

'I'm here with you, Papa,' I whispered to him as he picked up his baton to begin the performance. He nodded.

In the minutes which followed God taught me what fear can really be like. Every heartbeat, every breath I took was immersed, drowning, in a sea of fear, fear mixed with an almost metaphysical horror at what I knew was going to happen. And then it happened.

My father's right arm suddenly dropped limply in mid-stroke, his baton fell clattering to the floor, and he lurched over to one side. But before he could fall to the ground I had jumped up behind him and wrapped my arms around him.

'Help me, hold him!' I shouted to the musicians in the front row of the orchestra pit, 'Don't let him fall!' Two of them jumped up and grabbed him, and I rushed out into the foyer and shouted to the ushers that they should call an ambulance. Then I ran back into the orchestra pit again, through the rear entrance.

I held my father in my arms and waited for the ambulance, crouched down on the floor of the orchestra pit among the musicians. They had to play on, of course. I was sure he was dying. He couldn't speak, and even if he had been able to it would have been impossible to hear him above the infernal noise of the orchestra all around us. I don't think that any of the tortures of hell could even come close to the torment I experienced there with him in the hour it took for the ambulance to come.

When the ambulance men finally came in with the stretcher they had to carry him out through the auditorium, as the rear entrance was too narrow. That was Louis Ital's exit. The finale of his great career.

He lived for another four months without regaining the power of speech, even though he was fully conscious all the time. His life energy dwindled away slowly and peacefully. But that wasn't important – his real farewell to this world had been up there on the conductor's podium, the place where he had spent the most creative moments of his life.

Notes

1. The Pan-Germanic Association of Conductors.
2. *The Master, the Monks, and I*, by Gerta Ital. English edition published by the Aquarian Press, June 1987. These quotes taken from the galley proofs of this edition.

3

Heaven's Kōan

In all I haven't had more than six visionary dreams in the space of around twenty-five years. Visionary dreams are very, very different from ordinary dreams. They are so overwhelmingly intense that it seems as though every single tiny detail of the experience has been graven deeply and indelibly into one's memory, indeed, into one's very being.

Everyone dreams every night, of course, whether they are aware of the fact or not, but the rare experiences which I am talking about have nothing whatsoever to do with ordinary dreams. Anyone who has ever had such a dream will know exactly what I mean, for they are unmistakable, and the experience is something which one can never ever forget, at least not as long as one is on this earthly plane of existence. The reality of the so-called 'real world' pales in comparison.

These visions are usually messages, having to do with something which is going to happen to the 'dreamer' in the future. But where do these messages come from? Who sends them? I am personally convinced that they are revelations of the Divine Self which is within all of us. Sometimes the revelation is a warning, sometimes it has the function of a mirror held up to reveal imperfect qualities which can be improved, and sometimes it is simply a mental picture of that which is to come.

People who are fortunate enough to have such visions are sometimes rather perplexed, for they often seem completely incomprehensible at first. There is no need to worry, however.

Even though it can take years, their hidden meaning always reveals itself in the end. One's life provides the answer.

Sometimes 'It' chooses to speak to (or through) the seeker directly. The quality of such experiences is similar to that of visionary dreams.

More than twenty-five years ago a monk lent me an ancient copy of the original writings of Saint Teresa of Avila from his monastery's library. Her account moved me very deeply, and left me filled with an overwhelming feeling of gratitude and happiness. Gratitude that she had taken the trouble to write down what she had experienced on the path, and happiness because every chapter was filled with confirmations that I was on the right track.

I was particularly moved by what she wrote about the way in which she had received her messages from the beyond, for it coincided precisely with my own experiences. She would usually receive no more than a single sentence or command, which would then be repeated again and again for a long period, either until the prediction which had been made had come true or until she had met the demands which had been made of her. My sense of wonder and astonishment was even greater when I reached the passages in which she describes her experiences of the ultimate, which she refers to as the 'innermost circle', for it became clear to me that she was a mystic of the very first order.

When one reads these accounts of Saint Teresa's one should bear in mind that they were not written for the general public, but for the nuns who lived with her in the nunnery. They are records of Teresa's own path to union with God, and their purpose was to give the other nuns new courage and strength in the moments when they doubted the reality of their own experiences. There was no need for her to go into great detail when it came to the ultimate, which she describes in hesitating, shy terms, for she was writing for people seeking God, not for the merely curious. (I should also mention that the very old version of her writings which I was lucky enough to be able to read, and which consisted of several volumes, was much more detailed and comprehensive than the new, edited editions which have since been published. The language of the new editions is also very far removed from that of the original, which is delightfully archaic.)

In my own early years on the path, no matter how much I searched, strove, struggled and prayed, the only message which

I received from the beyond was a single, laconic sentence, repeated again and again and again:

'You are too zealous!'

The voice was right, of course. Once I had got my first taste of the divine there was no stopping me. I was completely enraptured by the new, unknown vistas which had opened up before me, and I simply couldn't get enough. I was mercilessly harsh upon myself in my efforts to experience more, living according to the very strictest precepts of the most exacting discipline which I could find, Raja Yoga. Nothing I achieved, nothing I experienced, was enough to satisfy my thirst. I wanted to *know*, and I wanted to know everything.

This admonition, 'You are too zealous!', was to follow me like a shadow for the next few years. None of my attempts to be vigilant and alert was enough to satisfy Heaven's great task-master. The warning was simply repeated, again and again and again. And then, quite suddenly, it stopped coming. Its disappearance was so undramatic that I didn't even notice it was gone at first. It was only when it was replaced by a different message that I realised that I had entered into a new phase of my spiritual work.

The new message was: 'Do nothing!' At the time I didn't know what kōans were, but now, many years later, I am convinced that this order which I received from the beyond was in fact a kind of kōan, given to me to solve by Heaven. I accepted it, absorbed it and lived with it, right up to the bittermost end, in every sense of the word. When Heaven decides to start testing someone who has embarked upon the path of realisation it is more strict, more unerringly accurate in its aim and more absolute and unconditional than any human Master can ever be.

Kōans were invented by the great Zen Masters of ancient China to help their disciples to attain enlightenment. What does the word kōan really mean? In his book *The Great Liberation*,[1] Dr D. T. Suzuki writes:

> Literally translated the word 'kōan' actually means 'statute' or 'decree'. It is an expression which came into use towards the end of the Tang dynasty. Nowadays it is used to describe a device designed to help open the mind of the disciple for the truth of Zen. This device can take the form of an anecdote about an ancient Master, or of a dialogue between a Master and a disciple, or of an observation or a question made or posed by a Master.

By definition, it is impossible to understand or solve a kōan intellectually, for they have no rational solution and they render even the most sophisticated instruments of the human mind completely helpless. The only option open to the seeker who receives a kōan is to live with it, absorbing it into the very fabric of his or her being.

At first I was completely thunderstruck, for the order came at a time when a terrible period of forced inactivity was just coming to an end. For the last seven years I had been suffering from a throat tumour, which had almost completely destroyed my vocal cords, forcing me to give up my beloved profession. As it grew the tumour had also enclosed a facial nerve, causing the most terrible pain for years on end. Now, after two operations, I was finally beginning to regain my health. My voice was coming back, I had just made my first comeback performance in a radio play (for which I had, to my great delight, received very positive reviews), and I was busy learning stage parts again. And now this!

Nor did I receive any more specific explanation of what the divine taskmaster meant me to do or not to do, no matter how deeply I delved within myself in my daily meditations. Forcing myself to obey was a battle, day in and day out, but obey I did, even though I was unable to understand the hidden purpose of the command at the time.

'Doesn't Heaven realise that I have to earn money in order to be able to go on living?' I asked myself. The answer to this question was that Heaven either didn't know or didn't care. The command was simply repeated again and again, without the slightest variation. Now I can see that the object of the exercise was more than simply putting me to the test (and that every minute of every day); Heaven also wanted to transform my impetuosity by forcing me to curb it and to ignore its urges and desires. As time went on it got weaker and weaker, and then, finally, the point came where it simply dissolved completely. Heaven had succeeded in its aim.

I should also stress that the command that I should do nothing did not in any way encourage me to become lazy or indolent. On the contrary, I worked harder than I ever had before. In addition to meditating for several hours every day I also took up my artistic studies again, devoting a great deal of time and effort to them, for I had no idea what the final outcome of this test was to be, and I had decided to do my best to be ready for anything. The only thing which I was not allowed to engage in was any kind of professional activity in the outside world, despite the fact that I was constantly bombarded with tempting offers to act in plays.

I don't think there is any way of expressing just how difficult it was for me to refuse all those offers. Although I did it with a sunny smile on my face there were tears in my heart, and financial disaster was looming larger every day. Despite my doubts I was driven onwards by a strange combination of despair, anger and curiosity. I had the stubborn desire to *know*. I wanted to see just how far the divine taskmaster was willing to go, and where he would take me. He took me to the very brink of total disaster.

This account is not a figment of my imagination. Every single word of it is true.

'I have entrusted my will to Him,' I told myself again and again, 'I simply do not believe that He can abandon me completely. It is not possible.' But it *was* possible. He did not lift so much as a finger to help or guide me, He simply stood by and watched. Every day I was broken and cast down afresh, and every day I had to find the strength to stand up again and go on. To my own surprise, however, I did not falter. On the contrary, I grew and flourished in the discipline of this 'non-doing'. It was almost as if the practice of unswerving obedience had become a kind of challenge to me.

Finally the day came when all I had left in the world was one 50 pfennig piece. I laid the coin on the table, sat down in the lotus position, closed my eyes and called out silently to the divine taskmaster, concentrating all of the energy which I had collected in long months of ascetic practice into the call.

'What do you want?' came the voice. I did not beg or plead this time. This time I rebelled openly.

'I thought you were God, or at least some aspect of Him,' I replied fearlessly, 'and if that is truly so then you know perfectly well what I want. I have followed your command to the letter. Now I have nothing. And I know what you are going to say now. You are going to tell me that I still have the 50 pfennig piece there on the table. Save your breath. Would you like to know what I am going to do with that money? I am going to buy birdseed with it! The tits and sparrows here trust me. It is winter, and they cannot go without food as long as I can. They know that they can depend on me to put food out on my balcony for them in the winter, and I am not going to betray their trust. This is your doing.'

'And what do you want?'

'Now it is up to you to do a miracle,' I said firmly. 'I have done everything in my power, for as long as I could, to obey your command. Now it is your turn. Now *you* are going to have to come up with something. I am giving you three days. I can hold out for another three days, but if your miracle does not come by the time the three days are up then you should know that I am going to stop obeying your command. I shall act, to prevent myself from falling into debt and doing injustice to others. Remember, three days, and no more!'

Even now, looking back, I feel that this exchange has something splendid and magnificent about it. After it was over I felt completely relaxed and at ease, despite my desperate situation. I hadn't budged a single inch, and this knowledge gave me a wonderful feeling of quiet exhilaration.

I waited. The first day passed. Nothing happened. The second day passed. Nothing happened. On the morning of the third day my telephone rang, and to my great astonishment the gentleman at the other end of the line turned out to be someone who owed me money. I had almost completely forgotten about him. His son had been responsible for a serious accident in which I had been involved some time before, and in strict legal terms this man was required to pay me an annuity for the rest of my life. There had been no reason to believe that he would refuse to pay the annuity – he had paid all of my doctor's fees and hospital bills without the slightest hesitation or objection – but when I came out of hospital I had felt so grateful at having survived that I hadn't bothered to take any further steps. I had never heard anything more from him since then, and I had put the matter out of my mind. And now here he was, calling me on the phone, on the third day after I had presented Heaven with my ultimatum!

After telling me who he was Mr W. said that he would very much like to come round and see me to discuss the subject of my annuity. I replied that I had no objections. 'I shall come right away then,' he said, 'if it is convenient.'

He arrived an hour later. Before saying anything else he apologised profusely for not having contacted me sooner, explaining that his business affairs had been going so poorly that it hadn't been possible.

'But all the time,' he went on, 'the question of the annuity was like a sword of Damocles hanging over my head. Both I and my wife are very grateful to you for not coming forward with any claims, but at the same time we have lived in constant dread, for there was always the possibility that this pleasant state of affairs might suddenly be changed. And so I have now decided to come and see you to discuss the possibility of coming to a mutual agreement of some sort.' If only he could have seen how my inner being had started to smile at hearing these words!

'What sort of agreement did you have in mind?' I asked, my face relaxed and impassive.

'Well, to begin with my wife and I will undertake to pay for any medical treatment which you may need to alleviate the after-effects of the injuries which you suffered in the accident for the next five years. As far as the annuity to make up for our son's terrible mistake is concerned, it is difficult for us to say whether we will be able to pay it for the rest of your life or not. Who knows what may happen? We thought we might discuss the possibility of settling the matter with a lump sum payment, if you are agreeable . . . ' He looked at me uncertainly.

'Yes, and?'

'Yes, well, if you are willing to renounce all further claims then we would agree to pay you a sum of two thousand marks now. That is all we can afford.'

I remained silent for a few moments before answering. I didn't want to prolong the poor man's agony, but I was unable to say anything before I had centred myself inwardly and sent a message to Heaven. 'Very well,' I said to my divine taskmaster, 'if you think that this is enough for the time being then I have no intention of trying to disagree with you. Thank you.' I turned back to Mr W.

'Yes,' I said finally, 'I am willing to accept your offer.'

'My wife will be very happy to hear that,' he replied, audibly relieved. 'And,' he added a little stiffly, 'I should also like to say that I have never got on with anyone so well as I have with you.' Then he got up with a jerk, picked up his briefcase, opened it, and counted out twenty 100 mark notes on to the table.

I glanced at the clock on the wall. In one hour's time the three days would be up.

The kōan had been solved. I had lived it out to the very end. 'Do nothing' was a message which I never received again. Now I was free to 'do' as I wished, but my doing had become radically transformed. Despite the fact that I was a fighter by nature I had learned to curb my instincts, and I had taught myself unconditional obedience. My own doing, as the activity of an individual will, had disappeared completely, and it had been replaced by a sense of 'doing without doing'. I no longer had to concentrate on the 'how' of doing, doing simply happened of its own accord. I am reminded of Erwin Rousselle's discussion of the 'circulation of the light' meditation in one of his works on Chinese yoga:

'If the exercises are successful the light begins to circulate of its own accord, and there is no need for any further meditation. This phenomenon is extremely significant, for it means that everything which is raised to the level of consciousness by such profound, shattering experiences can never again be lost.'

When one reaches this point one's actions become free of desire and egocentric considerations, and this results in the total transformation of the seeker. This state of 'non-doing' is also the goal of all of the many disciplines which are practised in Japan within the context of Zen, such as the arts of swordsmanship and archery.[2] I knew nothing about such things at the time. On the path of Zen and all of its associated disciplines the disciple must work long and hard to exterminate the weed of impurity, pulling it out by the roots. This is not something which can be done easily or quickly. It is a slow process of spiritual unfolding which usually takes many years, and which sometimes takes a lifetime, or even many lifetimes. And it is always a matter of life and death, at least as far as the seeker's ego is concerned, for the gateway to true life can only be opened after the personal, individual ego has been dissolved. The ego is incapable of understanding this, of course, and it battles for its survival with all of the weapons and tricks at its disposal. All that the ego can see is what it is losing. It too wants the joy of the promised 'enlightenment', but it wants it quickly and easily, and it does not want to die in the process. It isn't willing to take too many risks, and it demands constant encouragement in the form of small successes along the way.

Needless to say, allowing oneself to be guided by the wishes and fears of the ego is a complete waste of time. The only attitude which is of any use on the path to God is one of utter choicelessness and unconditional, desireless surrender. Only then is it possible to find one's way to Him, and then too only after a long and hard journey.

This is something which all of the great Masters of the East have repeated again and again for centuries. Many hundreds of thousands have read their words in the scriptures, and have been filled with longing and joy at reading them. Unfortunately, however, longing and joy are not enough on their own, one must also be willing to work and wait and suffer. The situation of the majority of seekers after God is the same today as it has always been. Everyone is hungry to behold the luminous goal, glowing far off in the distance like some enticing Shangri La of the heart, but only a tiny minority are able or willing to see the path which leads to it.

It is the path which is important, not the goal. What I experienced when my kōan ('Do nothing!') dissolved is far less significant than the path which I had to travel in order to make that experience. Continuing on one's way without being able to see what lies ahead, taming the ego, going on and on tirelessly until the last vestiges of thoughts of 'I' and 'I want' have been completely dissolved, these are the only things which matter.

The seeker who is able to persevere until Heaven decides that the time has come to liberate him becomes invulnerable. I should hasten to add that this doesn't mean that his daily life changes in any way, or that he is then spared the blows of fate. Life remains life, and karma remains karma. The really significant change is inward. The seeker's serenity can no longer be disturbed by anything. In the words of the beautiful Sanskrit saying:

> 'Even when joyful he is not joyful, even when tormented he is not tormented. Only those who are like unto him can fathom his wondrous demeanour in this and that situation.'[3]

Notes

1. D. T. Suzuki, *Die große Befreiung*, Zurich 1969. (According to the publishers, O. W. Barth Verlag, this book was an original translation into German from the Japanese, and to the best of their knowledge no English language edition of the book in this form exists.)
2. See also: R. Kammer (ed.), *Chozan Shissai, Zen and Confucius in the Art of Swordsmanship*; Eugen Herrigel, *Zen in the Art of Archery*; Eugen Herrigel, *The Method of Zen.*
3. Taken from one of the works of Heinrich Zimmer (all of which were originally published in English). The cited title, *Indische Offenbarungsworte* (Indian Words of Revelation), does not exist in any catalogue of H.Z.'s work.

4

Visionary Dreams

> You could not discover the limits of the soul even if you travelled every road to do so – such is the depth of its Logos. (*Heraklitus, Fragments, No. 43*)

There is something very mysterious about genuine visionary dreams. As I already mentioned in the last chapter I am personally convinced that they are an expression of the divine spark hidden within each and every one of us, which wishes to bear witness to itself and express itself within its earthly vessel as soon as it is awakened.

The First Dream

(Roughly two years after the beginning of my practice of Raja Yoga)

I am at a seaside resort. The usual small white holiday villas line the promenade. I know that I am staying in one of them. In the background is a small town.

It is a beautiful day. I am on the beach, and I am completely alone. There isn't another soul to be seen anywhere. The deep blue endlessness of the sea is magnificent.

Suddenly the luminous colours start to fade. I look up into the sky, and what I see makes me freeze in horror. The sky has disappeared, and it has been replaced by a huge, looming range of mountains, a mass of ponderous stone hanging there where the sky was before, its sharp peaks and ridges pointing down threateningly towards the earth.

I am terribly afraid. The mountains are coming closer and closer. They seem to be falling, and I am sure that they are going to come tumbling down on to the earth, crushing everything.

No sooner has the thought formed in my mind than it starts to happen. The mountains crash down with an indescribable, thunderous roar, breaking asunder and shattering in a shower of stones and rubble. I am lying on the ground, completely motionless.

There is a sudden silence.

After a while I start coming to my senses, very slowly, amazed that I am still alive. I move my limbs carefully. I am unhurt. I stand up and look around.

The town and the villas have disappeared. Everywhere I look I see nothing but huge masses of stone and rubble, covering everything. Only one house has been spared. It is the house where I have been staying.

Suddenly I freeze in horror.

'The sea!' I shout in terrible anguish. 'Where is the sea?'

The sea is gone. It has been replaced by a stony desert.

Deep in my heart I am certain that it will be the end of me if I can't manage to find the sea again. 'The sea!' I shout out again in despair. 'Where is the sea?'

And then, suddenly, a shiver of joy courses through me. Endlessly far away on the horizon I can see a thin blue line. The sea!

I know immediately that I must go to it, that I must make my way to it, through this endless stony desert. I won't be saved until I have reached the sea.

I wake up from the dream, and yet within me the dream continues. I know that I am a little bundle of agony in the middle of a stony desert, exhausted, crawling forwards on all fours, my hands and knees bloody. I must go on . . . I must go on . . .

Even now, as I write, I can still feel the overwhelming sense of shock and horror which I experienced there in the desert. In fact, the shock which I feel now is even greater than it was at the time, for then I was still living in the 'world', and this prophetic dream was no more than a vision. Now I know what the vision meant, for I have experienced it as a harsh, bitter reality.

The path which I now had to travel on, alone, was stony,

hard and merciless. On the way the world in which I had lived, which had given me nourishment and had been my home, *my* world and with it my entire being as it had once been, was utterly annihilated by Heaven. There is no need for me to describe in all its details the cruel, implacable severity with which Heaven began to manifest itself in my life after this (a life which was already more than half over), never stopping to let me rest, for the 'dream' speaks for itself.

The Second Dream (Two years after the first)

In a sense this dream is the continuation of a long conversation with my deceased mother, in which we have discussed my 'initiation'. I am fully aware of everything we have said to one another, even though the dream begins after the conversation is over.

We are both very grave and solemn. We enter into a vast, circular courtyard. There are many churches around the circumference of this courtyard, all of them very different from one another. I am wearing my ordinary worldly clothes, my mother is dressed in a long white robe.

We turn towards the church on our right and enter. As I cross the threshold I feel myself being held back by an unseen power, and then I am kissed by invisible lips. I realise that this is the ritual blessing, preparing me for that which is to come.

Inside the church we turn to one side and enter into a chapel. A bishop in robes of red and gold is standing in front of the altar. I know that he is waiting for me.

I kneel down, and my mother kneels down behind me. The bishop blesses me. Then he leans down and kisses me.

'How do you intend to help?' he asks me, speaking for the first time. I look up at him in confusion.

'Perhaps I should only give benefit performances from now on?' I ask hesitantly.

'That is not enough,' he replies, his voice stern.

Then a woman dressed in grey steps forward. She is the bishop's assistant. I know this, even though I haven't noticed her up to this point. She says that she will explain everything to me and that she will show me the way.

The bishop nods, and then, suddenly, he is gone.

My mother and I leave the church and step out into the huge, sunny courtyard again. We walk towards the gateway leading out of the courtyard in silence. There is a kind of washing line stretched out near the gateway, and a pair of snow-white gloves is hanging on the line. I know that they are meant for me, and I take them down as we pass.

On the whole this dream speaks for itself. For the sake of clarity, however, I should point out that I was still very deeply involved in my work as an actress and a musician at the time, and that I regarded this work as something sacred and holy. I was still convinced that it would be possible for me to continue on the inner journey to God without giving up my artistic calling. That is why my answer to the bishop's question was so confused, and so unsatisfactory.

A Waking Dream (Two years after the second dream)

I wake up with a terrible feeling of fear. Fear . . . fear . . . fear . . . The entire room, my bedroom, is filled with this fear, with an almost tangible atmosphere of cosmic terror.

I go in search of help, floating through the closed door into the guest room, where I know that a trusted friend of the family is sleeping. I crouch down beside him and shake him desperately, trying to wake him up, and I beg him to help me. But he flings out his arm and pushes me away violently. 'Go away!' he snarls, furious at being disturbed, 'Go away!'

The room is in total darkness. Suddenly an area of light opens up in the darkness in front of me, as though an invisible curtain has been pulled back. I see many monks in dark robes, walking slowly down a very high, broad flight of stairs. I sit there on the edge of the bed, speechless, and observe the scene. One of the monks, in the middle of the group, is wearing a lighter-coloured robe. I know that he is more senior than the others. None of the other monks seems to notice that I am there, but he smiles at me and waves encouragingly.

Then a luminous being in silver armour suddenly appears on the right hand side of the group of monks. He looks something like the traditional pictures of the Archangel Michael.

He too smiles at me, and his smile is as radiant as the aura of light around him. He raises his right arm and waves to me, smiling all the while. I have the feeling that he too is trying to give me courage. Then the curtain closes and everything is dark again.

A few seconds later, however, the curtain in the wall of darkness opens again, and the entire scene is repeated. It is as though that which I have seen is being confirmed. As the silver figure smiles and waves again I suddenly have a strong desire to help the poor sleeper lying there next to me to share the blissful vision with me, and I shake him, trying to wake him up.

At that very moment the entire room is filled with the silent presence of a single, overwhelming command, irresistible in its intensity. It is invisible and inaudible, but nonetheless it fills the entire room.

'Be still!'

And then the curtain closes once again.

A moment later I am back in my own bed in my own room. I get up and write down what I have seen.

As I understood it then this waking dream meant that I should follow the directions of Heaven, and of Heaven alone, not seeking help or support anywhere else, and I obeyed the unspoken command. Many years later, however, I was to discover that the dream also had a much more astounding, literal meaning. I described this moment of recognition in my first book about my experiences in the Zen monastery in Japan, *The Master, the Monks and I*:

> Then the chauffeur turned the car into a narrow, steep alleyway leading upwards and Mrs M. pointed straight ahead:
>
> 'The temple, Shofuku-ji.'
>
> I leant forward and peered through the curtain of water. All I could see was a broad, extremely steep flight of stone steps leading upwards, but at the sight of it a memory suddenly flashed through my consciousness like an electric shock . . .
>
> We got out of the car. I stood there in the pouring rain, wet through, almost completely blind and drunk with happiness. It seemed almost too good to be true, but now I was completely sure that I had found what I had been seeking for so long, beyond any shadow of doubt. I knew it, for I had seen the stone steps of the temple in a visionary dream many years before . . .
>
> In the years which followed I had visited many beautiful churches and cathedrals, and there were flights of stone steps in front of some of them. But none of them were like this, seemingly appearing out of nowhere, leading to a temple which was hidden somewhere in the background. This was the place.

More than thirty years lay between the waking dream and that moment at which I first set eyes on the steps of the temple.

The Fourth Dream (Four years after the last dream)

I am standing in the centre of a tiny, circular clearing in the jungle, surrounded by huge tropical trees with very thick foliage. There is no way out of the clearing. I am a prisoner.

I look up, and suddenly a shock of mortal fear runs through me, and my hair stands on end: a huge snake is slithering out of the undergrowth on the other side of the clearing in front of me and coming directly towards me. It has seen me. I am terribly, desperately afraid. Just before it reaches me it stops, and rears up in front of me. I stand there trembling, waiting for the snake to strike like someone awaiting their own execution. I know that this is the end.

And then something unbelievable happens. The snake suddenly turns off to the right and slithers away past me, its head still up in the air. It brushes my left arm as it goes, and disappears into the undergrowth behind me.

But before I can even manage to grasp the fact that I have been spared a second snake emerges from the same place in the undergrowth, directly in front of me. I stare at it in horror.

The second snake is even more frightening than the first. Its terrible, scaly head looks like the very incarnation of everything which is evil and ugly.

I am overcome by indescribable panic and horror. I look around desperately for some avenue of escape, but at the same moment the trees of the forest start to draw even closer together. I cannot see even the tiniest crack between the leaves and branches. There is no escape.

The second snake rears up its head even before it reaches me. 'Oh,' I feel myself thinking, my voice a desperate, silent cry within my heart, 'it is going to kill me! I am certain of it. My death is going to be terrible, loathsome!'

Suddenly I have the feeling that the trees around me are waving to me gently in encouragement and comfort, and in the rustling of their leaves I sense the whispering voices of my deceased parents and friends.

The snake's head is almost on the same level as my own. It approaches even closer. Now it is only a few inches away, and it gazes at me intently for a long time.

Paralysed with horror, I return its gaze.

We look into one another's eyes, and despite my fear I am able to see that the snake's eyes are wondrously beautiful, and deeply sad.

We both stand there without moving a muscle for many seconds, gazing into one another's eyes. Suddenly, without any warning, the snake turns its head and the upright portion of its body to one side and slithers past me into the undergrowth, brushing my left shoulder gently as it passes.

I breathe a sigh of relief, thinking that I am out of danger. Then I glance over to one side and see three more snakes coming towards me. They emerge from the undergrowth on the left this time, not from directly in front of me like the others. These snakes are not nearly so terrifying as the first two. They are much smaller, and in comparison they look almost friendly. I am no longer afraid. They slither past me and disappear into the undergrowth behind me just as the first two did, brushing my left leg as they pass.

Now I know that I really am out of danger. In the same moment the feeling of paralysis which had overcome my body disappears, and I am able to move again.

I turn to the right, and to my surprise I see that the wall of jungle there has disappeared, and that it has been replaced by open sky. I walk a few steps, and then I stop again.

Suddenly I see a small, thin, snow-white snake swooping down out of the sky towards me at a terrific speed. There seem to be little wings fluttering at its sides.

A moment later it lands on my left foot and crawls inside my shoe. I feel a small, hot jab in my foot, but I don't dare move. I am unable to say anything.

I look up again and see my mother standing there next to me, dressed in a white robe. I am not at all surprised to see her, and I tell her all about the wondrous appearance of the white snake from the sky. She doesn't say anything. When I have finished speaking she turns around, and I see that the wall of trees on the left hand side of the clearing has disappeared as well. We walk out of the clearing to the left together and into the jungle, which no longer seems strange or threatening. On the contrary, it now seems tame and friendly, and I see that we are walking along a broad promenade.

Neither of us speaks a word. But the whole time I am aware of the small, white snake, curled up on my left foot inside my shoe.

Zen Masters say that once one has overcome the 'barriers erected by the ancient Fathers' and become one with the Original Source the world which one abandoned in order to set out on one's spiritual quest once again returns to normal – in overcoming the 'barriers' one has also overcome the restrictions and limitations of the world, and one is free to come and go in it as one pleases. I wasn't aware of this adage at the time, but I think the reader will agree that the message of the above dream is very similar; at the same time, of course, the dream also gave me a very clear indication that the tests to which I was to be subjected were going to take me to the very limit of human endurance.

The Fifth Dream (Six years later)

At the beginning of the dream I am sitting on a windowsill. The window is wide open. I am looking out of the window, and I have my back to the room. I don't know what is in the room itself, nor does it matter.

I know that I have experienced many terrible things in the recent past, and that I have been in great danger. But I also know that I have finally managed to escape to the safety of this windowsill. I am acutely aware of the fact that I have 'escaped'.

I sit there quietly and gaze out of the window. There is no way I can possibly describe what I see there, or rather, what I don't see, for what lies there before me is simply nothingness.

I can still feel the awesome dread of that sight now as I write these words. There was simply nothing at all outside the window, it defies all description. It was not only that there was nothing material to be seen, there was no sky, no horizon, nothing visible at all; there was only an endless emptiness. But even the word 'emptiness' is nothing more than a word, and there are no words which can come anywhere close to what I saw there, or rather, what I did not see. I was sitting on the very threshold of non-being.

Suddenly, as I sit there staring into this nothingness as though bewitched, I sense the approach of a being from this invisible world. It comes closer and sits down on the windowsill, to my right. Even though this being remains invisible I am aware that it is a boy, although I know at the same time that he is no child, and that he and I are in perfect harmony.

A moment later – I have only just managed to grasp what has happened – I sense that this 'boy' is commanding, wordlessly, that I should leap out of the window with him.

A feeling of nameless horror overcomes me. I gaze into the nothingness and say, 'But we will plunge into the abyss if we jump, won't we?' Suddenly a realisation flashes through my mind, and I ask, 'Are you the Star-Boy?'

I receive no answer, but I suddenly sense myriads of people and events from my past appearing like ghostly forms behind my back. They are reaching out towards me, trying to grasp me. I cry out, as though all the hounds of hell were after me:

'No, no! I don't care what happens, but I shall never never go back!'

The 'boy' and I leap out into space.

A moment of fear, of terror. But it does not last long. The arms of the 'boy' are wrapped around me so tightly that all my fear dissolves. And in the very moment in which my fear dissolves we stop falling. We stand there, motionless. But not on solid ground – we are standing in empty space.

And then we start to rise upwards again!

All my fear is gone. It is as though fear is something which I have never known. I am filled with bliss. I hear my own voice asking, again, 'Are you the Star-Boy?'

Again I receive no answer. But the arms of the 'boy' enclose me even more tightly.

We continue to rise upwards.

I hear my own voice again. It sounds jubilant and exultant this time: 'Are you the Star-Boy?'

A divine face approaches close to mine, and a feeling of bliss courses through my entire being, it is as though I am completely filled with a great 'yes' to everything in existence.

We continue to rise upwards, endlessly, into endless space.

In this wonderful dream too the *conditio sine qua non* of the spiritual path is made very clear: it is not enough to overcome the world. So long as the seeker is not willing to leap into the abyss, no matter what may come, the material world can still reach out and regain its power over the traveller standing at the boundary. On the other hand – and this is the truly wonderful side of the whole story – those who see the path and accept it as their own truth, going on unerringly through times of hardship, death; and happiness too, are always helped by Heaven.

This last is also a truth which is confirmed by every single one of these visionary dreams.

When I say this, however, the reader shouldn't misunderstand me: I don't mean that any freedom or responsibility is ever taken away from the seeker. Even the decision to leap into the abyss is a decision one must make alone, on one's own responsibility. But once one *has* taken the great leap one is then in harmony with Heaven, and one receives its support.

Before finishing my account of this particular dream I should also like to describe a strange coincidence which I became aware of later on: there is an old Chinese legend that on one day of the year, 7 July, the 'Divine Cowherd' or 'Star-Boy' crosses the Milky Way to consummate his marriage with the 'Spinner-Woman'.

In Japan 7 July is an important religious feast-day, even though it is an unofficial one. It is referred to as Tanabata Matsuri, and is held to celebrate the meeting of two stars, Kengyu and Shokuya, which only takes place once a year. Their names are written on colourful strips of paper or cloth which are then attached to bamboo poles set in people's gardens, and offerings of flowers and fruit are placed on altars in homes and temples in their honour.

I was born on 7 July.

The Sixth Dream (Six years after the previous dream)

I am sitting in a meadow, in the lotus position as is my usual practice, gazing out at the landscape in front of me. Green meadows stretch out all the way to the horizon. To my left, quite a long way away, is a gently winding river. To my right, in the background, is a huge mountain.

Suddenly I notice that the mountain is moving. It is coming closer, very slowly. I watch its approach in horror. Then I notice that the face of the mountain, which is getting closer and closer all the time, is a human face. It seems to be a man's face. At the same moment I sense, with a feeling of panic and fear, that this mountain desires physical union with me . . .

Even so, I remain where I am without moving, and when the mountain reaches me it simply dissolves into me.

I am paralysed with shock at the unbelievable event which has taken place, even though my outward form has not changed at all.

Then my gaze happens to fall on the river, and now my sense of horror is even greater than it was before, if that is possible, for the river has changed its course and is flowing towards me . . .

'It's going to swamp me completely, I shall drown!' I cry out in anguish.

But then I hear a voice speaking out of nowhere. 'Do not be afraid,' it says, 'look into it. You *are the river.' I look at the river. For a single second I see my own face within the water, and then the river too dissolves into me.*

I sit there in the meadow, no mountain to my right, no river to my left. Both of them are within me. And again the voice speaks:

'This is the way to unity, to perfection.'

I am reminded of the words of my Rōshi, or Master, in the Zen Buddhist monastery twenty years later, repeated again and again in *sanzen*:[1] 'You are it! You are it!' No matter what the 'it' is, Buddha or other beings or even inanimate objects, and no matter whether they belong to this earthly plane or other planes, you, I, we, everything, are it, for nothing else exists. According to Zen only the One, or the Whole, if you like, exists, and it is everything which exists, without exception. This truth is one aspect of the message of the above dream. Another aspect is the dissolution of the barriers between *yin* and *yang* (female and male), symbolised by the river and the mountain.

I was granted my seventh and last visionary dream about ten years after the dream about the river and the mountain. I can only assume that the cycle has ended with this last dream, for it was about something which is to take place far away from this earth, after my own physical death. I do not feel that it would be right to disclose anything more about this vision here, however, for it deals with events which do not have anything to do with my earthly existence.

Notes

1. *Sanzen* is a private dialogue between Master and disciple in Zen Buddhism, in which the Master gives instruction to disciple.

5

Transcendental Experiences

In the course of the last two years I have examined my conscience again and again, trying to decide whether it is right to write about the things which I experienced during my first fourteen years on my path back towards God. I am not talking about the visionary dreams which I described in the last chapter. The experiences to which I am referring now were truly extraordinary, of a type which have become exceedingly rare in our modern age.

The reply which I have received is very clear: the time has come to write an account of these events. Once again, I shall obey the command of the great taskmaster. He, or It, surely has a good reason for asking me to do this.

The most decisive experience of my entire life took place between the second visionary dream and the third, exactly five years after I had set out on my search for God, a search to which I devoted all of the passion and ardour of my heart.

It was a mild May night. I woke up suddenly with a violent and painful jerk, which shook my body to the core. A moment later the pain was gone. Although I hadn't yet realised it the 'jerk' had catapulted me out of my body. I was still lying on my back, but I was floating just above my physical body.

It is impossible for me to find the right words for what I saw and felt in the moments which followed, for our language contains no words adequate to describe such things. My bedroom was suffused in radiant, otherworldly light. A divine being, enveloped in what seemed to be robes of flowing silver, stood in the very centre of this light. His radiance was infinitely more intense than the light in which the room was bathed.

His beauty was beyond description. His aura, the aura of utter love, filled the room. These words are pale, miserably poor in comparison to that love. The energy and light which flowed out of this being were an expression of the Whole, the Undivided, the Divine.

Human beings living on the earthly plane of existence are not usually capable of seeing and feeling such things, and I can only assume that it was possible for me because I was no longer in my physical body.

I lay there motionlessly and watched the events unfold. Sitting at my side on my right was my mother, dressed in a simple white robe. I assumed that the luminous being had brought her with him – it had been four years since she had passed away. She stroked the right side of my neck gently, again and again, without stopping. I paid no attention to her, nor did I notice when or how she finally disappeared again. I only had eyes for the glory of the divine being standing there in front of me, towering all the way up to the ceiling.

He stood there without moving. The eyes in his wonderful face shone like suns, gazing into mine commandingly, full of solemn admonishment and warning. I returned his gaze, saying nothing.

Then he turned away from me, rose into the air and disappeared through the window. I was crestfallen. A great longing arose in me to follow where he had gone, and in the very moment that the desire arose I started to float up into the air, unhindered by the shackles of gravity, and I flew through the window. There was only one thought in my mind, to go to him, to be near him! I must have been carried up on the winds of my own despair and longing, for I reached my objective.

The radiant being paused in his flight and turned to face me. I gazed up at him, shyly, imploringly, offering myself up to him.

And then something happened which was so supernaturally beautiful that I scarcely dare to write it down: the serious, beautiful face of the being started to smile. No human words can come close to describing that smile; no words at all can describe what it is like when Heaven smiles. Love coursed through me like supernatural electricity. And then the radiant being took me in his arms, drew me close to him and kissed me on the lips.

Language is too poor a medium to express the bliss which was bestowed upon me in that moment. Anything which I could say would be no more than a kind of helpless stammering, and that would not be fitting.

A little later I found myself back home in my bed. My body was stiff and motionless, but my spirit was radiant and wakeful. After a while I was able to move my eyelids again, then life and warmth gradually returned to my entire body, starting at the tips of my fingers and toes and moving slowly upwards.

After one of her transcendental experiences the great Saint Teresa of Avila wrote, 'The next day my entire body hurt all over, it was as if I had dislocated all of my joints.'

The next day, it was Whit Sunday, I was in such extreme pain that I was unable to get up. I called the doctor, who said that my pleura were severely inflamed. It wasn't until two weeks later that I started to recover. Even so, this understandable physical reaction to my encounter with the beyond was nothing compared with the trials which were to come.

The part which my deceased mother had played in the vision as she had sat there and stroked my neck had seemed of secondary importance to me at the time, but as things turned out it was this 'treatment' which was the seed of the disaster which was to turn my outward life upside-down. And I know that this catastrophic transformation of my life and affairs was in accordance with the wishes of Heaven – it cannot be otherwise, for I had offered myself up to Heaven, asking it to do with me as it pleased.

A gland in my neck, on the side my mother had stroked, started to swell up disproportionately, and a mere three months later it was so large that Dr Sauerbruch had to remove it. Soon after the operation I was offered a very attractive part in a play. I was already feeling much better, and since I assumed that the strange inflammation in my neck had now been dealt with for good I accepted the part and signed the contract. The premiere of this play was on Christmas day. It was to be my last performance.

Several new lumps started to form in the place where the gland had been removed. I went to the well-known X-ray specialist, Professor Chaoul, and he gave me a course of radiation treatment. This treatment was doubly unsuccessful: it failed to halt the spread of the disease, and the powerful X-rays almost completely destroyed my vocal cords.

It was a while before I grasped the true extent of what had happened to me, and the realisation was like the onset of a slow, inexorable death: singing had become completely impossible, and I was unable to speak for more than five minutes without becoming painfully hoarse. My career was finished.

The disease continued unabated. I was in terrible pain all the time, and it was to be seven years before I was to be released from its cruel grip. Dr Sauerbruch finally decided to operate again. We both knew it was now a question of all or nothing, for the tumour had grown around a facial nerve, enclosing it.

The operation was a success, and I started to get better again. Or perhaps it would be more accurate to say that Heaven now permitted me to start getting better again.

The results of this divine intervention in my life were many and varied. However, since most of them were of a spiritual nature I should first like to describe a few of the more significant supernatural experiences which followed in the wake of this first encounter before I go on with my description of my spiritual journey, in order to make the path which I had to travel more comprehensible to the reader.

The second 'visitation' took place a mere three weeks after the first. Once again I woke up in the middle of the night with the same sudden jerk, although it wasn't painful as it had been the first time, and once again the entire room was filled with the same overpowering aura of love. But there was no light this time, everything remained dark. I couldn't see anything, I could only 'feel'.

The divine being which had released me from my physical body floated directly above me. I felt the heat of his breath on my face, and as this hot current filled my head his hands stroked my forehead, starting in the middle and stroking outwards towards my temples, ceaselessly.

I was overcome with a feeling of enormous bliss, but at the same time I was also very wide awake, and fully aware of everything which was taking place. After a while the procedure, or perhaps I should say the treatment, was once again terminated by the same divine, indescribable kiss, which penetrated every single layer of my being.

This was the last 'treatment' of this kind. The next meetings (three in all in the course of the next year) did not take place on our earthly plane. Nothing much 'happened' in the course of these meetings, at least, not in the normal sense of the word. But the indescribable state of bliss with which they were always accompanied made it clearer and clearer to me that our normal state of consciousness on this probationary planet we call Earth is actually a spiritual prison.

Seekers and scholars who know something about the Indian system of Kundalini Yoga or the Indian sages' doctrine of the seven energy centres or *chakras* in man's being, which must be activated in the course of his spiritual development, will have realised that the purpose of the 'treatment' to which I was subjected was the awakening of the two-petalled lotus *chakra* in the forehead, sometimes known as the third eye.

The lowest of these seven *chakras* is called *muladhara*, and it is located at the very bottom of the hollow spinal column. Coiled up like a sleeping snake in the *muladhara* is an energy referred to as *kundalini*. After one has travelled on the spiritual path for countless incarnations the *kundalini* starts its inexorable journey upwards through the other *chakras*. In his book *Raja Yoga*[1] Swami Vivekananda describes this process as follows:

> As it [the *kundalini* energy] rises upwards, step by step, one level of consciousness after another opens up.

The German scholar Werner Bohm has done the lay reader a great service by drawing up a brief, but very useful summary of Arthur Avalon's monumental work *Serpent Power*. The following description of the two-petalled lotus, which is the sixth *chakra*, is taken from this booklet of Bohm's:

> Each and every impulse on the part of the Awakened One issues from the luminous two-petalled lotus centre. The nature of this centre is described by its name, *ajna*, which can be translated as 'command', or 'instruction' or 'precept'. It is located approximately three quarters of an inch behind the forehead, directly between the eyebrows.
>
> The spiritual rebirth of the disciple takes place in this command-lotus, the *ajna chakra*.
>
> It can be compared to the spiritual rebirth which takes place in the holy night of the winter solstice in the sign of Capricorn. The Yogi becomes spiritually free, he becomes the master of everything within his body, all the way down to the four-petalled lotus. He becomes the master of the legion of beings which are within him. The brilliant light of realisation illuminates all the depths of his

being; the serpent has been overcome, the dragon has been conquered. From now on the only commands which have any validity for the Yogi are the commands which issue from this union with the divine cosmic spirit, the commands of true intuition.

A clear sense of discrimination and the ability to think logically are preconditions for the development of the two-petalled lotus. The centre in the forehead is brought into being by discrimination between Truth and the *maya* of appearances, and it is activated by right meditation.

Once the two-petalled lotus has been activated currents of energy start to flow from its radiant centre, along the arms and into the hands, setting the etherial body into motion. The higher Self is then born, in freedom, and comes into contact with beings from the spiritual world. The two-petalled lotus is the gateway to the spirit.[2]

All I should like to add to this exposition is that with the help of meditation it is possible to make the two-petalled lotus in the forehead vibrate in harmony with the seventh chakra, the thousand-petalled lotus in the crown of the head, thus connecting both of them with the very highest cosmic energies.

The next year was hard, and many very much harder years lay before me. Nonetheless, I knew that these trials were Heaven's will for it had given me the following message to comfort me on my stony path.

One night I was woken up by the sound of rolling thunder in my bedroom. I sat up in bed, terrified.

Floating before me in the middle of my bedroom was a snow-white cloud. And then three things happened at the same time, all within the space of a couple of seconds: There was a violent clap of thunder, a flash of lightning shot through the cloud, and at the same instant It spoke, saying, 'You shall be helped!'

I say that It 'spoke' for want of a better expression. It wasn't that a voice spoke the words, they were simply there in the room, an overwhelming, hard and powerful presence in the midst of the thunder and lightning. It was a shattering experience.

At the time that this happened I was still naïve enough to believe that the help which I was to be given would also make my earthly existence easier, but that was not to be. On the contrary, the help was only ever given when I was in the very direst of predicaments, at times when it seemed as though everything was finished and disaster was unavoidable. Then the shackles which bound me would simply fall away of their own accord (at the end of the years in which I had received the constant command that I should 'do nothing', for example).

Ten years later I was granted a truly great visitation. It took place at about the same time as my fifth visionary dream, which I described in the previous chapter.

On the night it happened I had spent the entire evening reading the dialogues of Socrates, which I loved very dearly. I turned off the light and went to sleep, but a while later I woke up suddenly with a fright. The earthly part of our beings is always afraid when the unknown approaches.

'His' aura was there, filling the room. But this time it wasn't the aura of love, which I already knew so well, it was the aura of wisdom. It was indescribable. It filled everything, penetrated everything, and at the same time I was enfolded within it. I knew, without a doubt, that I was in the presence of Wisdom itself.

I lay in bed facing the wall, unable to move a muscle. The room remained dark. I felt myself being turned over gently by the presence, so that I came to lie on my back. And then Wisdom kissed me. It was a powerful, passionate kiss, that touched the very core of my being.

In the very moment that the overwhelming bliss of that kiss filled me I suddenly became aware of the fact that I could not and should not stay here with this being of Wisdom for too long. I knew we would soon have to part and go our separate ways again, and at this realisation I felt a sharp pain deep within me. At the same time, however, in that moment of union, I also sensed that the being of Wisdom was experiencing exactly the same pain as I was. (To paraphrase Zen: when you weep it is the universe which is weeping.) And so we parted, in pain and bliss, both at the same time.

It is not really possible to communicate the deeper reality of experiences of this nature to those who are still living on the earthly plane of existence without falsifying what has taken place. It may be possible to describe the state of consciousness in comprehensible words, it may sound simple and even straightforward, but nonetheless the very process of description distorts the reality of it. It is best to remain silent.

This visitation was the last. From that moment onwards I was alone. This too was a trial which I had to endure, for the human mind has a tendency to hope that moments of bliss will never end, and it has to learn to accept and endure the end of something to which it has become attached when the end comes.

From another point of view, however, I was not alone, for the divine spark which is to be found deep within each and every one of us had been awakened. It slowly became stronger and brighter, until, finally, it illuminated my entire inner world.

No one is really alone so long as they are aware that 'It' is within them. Then, no matter where one is, no matter how profane and worldly the situation, all one needs to do is to turn and look within and one is once again united with the Source.

There is only one prerequisite: one must continue with the practice of one's daily meditation exercises, otherwise everything which one has gained will start to fade away again. It is not possible to stop and rest once one has 'attained' some small success. Another fatal error is thinking that one has 'got' It, in the sense of possessing It, for It cannot ever be possessed.

The seeker who continues unerringly and untiringly becomes more and more humble the further he advances on the path. Ultimately, he must become Nothingness itself, for only when he is utterly empty is it possible for Heaven to use him as a tool. Then, even amid the hustle and bustle of the world, his innermost being will remain untouched, and when he acts he is no longer the 'doer' – the action simply happens.

In the tradition of Taoism it is said that such a one becomes 'one with his dust'. But, one could add, the emptiness which he has become wears a kingly robe, even though it is invisible.

At this time Zen had not yet come to play a central role in my spiritual development. That was to come later. For the time being India and the Indian system of Yoga were an inexhaustible source of wisdom and inspiration on the path. And this is still the case today, despite my profound experiences on the path of Zen, or rather, *because* of these experiences. India was the original source of the teachings which were later to become Zen, including the doctrine of Non-Being and of the world as *maya* or illusion. Zen Buddhism is simply the strictest and straightest way of attaining union with the Original Source. It is a mercilessly direct path, one which does not permit any detours whatsoever.

The next experience which I wish to describe was very different from the previous ones. There was no encounter between two beings this time: 'It' simply spoke through me, using me as Its mouthpiece. This experience was not in the least bit blissful; on the contrary, it was extremely frightening.

It happened in July 1950. By this time I had long since given up hoping that the beyond would reveal itself to me once again, for I knew that there was nothing left to be revealed. If it did contact me again, I was certain that it would no longer be in the form of a personal encounter, and as it turned out I was right.

It was the middle of the night. I suddenly sat up bolt upright in bed, wide awake, even though I had been fast asleep a moment before. 'It' was speaking. There was no thunder or lightning this time, in fact there was nothing in the room at all. The voice was speaking from deep within me.

'It' spoke unbelievably quickly. I had to grasp what it was saying in the space of a few seconds, for I was certain that nothing would be repeated.

Being used as a channel in this way is a very strange and alarming experience. I listened breathlessly, doing my best both to understand what the voice was saying and to memorise it word for word. It is essential that the vessel used by the beyond should remain absolutely alert at moments like this, for if one hesitates, even for so much as a fraction of a second, 'It' will be gone forever, and one can be sure that the opportunity will never be repeated.

This is what the voice said:

> I am Existence. I am everything which is encompassed by Being.
>
> Being is divided into two: into the Being which is both there and not there, and the Being which *is*, and which cannot exist without the Being which is both there and not there.
>
> And then there is also the third Being: the Being which can only be revealed through the Being which *is*. This third Being can only be known by being manifested. But that which is then known is nothing other than the Being of the *manifest* world. And its lights, suns and stars are the manifest Being of the present.
>
> You must know this, in order that you may also understand that Non-Being exists.

Paper and pencil lay on my bedside table. I grabbed them as soon as the voice had finished, and wrote everything down at the same breakneck speed with which 'It' had spoken. This old piece of paper, yellowed with age, is lying in front of me on my desk now as I write. I haven't changed a single word.

What was the purpose of this nocturnal 'lesson'? What was it that 'It' wanted of me?

First of all, it was a signpost pointing to that which was going to come, to the realisation that Non-Being exists. And, amazingly, the voice of Existence which spoke to me also made it clear that the only way to know Non-Being is through manifest Being. This means that we live on this plane in order to know and realise.

Manifest Being, our universe, was created by the 'second' Being, 'that which cannot exist without the Being which is both there and not there', which one could also refer to as Creative Being or God the Creator.

It thus becomes clear that all of us and everything which is, right the way down to the very last blade of grass, are an inseparable part of the Original Source of all Being, no matter whether we know it or not, no matter whether we behave in accordance with this truth or not. There are no exceptions.

Or, as Zen would say, 'From the very beginning, all beings are Buddhas.'[3] (The Buddha referred to here is the Cosmic, or Original Buddha, not the historical Buddha.)

This is something which all the great enlightened ones of all ages, races and religions have known.

In the course of time I became one with the revelation which I received in those unforgettable moments. Now I live in, from and with this Being all the time, every single moment of my life. In actual fact everyone does this, for they cannot help doing so, but the majority are unconscious of it. It is the will of Divine Being that its creations should learn to become conscious and realise the true nature of their existence.

Of course, the next obvious question is, how can one attain to this realisation? How can one learn to experience it? For it must be *experienced*; understanding it intellectually is not enough.

Before I try to answer this question I would like to draw the reader's attention to an important sentence in the message which I received eighteen years ago today, a phrase which I have never been able to forget since then: 'And its lights, suns and stars are the manifest Being of the *present*.'

I have stressed the word 'present' here for a particular reason. The obvious implication of this statement is that other universes have already existed before ours, and that others will arise after ours passes away and disappears into Primordial Being.

This insight is nothing new in India – it has been an integral part of Indian cosmology and the Indian way of looking at life and the world for thousands of years. Nothing was static in the ancient Indian view of the world, everything was in a constant state of flux. Each cycle of the creation and destruction of the universe was referred to as a *kalpa*, and each of these *kalpas* was divided into a large number of smaller units of time referred to as *manvantaras*. For the Indian of 4,500 years ago the answers to the fundamental questions of human existence were very simple and self-evident. Modern man on the other hand, with his rational mind, is incapable of grasping these concepts simply by thinking about them, and if he does manage to begin to understand them he finds them outlandish and strange.

How did the Indians arrive at these insights into reality? They are the legacy of the ancient Indian seers and saints, whose close connection to the divine plane of existence would seem all but incredible to us today. It is our great good fortune that we have records of what these great Masters said, written down either by the Masters themselves or by their disciples. These records, from the Vedas to the Upanishads, many of which are written in the form of dialogues, are a magnificent, unparalleled document of the overwhelming fruits of constant contemplation and meditation.

In a very early Vedic text, for instance, we find the statement:

> The world does end, but in such a way that certain energies are left over after it ends. These energies are then the root, the seed from which the world is then born again. If it were not so we would have an effect without a cause.

In another passage the same idea is explained in a little more detail. The energies of the last universal cycle, say the Vedas, do form the roots of the next cycle, and to a certain extent everything which has been in the old cycle is thus repeated in the new one. On the other hand, something is added to the new cycle which was not there before: a new state of consciousness, as the object of new experience and realisation.

A planet such as our earth does not necessarily have to 'live' for the entire length of a *kalpa*, but it is very important that all of the beings living on such a planet should reach the state of liberation or enlightenment before the planet 'dies'; if they do not manage this they must then repeat the entire process of spiritual evolution right from the start, on another planet which is still in the early phases of its own development.

In India and China literature which refers to both past and future universes is so common that it cannot be ignored. These texts speak of these things in the same matter-of-fact way in which we would talk about what life was like during the Renaissance, or what it might be like in the twenty-first century.

In this context I should like to quote a delightful passage from Erwin Rousselle's book of collected essays, *The Buddhist Visual Arts in China – Their Meaning and Significance.*[4] The Buddhas of the Three Ages to whom Rousselle refers in this passage are Buddha Dipamkara (literally 'The Lighter of the Lamp'), the Buddha of the Past Age, who is said to have lived to an age of 100,000 years four unmeasurably long ages ago; Sakyamuni Buddha (Gautama), the Buddha of the Present Age and Teacher of Gods and Men; and Maitreya, the present Bodhisattva and Buddha of Love and Friendship, the Buddha of the Future Age, whom Sakyamuni Buddha named as his successor.

> If one examines the concept of the 'Buddhas of the Three Ages', if one plumbs the true meaning of the *Lotus Sutra*, that glorious vision in which the Original Buddha of a long forgotten universal cycle, Prabhutaratna, arises once again from the womb of the ages and countless Buddhas from many far-distant worlds illuminate the depths of endless space, then one cannot help being moved by one of the most noble and sublime themes of Buddhist philosophy: the concept of eternal Truth, a Truth which encompasses everything, which is always valid, everywhere, without exception – *philosophia perennis.* Buddhism, and particularly Mahayana Buddhism, is utterly at home in the vast expanses of time and space, more so than any other religion.
>
> In a world in which the gaze of the majority does not rise beyond the dust at their feet the spirit of Buddhism is like a flaming beacon in the darkness, illuminating the peaks of eternity; it draws our gaze up into the heights, from where the birth and death of entire universes seem like nothing more than the momentary twinkling of a spark struck on the stones of the path at night by the staff of the Universal Dharma, held in the hand of the Original Buddha on his pilgrimage[. . .].
>
> And yet at the same time we hear the soft strains of that comforting, eternal song – whence it comes nobody knows – singing to us of the path, telling us that there is meaning in this procession of twinkling sparks and the seemingly endless journey through the night, telling us that they make it possible for the pilgrim to reach

> his goal, and for the journey to have an end; for at the end of the journey the last spark in the procession will be like a morning star, the harbinger of the new, eternal day, the day whose sublime light shall know no darkness[. . .].
>
> These Buddhas encompass the entire expanse of time, past, present and future: flanking Sakyamuni, 'The Teacher of Gods and Men' and herald of Nirvana in the centre we find Maitreya, 'The Friend' and incarnation of love on the one side, and Dipamkara, 'The Lighter of the Lamp' and embodiment of light on the other. Dipamkara and Maitreya reach out into Sakyamuni's domain from the depths of the past and the future, Dipamkara symbolising the initial setting of the scene (the lighting of the lamp at the beginning of time) and Maitreya the attainment of ultimate perfection (the universal, liberating love at the end of time). Sakyamuni, however, encompasses both of them, and it is for this reason that we find him enthroned in the centre in Buddhist temples. His position is in the centre of time, the present age, and his role is to enlighten this age and point the way to its liberation.
>
> This monumental vision of Eternity, in which all worlds and ages are as nothing, makes it possible for the spirit to feel at home in the universe, bestowing the gift of detachment and *sancta indifferentia*, while the great, echoing promise of freedom awakens enthusiasm, vigour and the spirit of love, calling everyone to take part in the task of liberation and filling each ephemeral moment with the holy aura of Eternity.

It is easy to dismiss these ideas as 'mere' mythology, but they are more than that. They are the profound expression of a heart overwhelmed by its own living realisation and overcome by the influx of the unknown, for the author is a man who has experienced that of which he writes. Erwin Rousselle and I often used to exchange stories, and in one of these conversations he told me about a decisive mystical experience which he had had in the course of his long sojourn in China. This experience took place while he was meditating on the *kōan* given to him and the other monks in the monastery by his Master, and it was very similar to another experience I had.

The amazing discoveries which are now being made in the sciences of physics and astrophysics are also very significant, even though these discoveries still have, for the moment, the status of scientific hypothesis rather than proven fact. What is significant is not only that new picture of the universe which is being revealed by these sciences is very similar to the religious cosmology of the sages of ancient India; the scientists are also coming to exactly the same conclusions about the ultimate nature of reality. Of course, the scientists and the sages express their insights in very different languages, but that is only because the paths on which they are travelling are different – it doesn't alter the essential nature of the truths which they are expressing. Western science is moving closer and closer to a meeting with the doctrines of the ancient Indian sages, which have never lost their validity in the East. And even though it will not be possible to go beyond the point at which they meet it is a meeting which is going to bring great illumination to our civilisation.

How does one arrive at the insight that 'from the very beginning all beings are Buddhas'? It is an insight which must be attained by dint of experience, and the ultimate outcome of this experience is union with the Cosmic Buddha, or, in Christian terms, union with God. In my own experience, which is confirmed by the teachings of Zen, the process of union with the 'Being which is both there and not there' results in the experience of enlightenment, in which one sees that all beings are That, or It, and that they always have been, from the very beginning. However, I should also stress that even though such an experience of enlightenment (called *satori* in Japan) can sometimes take place at breathtaking speed, like a bolt of lightning from the blue, it is always preceded by a very long process of inner growth and maturation.

In the Indian tradition it is said that aeons must pass before the individual can finally return to the state of union with Original Being. This means that everyone must pass through the entire spectrum of possible experiences, both blissful and terrible. Only then, when they have reached the sum total of all experience, which is ultimately equivalent to Non-Being, can one return once again to the plane of Being itself.

Looked at this way the process is like an equation, an equation which balances perfectly. The seeker who attains to enlightenment can no longer be measured by human standards, even though he lives within the confines of a human body like everyone else. Even after the experience of enlightenment, however, the seeker must perform yet one more task before he can attain to the ultimate state of balance. This task is the last, and at the same time the most difficult of all: The seeker must come to accept the *non-existence* of even his most supernaturally blissful experiences, his encounters with divine beings who are the guardians, planners and rulers of 'manifest Being', and he must let go of his attachment to these experiences and leave them behind him. This is the last great test.

Before one can return to the Original Source (and no matter how hard and sincerely one strives there is no way of saying when this will happen) every last vestige of duality must be destroyed. Even the division between God – Being itself – and the seeker must be broken down and dissolved, so that the seeker is God and God is the seeker.

That is the goal. The journey to this goal is very long, and at first it seems overwhelmingly hard. But when the seeker realises that to travel on this path means to act in accordance with the will of his own true being, his original will, so to speak, everything becomes very much easier. In accepting his own original will the seeker takes the first step towards living consciously. Living consciously means watching and observing oneself all the time, alert to every detail. 'Know thyself', the motto inscribed above the entrance of that most famous of ancient Greek temples, is just as essential an axiom today as it was then.

To live consciously, watching one's own thoughts and actions alertly and critically, is to embark on a journey of discovery which is more full of unexpected and unbelievable adventures and revelations than anything ever experienced by the most daring and intrepid explorers of the outward world. For the traveller in search of himself soon discovers, to his dismay or delight, that he himself is everything which is, positive and negative. He is both evil itself in its purest form and, at the same time, the very incarnation of goodness and love. He carries the entire universe within himself, he *is* the universe, and there is thus nothing, potentially at least, which he could not be.

When the seeker reaches this point he must then make a fateful decision: he must decide which of the two paths he is going to take. The man of knowledge becomes his own guide.

This has nothing to do with the normal concept of being 'good', which involves no more than living in accordance with the accepted precepts of duty, honesty and ethics and doing one's best to avoid coming into conflict with the laws of one's country. This kind of goodness is simply the basis, without which civilised life on this planet would not be possible, and the true seeker will have made the decision to live in accordance with these precepts many, many years before he is faced with the decision I am talking about here. This latter decision is of a much higher order, for it has to do with the stony path back to God.

Since the publication of my first book I have often been asked if it is necessary to travel to Japan in order to attain to the state of 'unity' or 'enlightenment' which I described in my account, and one of the main reasons I decided to write this second book was because I wanted to try to clear up misconceptions of this type once and for all.

No one needs to leave his own country or give up his home or his profession in order to embark on the great homeward journey. Being is omnipresent and eternal, and to think that one must go somewhere else in order to find it is to reduce it to something small and petty. It is always to be found wherever one happens to be, at any time. All one needs to do is to open one's heart to it.

It is certainly true that desires are the greatest enemy of the seeker and the greatest obstacle on the path. But in order to rid oneself of one's desires, which is a slow and difficult task demanding constant, tireless work and sacrifice, there is no need to travel to another country or to enter into a monastery. It is the law of *karma* that everyone is exactly where they need to be, and the right place to start with the great task of self-transformation is thus wherever one happens to be right now. For no matter whether we are willing to admit it or not, the biggest surprises are usually to be encountered in those situations and surroundings in which we have learned to take everything for granted.

Seekers who are honest, strict and merciless with themselves always receive help on the path. The divine spark within, awakened by their tireless efforts, will guide them on their way and draw their attention to the seemingly endless faults which must be recognised and obliterated before realisation can take place.

Notes

1. Swami Vivekananda, *Raja Yoga: The Yoga of Conquering Internal Nature*, Advaita Ashram Centre, 1970.
2. Werner Bohm, *Chakras, Lebenskräfte und Bewußtseinszentren* (Chakras, Life Forces and Consciousness Centres), O. W. Barth Verlag. No English translation of this work appears to be available.
3. Hakuin, *Song of Meditation*.

4. Erwin Rousselle, *Vom Sinn der Buddhistischen Bildwerke in China*, Gentner Verlag, Darmstadt. According to the British Museum Catalogue no English translation of this work exists.

6

Experience and Realisation

As far as the actual practice of *zazen* meditation is concerned I have already provided detailed and comprehensive instructions in my first book, and there is thus no need to repeat them here. I refer those readers who have not yet had any experience with this type of meditation to that book. The instructions provided there include descriptions of the sitting position and of the first breathing exercises which one needs to learn in order to get off to a good start.

However, I would nonetheless like to take this opportunity to answer a question which is often put to me regarding the practice of *zazen*. The question has to do with the proper sitting position for *zazen*, either *kekka* or *hanka* (very similar to the lotus posture of yoga), which is extremely uncomfortable for many Westerners, especially at first: are one's efforts doomed to failure right from the start if one is unable to sit in this posture?

The answer to this question depends entirely on the reason for the alleged inability. Is it simply laziness, a disinclination to put up with the pain caused by the posture at first? If this is the case then the answer is yes, dispensing with the proper sitting posture will create formidable obstacles to spiritual progress. I would be the first to admit that the pain can be extreme, and that the process of getting used to the posture can take a long time; nonetheless, healthy people simply have to learn to bear it, for this posture has proved its inestimable value in thousands of years of practice. Not only does it provide the body with a firm foundation to rest upon, ensuring that all its parts are in the optimum position for meditation, it also makes sure that the seeker's functioning as a spiritual 'transmitter' and 'receiver' is made as easy and effective as possible. It is also, relatively speaking, the best possible posture for awakening the functioning of the *chakras* or 'lotus centres'.

However, it is another case altogether if the seeker is prevented from sitting in the posture by illness or some physical disability. That is karma. The first thing which someone in an unusual situation like this must do, and this cannot be repeated too often, for it is extremely important, is to *accept* the condition rather than complaining about one's fate.

If the acceptance is unconditional (without any hidden motivations, such as the hope that Heaven will do such and such if one makes an outward show of willingness to accept one's fate) then this act of surrender can become the first important step, or even the first leap, in the right direction. The first thing to do is thus to accept one's fate. The next step for seekers who are afflicted with a physical disability is to find a position (sitting on a chair) which makes it possible for them to keep their back and spine absolutely straight and perpendicular. This is very, very important – the back *must* be straight. This position must then be practised regularly, until it is possible to sit in it comfortably and easily for longer periods. Then the real work can begin.

But what about people who are completely unable to sit, even in a chair or in bed, and whose disability makes it necessary for them to lie down all the time? For them, normal yoga exercises are impossible. They must take a completely different approach, even though the first and most important step, accepting one's *karma*, is still the same.

Once this inner process of acceptance has been completed bedridden seekers should concentrate their energy on spiritual exercises of which they are capable, not wasting their time worrying about positions and postures which are in any case completely out of the question.

Prayer is a great help. Not prayers repeated by rote, but a silent, inner prayerfulness. Done properly, prayer is really a kind of meditation.

How does one pray properly? Here too, the right position is important. Lie down flat on your back – the bed or mattress should be firm and flat – placing a small cushion at the back of your neck. This position ensures that the spine is as straight as possible so that the breath can flow freely and without obstructions. Then fold your hands over your lower abdomen (without exerting any undue pressure), roughly at the level of the navel, with the left hand resting in the palm of the right and the thumbs together in the same way as in the normal *zazen* posture.

The next step is a breathing exercise. Inhale as deeply as possible through the nose, slowly and without forcing it, directing the flow of the breath gently downwards into the solar plexus. Then exhale again, just as gently and slowly. This should be repeated several times. You may find it a little difficult at first, but if you persist patiently for a few weeks the day will come when you find that you are doing it right automatically.

This process of directing the breath down into the solar plexus is a preparation for the actual prayer, which must also be directed into the solar plexus. The solar plexus is the seat of the third *chakra*, also referred to as the ten-petalled lotus. This is the point at which all the unconquered desires from our previous incarnations enter into our present lives, bubbling up from the depths of our innermost memories (psychologists would say, from our unconscious or subconscious). And remember, all evils, even the smallest and most 'insignificant', are caused by desire.

The prayer which you now direct downwards into this centre is a prayer to your own divine Self, which is both the sum total of all your countless previous experiences in countless incarnations, and, on a deeper level, the original source of your existence: God.

It would be a mistake to assume that people who suffer from illnesses or physical disabilities which make it impossible for them to move about are free of what we refer to as 'greed'. They are not; their faults, small and large, simply adapt themselves to the new situation. Take the desire to go for a walk in the park, for instance, something which is perfectly normal for a healthy person. For someone who is bedridden this simple desire can be a source of unbearable torture, and this torture is nothing other than desire.

The prayer which you address to the depths of your own being should thus go something like this: 'My True Self, release me from the desire for . . . ' This prayer, spoken inwardly, should have all the force of a command. Remember, it is *your* self which you are speaking to, even if it is your divine self.

After this you should then turn your prayers away from your

own depths and towards Heaven, or Universal Being. As everyone experienced in praying knows, the best way to do this is to direct one's thoughts upwards through the *chakra* in the forehead, the two-petalled lotus. The process is rather like transmitting a message with a radio transmitter, and if your thoughts are pure you can be sure that they will be received.

This time the prayer should be a prayer of humbleness, asking for help and support in your work on your own liberation. And remember, no matter where one is, no matter whether one is healthy, sick, moral or immoral, it is always possible to contact God. Even if one were in the darkest depths of hell the call would still be heard – there are no barriers which are strong enough to hold back the cry of a heart longing for God. All one needs to do is utter it.

At this point I must stress something very important, which applies to all seekers on the path, both the healthy who are able to work tirelessly on their own development and those who are hampered by sickness and disability: one should never ever hope for or expect either success or any kind of reward for one's efforts to attain purity and realisation. That is the worst form of greed, and one of the most essential things which the seeker on the path to God must understand.

The only acceptable reason for doing what is good is for the sake of goodness itself, just as the work on one's own growth towards purity must be done for its own sake, and not for gain of any sort. The seeker who is motivated by the desire for recognition, even if that recognition is divine and not human, forfeits his reward. The only path which leads to God is a path of unconditional and choiceless action.

Whenever the subject of the role of *karma* in human life comes up I cannot help thinking of all the innocent people who have suffered in concentration camps, and of those who must serve time in prisons for crimes which they never committed. This is a particularly cruel fate, one which can be so shattering to its victims that it can be enough to literally drive them insane. At a single blow everything good which they have ever believed in seems to have been destroyed: justice, humanity and the triumph of goodness and honesty over evil.

But even when everything seems utterly hopeless, when no one but you yourself know that you are really innocent and all the evidence speaks against you, even then you still have one last hope: God. It doesn't matter if you have never had any interest in religion, for it is a hope which everyone is born with, and, in desperate situations like this which shake us to the very core, our hope in God is always awakened. It is simply not possible, we think, that He can allow such a monstrous injustice, and we pray to him for help.

And yet God is silent. He allows the injustice without so much as a word. Where is He, why doesn't He help? Explaining the spiritual context of such seemingly unjust suffering to someone in a situation like this is not an easy task.

What is *karma*? It is simply the law of cause and effect. Whatever happens to us, good or bad, is the result of our actions in past incarnations. In each life we 'work off' some of our past *karma*, laying with our actions and attitudes the foundations of our future fate. Thus, according to the law of *karma*, the innocent person languishing in prison is not actually the victim of injustice, he is simply working off past *karma*.

On the plane of the cosmic memory, where all the actions of each individual person are recorded, mercy, compassion and 'fair' judgement do not have any meaning. The only thing which counts there is the law of balance.

In our case in point, that of the innocent prisoner driven to desperation by the apparent injustice of what has happened to him, an understanding of the law of *karma* can be a great help. If he can learn to see that the error of the earthly court in fact represents a just sentence passed on him by his own *karma* for wrongs committed in past lives, knowing full well that Eternal Justice knows no statute of limitations, he may find it much easier to bear his fate.

However, it is also possible to go one step further: if the prisoner manages to overcome his own limitations by accepting his lot with a glad heart and actually welcoming the punishment for the unknown crime he will find that he has reached an important turning-point on the spiritual path. I don't mean to say that he will suddenly be released from prison, although that is something which *can* happen in the course of this process of inner trials and growth; the turning-point which I am talking about doesn't have anything to do with the outside world. It is a process of inner realisation, of seeing the Truth. The initial despair and suffering of the seeker who manages to reach this point are replaced by a bliss which is beyond description. Heaven rewards such lonely conquerors richly, showering them with sublime happiness and joy.

Unfortunately, most people who have decided to start working on themselves are usually too impatient. They want to see 'successes' as soon as possible, otherwise they feel that Heaven hasn't taken note of their efforts. It is a strange paradox: nobody objects to the long years of training and study which are necessary for most professions (in the case of academic professions this period of study never really ends), nobody finds it strange that famous actors, writers and artists have to sacrifice their lives to their vocations, but everyone seems to expect instant success on the spiritual path, which is the most difficult and arduous undertaking in the world. It is extremely important to nip such wildly unrealistic expectations in the bud, for they present a very serious obstacle to progress.

A frequent objection raised at this point, even by very well-educated people, is that 'one often reads that it (enlightenment) happens terribly suddenly, just like that, even in the case of children . . . '.

It is important to point out that what is often described as 'sudden enlightenment' in Zen literature is not something which is ever attained suddenly, or even quickly, not even in the case of children who become enlightened. It is always the result of hard, untiring spiritual work, in many many incarnations.

Not even the Buddha of our age, Gautama, was an exception to this rule. Even in his last incarnation he had to devote many lonely years of struggle and unbelievable sacrifice to ascetic exercises and meditation before he could attain the perfect, cosmic enlightenment which finally made him a World Teacher.

Bodhidharma, who brought Buddhism to China from India in the year A.D. 520, and who lived a life of almost inconceivably strict asceticism himself, made no bones whatsoever about the discipline necessary on the path. When Eka, a very wise and scholarly monk who was later to become his successor came to him for instruction, under exceedingly difficult circumstances, Bodhidharma is reported to have said the following words to him:

> The incomparable doctrine of Buddha can only be understood after a long and hard training, through bearing that which is hardest to bear and through the practice of that which is the hardest to practice. People of limited virtue and wisdom whose hearts are shallow and full of self-conceit are not capable of realising the truth of Buddha. All the efforts of such people are certain to be wasted and worthless.

There is no end to the examples one could cite of the extreme hardships which the great Chinese Masters, and the Japanese Masters who were to follow them, voluntarily bore for the sake of their great goal. But even such examples, legion though they may be, are not enough to convince those who stubbornly cling to the occasional reports of 'sudden enlightenment', and who are not capable of understanding that such breakthroughs can only be the culmination of endless years of rigorous spiritual discipline. This discipline is an absolute precondition, there is no way around it.

If this were not the case there would be nothing to prevent the fortuitously enlightened individual from leading a dissolute and worldly life, for he would not have the maturity which one needs in order to be able to cope with the ultimate experience.

Even after their enlightenment all the great Masters have lived very simple, strictly ascetic lives. Nor is it enough to dive into the sea of enlightenment once only, and then never again. After the first experience of enlightenment the connection with Eternal Wisdom must be refreshed every day thereafter, in order to ensure that it is never ever broken, not even for a single day. This does not mean that the actual moment of 'contact' with the Original Source, something which only takes place after a long period of incredibly strenuous and sincere spiritual exercises, is repeated again and again; it simply means that the seeker's connection with this eternal and absolute plane of Being must be deepened and made more complete and perfect by daily meditation.

It is only through this ceaseless process of deepening one's connection with the Absolute that one is able to become, and remain, a vehicle for 'Him', or 'It'. The objective is not one's own happiness and bliss but to create a stage on which He can manifest Himself in this world, no matter how small that stage may seem to be in relative terms. Becoming a vehicle for the Absolute means that although one still thinks, one is no longer the thinker, and although one still acts one is no longer the doer. The confidence and detachment from worldly matters which are associated with this state of consciousness are something which can only be fully understood by those who are themselves in the same state.

I have already described my own mystical experiences in the previous chapter, although as far as I was concerned they were not really mystical in the sense of being mysterious or fantastic, they simply went beyond our normal limited concept of reality.

For all those who still doubt the words of the great mystics I can say from my own experience that there really is more to reality than meets the eye, and that divine beings are just as real as we are. Even so, they too are not the ultimate, they are simply shining signposts along the way, pointing towards the true Ultimate, which is nameless, formless, immaterial Non-Being.

Why is it that Zen Buddhism dismisses such mystical experiences? This is an attitude which goes all the way back to Sakyamuni (another name for the Buddha of the present age, Gautama). Almost all Western commentators have interpreted it incorrectly, and since I have experienced both sides of this particular coin on the path to enlightenment, both mysticism and Zen, I should like to say a few words on the subject:

When he was asked directly Buddha never made any attempt to say that gods and divine beings do not exist, nor did he dispute the existence of Brahman, which one could also refer to as Original Being. In essence his answer to such questions was as follows. The desire for knowledge of this kind is of no help in the attainment of liberation. It simply distracts the attention of the seeker from the pure path, whose purpose is the extinguishing of greed and desire. Only tireless effort on the part of the seeker leads to freedom from suffering and thus to Nirvana.

Nirvana is something which seekers who have freed themselves of all desire can experience here on this earthly plane. It is not a place, it is a state.

When Buddha spoke of his own earlier incarnations he often mentioned encounters with divine beings, or gods. According to one story which he is reported to have told his disciples, he also had such an encounter in his last incarnation on this Earth, as Guatama. He was meditating under the bodhi tree shortly after attaining perfect enlightenment, and his spirit was inclined to remain silent and not proclaim the *dharma* to others. Seeing this, Brahma Sahampati came down from heaven to ask Buddha to proclaim the *dharma* for the sake of those beings whose hearts were almost free of worldly desires.

Finally, in order to provide an illustration of the way in which Buddha himself explains his reasons for remaining silent in response to such questions, I should like to cite a passage from a dialogue which he is recorded to have had with the venerable Malunkyaputta:[1]

Malunkyaputta: Lord, as I was meditating here the following thought arose within me: 'With regard to the world's eternity or its transience, its finiteness or its infiniteness, and also with regard to the relationship of life to the physical body and the fate after death of one who has attained perfection, on all these subjects the Tathagata has remained silent. This troubles me, and I shall thus ask him to speak on these subjects' . . .

Buddha: . . . The way of virtue is not served by the opinion that the world is eternal, nor by the opposite opinion, nor by the other opinions which you have brought forward. It may be that one or the other of these opinions is true, but what is certain is this: Birth, old age and death, sorrow, misery, pain, grief and despair exist in this world, and I teach the way to end them in this very life.

Thus accept that which I have not explained as unexplained, and heed that which I have explained.

That which I have not explained I have not explained because it does not serve the perfect way of virtue, because it does not lead to renunciation, nor to freedom from passion, nor to the ending of suffering, nor to calmness, nor to higher wisdom, nor to enlightenment, nor to Nirvana.

Buddha simply rejected all questions which had no relevance for the spiritual development of the questioner and his efforts to extinguish his passions and attain enlightenment. For the root of these questions is desire, the desire that reality should be as the questioner wishes it to be, and there can be no liberation where there is desire, be it ever so sublime and subtle.

Buddha made it very clear that the time would come when the seeker on the path would have to do without the help of divine beings. Only then, he said, would it be possible for him to attain complete freedom. However, in saying this he was not denying the existence of these beings, he was simply pointing out that those who are on the path of awakening to the Truth must abandon all supports, including these. And when he said that the seeker should abandon *all* supports he did not exclude himself from this statement.

I know that the superhuman sacrifices which Buddha demanded of his disciples will seem almost incomprehensible to many readers, but one should remember that these disciples were not just anybody. They were the spiritual élite of the India of the Vedas and the Upanishads, a country which was the womb of the most advanced spiritual culture which has ever existed on this planet. His disciples were highly educated and cultured, and even before they had come to gather at his feet they had already lived lives of strict asceticism and discipline. If Buddha had not been the most perfect liberated and enlightened one, and if they had not recognised him as such, it is hardly likely that these men would have bowed down before him.

These conditions were laid down for seekers who were already very advanced on the path of liberation, and they were very different from the precepts with which we are more familiar, laid down by Jesus the Christ. The disciples around Buddha understood what he meant, and they immediately transformed his teachings into spiritual practice and realisation.

The Masters of Zen Buddhism are the direct successors of Buddha, and the path of Zen is Buddha's 'direct' path to realisation, in its purest and strictest form. The Zen tradition is still alive today, in a few small, out-of-the-way monasteries. But more of that later.

Of course, no Master, not even a Zen Master, can prevent his monks from having visions and other mystical experiences in the course of their strict ascetic training. As far as the Zen Master is concerned, however, such experiences are, at the very best, nothing more than neutral signs of progress and indications that the monk in question is practising hard.

The rather deprecating Zen name for such experiences is *makyō*, or 'disturbances'. Before their enlightenment many Zen Masters had *makyō* of such intensity that they were all but defenceless against them. The reason for Zen's deprecating, dismissive attitude is that these experiences are of no help to the seeker in his development. On the contrary, he must exert himself to become free of them if he wishes to progress any further.

These 'disturbances' are not the same as the experiences with which we are familiar from the accounts of the mystics of India and the West. They are not considered to be helpful on the path: they are simply side-effects.

In 1963, after I had spent several months practising *zazen* in the Zen monastery of my Rōshi in Japan, I had an experience of this sort myself. When one sits in *zazen* one's eyes are half open and half closed, and one day I suddenly started seeing a procession of venerable figures passing before me, as if a relief had appeared on the white wall I was facing and had come to life. I sensed that they were Masters from the past. They were dressed in the long priestly robes of their time, and their heads were shaven. Almost all of them looked Chinese, and many had long, flowing beards, some of them black and some white. They walked slowly, and with great dignity, not paying any attention to me.

As soon as I became aware of the phenomenon I closed my eyes in an attempt to banish the illusion, but when I opened them again the venerable figures were still there, walking past in slow procession.

For the next two days I simply allowed them to be there, not paying any attention to them, and at the end of the two days they disappeared, never to return again. Now as I write these words, however, I can see the silent, noble procession passing before me again, just as clearly as I did then.

I didn't tell the Rōshi anything about this experience, for I knew that his only response would have been to say, 'Nothing', which is exactly how I had dealt with it myself. Nor did I ever tell him about my previous mystical experiences. There was no way I could dismiss these experiences as *makyō*, and it is difficult to speak about such things in a foreign language (the Rōshi and I always spoke English to one another), as misunderstandings are always possible. In any case, I didn't need any human commentaries – I knew what had happened to me, what it meant and what was required of me, and this inner knowledge was something much deeper than anything which could have been said in the course of a *sanzen* dialogue.

During my sojourn in the Zen monastery and in the course of my wonderful work with the Rōshi my only interest was to experience 'nothingness' (also referred to as 'the Void'), to penetrate it and to attain to the state of unity. In order to do that it was necessary to leave behind me all the divine beings in the realm of manifest Being, something which I did with their knowledge and permission. I forgot everything, even myself. Only so was it possible for me to become that which I have already described in my first book.

Once one has experienced this great breakthrough, however, 'trees are once again trees and mountains are once again mountains', as the famous Zen saying puts it. And not only that – divine beings are then once again divine beings. The only thing which has been transformed is the traveller himself, returning from the realm of that which he has experienced. The world is still there, just as it has always been, but there is no more division between him and the world. He is at peace. (In the last chapter of this book, which will be devoted to a more detailed discussion of Zen and the Zen tradition, I shall attempt to make this ultimate experience more comprehensible.)

Before ending my account of the spiritual experiences which I had before coming into contact with the ultimate journey known as Zen I should like to draw the reader's attention to an important unanswered question.

There is nothing in the observable, physical universe which the great scientists of our age have not made an object of their investigations, all the way from the microscopically small to the astronomically huge, and their methods and instruments are giving us an increasingly accurate understanding of all these phenomena. What the human mind has achieved is simply staggering: science has progressed so far that, in many cases, even the scientists themselves are unable to comprehend the route which they take to arrive at their results in its entirety, because of the staggering complexity of the instruments which they use (which are, in turn, also products of the human mind).

However, all of this scientific energy is still exclusively devoted to the investigation of the *outer* world. No matter whether they are breaking matter down into its last, tiniest component or making the preparations for a flight to Mars, it is still the outer, material world which the scientists are examining, not the inner world of the spirit.

The human spirit of enquiry is so endlessly creative – why shouldn't it be possible to combine the study of physics and astrophysics with an inner spiritual path? It is a combination which could lead to astounding new discoveries, and I am certain that it could help to save humanity.

Let us assume, hypothetically, that there are some scientists who are willing to drop the idea that people like myself and my illustrious predecessors on the mystical path are either frauds or mentally unstable, and to accept our accounts of what we have experienced at face value, as phenomena to be investigated. I have a question for these scientists, and this question was inspired by the experiences which I described in the previous chapter, in which I was visited by supernatural beings. (I should like to stress that my account of these visits was literal, and that I neither added anything nor changed anything.) In my own case there is no way that one could suggest that these experiences were 'mere' visions, as a specific physical action was performed each time. Thus, if one is willing to accept that I am telling the truth, one must also accept that these beings exist. My question to our scientists is as follows. Where, then, do these beings come from? Since they exist they must come from somewhere. But where?

My own feeling is that they come from heavenly bodies or planes which are invisible to us and which cannot be detected by even the most sensitive scientific instruments, because the substance of which both they and their inhabitants are composed is of an ethereal nature. A few years ago some eminent physicists introduced the hypothetical concept of 'anti-matter', a concept which implies the possible existence of entire 'anti-universes', and even though the idea is still a hypothesis the scientists are already able to use it to perform calculations which help to explain a number of problems in the realm of physics. Could it be that the answer to my question about the origin of these divine beings has something to do with the concept of anti-matter? I am not able to answer this question myself, but I feel that it is a fascinating hypothesis which is worthy of consideration.

One way or the other, one thing is certain: we are on the brink of making discoveries about the nature of the universe which are going to make even our most daring conjectures about what is possible seem conservative. Who knows, perhaps there are heavenly bodies which cannot be observed directly, whose existence can only be demonstrated by calculation?

Investigating this mystery, the origin of these rare and wonderful beings, must surely be a challenge to the spirit of scientific curiosity. Of course, it goes without saying that such work can only be carried out by genuine, serious and well-trained scientists, not by whimsical UFO enthusiasts. The scientist who embarks on such a quest must travel on two paths at the same time: in addition to his external, scientific research he must also be willing and able to follow a path of inner realisation. The technique of *zazen* is ideally suited for such an undertaking: it permits no illusions whatsoever, and at the same time it is capable of carrying the seeker to the highest possible experience of enlightenment; it would certainly provide a sincere and curious scientist with some very unexpected revelations.

From the spiritual point of view sending spaceships to the moon, or even to Mars for that matter, is of no interest whatsoever. It contributes nothing to inner development. But it would be something else again if a scientist were to manage to combine the precision of the scientific method with spiritual realisation, using the techniques of meditation, and to come into contact with worlds which cannot be detected by physical means. Such a breakthrough could completely transform the murky spiritual darkness in which the beings of this planet have been languishing ever since the time of Adam and Eve, finally releasing them from the evils which afflict them and bringing them the healing for which they have been waiting for so long.

One way of attaining this goal would be to make use of the energy which is dormant in the human brain.

The German Nobel laureate Wilhelm Ostwald was the first person to use the term 'energy' for a particular state of what we call matter. In order to clarify what I am getting at I should like to cite a short passage from Ostwald's work, *The Fundamentals of Natural Philosophy*, in which he explains his approach very clearly and concisely:

> It is not possible to produce matter without destroying an equal weight of some other form or forms of matter. Creating matter out of nothing is thus out of the question, just as it is impossible to make matter disappear into nothing. All that one can do with matter is to change its form.
>
> In order to make talking about the subject of our discussion easier I should like to give it a name, once and for all: let us call it *energy*. Naturally, we are not talking about the moral quality of energy, but about a precisely measurable quantity. The special property of this energy is that it can be transformed into work, all kinds of work, but only under the condition that a quantity of energy corresponding to the work performed is transformed in the process.
>
> Energy is thus a 'something' which is itself work, or which can be transformed into work or which can be produced by means of some kind of work.
>
> This something is just as uncreatable and indestructible as matter is, and we can think of it as a something which is similar to matter in some respects. The difference is that it is not necessary for it to have weight or occupy space, and the similarity is that it is not possible either to create it or to destroy it. It is thus a something which is significantly more subtle and more difficult to control than the usual forms of matter we are familiar with, and this is also why it is only relatively recently that we have come to understand the nature of this new being, energy, at all clearly. [. . .]
>
> Every process of any kind at all can thus be described as a process

> in which energies of one kind are transformed into energies of another kind. The quantity of the energies remains unchanged throughout, but their form and their properties undergo radical changes. [. . .]
>
> And thus energy proves to be the essential, decisive factor in all processes – all processes are in fact energy processes.

Ostwald's explanation of the subject – I am tempted to refer to it as 'Ostwald's Theorem' – is so clear and convincing that nothing needs to be added to it. I have quoted it here because it makes the ideas which I would now like to elucidate very much easier to understand.

The head of every living being contains an 'energy station'. The level of development of this energy station varies from individual to individual, but without it the existence of the individual would not be possible. Energy is the creative force out of which everything which is has been formed, by transformation.

Human beings use their brains both for thinking and for envisioning their world. The power of this envisioning capacity is tremendous. For instance, if one chooses to one can see the Alps, a Mediterranean landscape, terrible war scenes, friends and enemies all passing before one's inner eye and listen to a piece of music with one's inner ear, all within the space of a single minute. This is an amazing miracle, and if one thinks about it for a moment it becomes clear that a huge amount of energy must be consumed in order to make it possible. This process is very concentrated, and it takes place away from the outside environment, inside the human brain.

Why not try to reverse this process consciously, and transmit energy waves out of the confines of the brain in order to achieve a specific, carefully chosen objective? Our planet is filled with countless thousands of transmitters and receivers of all sorts, from simple transistor radios and walkie-talkies all the way up to huge radio telescopes. All of these instruments have been made possible by the advances of modern technology, they are products of technology in the service of technology, no matter whether their purpose is the investigation of the nature of the universe or simple entertainment. Despite all these advances, however, the most perfect transceiver known to man is still to be found hidden inside the human body.

The ability of this 'instrument' to send and receive messages over great distances has been amply demonstrated by many precise experiments performed by researchers investigating the phenomenon of telepathy. Up until now, however, all experiments of this sort have involved messages transmitted and received horizontally, that is to say between two people located at different points on the surface of the globe. But there is no reason why one shouldn't perform the same experiments vertically, so to speak, in order to demonstrate whether or not it is possible to transmit and receive messages to and from other dimensions.

I would like to stress that what I am suggesting is serious scientific investigation, not a new form of spiritualism. It has already been demonstrated mathematically that the existence of other worlds in dimensions invisible to our telescopes and other instruments is a real possibility; all I am suggesting is that a carefully controlled series of experiments should be carried out in order to see whether it is possible to contact such worlds on a spiritual wavelength. There is one proviso however: both the scientists performing these experiments and their motives would have to be completely pure, for the results of such work always corresponds to the character of the individual concerned.

This is a subject which has fascinated me my whole life long, ever since I embarked upon the strict path of yoga and total surrender to God. In those early years I often received silent messages and instructions, and the receiving point always seemed to be located in the very centre of my brain. I often asked questions in return (the replies came immediately), and when I did I 'transmitted' these questions from the same point, as though it were the most natural thing in the world. I was always astonished at the whole phenomenon afterwards. In the course of one of these communications I once managed to ask how it was possible that my mental questions could be understood at the receiving end. I received the following unforgettable reply:

> Mental transmissions appear in the form of luminous sparks which we receive and understand.

Even at the time I was aware of the mind-boggling implications of this statement; nonetheless, I never discussed the matter with anyone. I have now decided to break my silence, but this is not because I want to provide grist for the mills of the pseudo-occultists and dreamers among us – these are people whom I have always avoided. In an age dominated by the seemingly limitless potential of our material technology I feel that it is important to draw attention to the endless possibilities presented by 'spiritual' technology, if I may be allowed to coin the phrase, which are as yet unused and uninvestigated.

Finding out whether moss and bacteria exist on faraway planets is something which is only of real interest to a handful of scientists. Such discoveries do nothing to transform the desperate spiritual pessimism of modern man. It would be more fitting to the spirit of our age, and more helpful, if our scientists could combine the investigation of the outer universe with an equally profound investigation of the inner universe. And to do this there is no need to travel to the most distant galaxies, which are millions of light years away. There is no need to leave our own solar system. If the existence of an anti-matter universe does turn out to be a scientifically demonstrable fact, then there is no reason why it shouldn't be just as accessible here as anywhere else. Perhaps there is a 'spiritual' sun right here in our solar system, as well as a physical one. The only way to find out is by empirical investigation.

In the course of the last few decades we have been forced to eliminate the word 'impossible' from our vocabulary, at least as far as science is concerned. If only spiritual research were to start making the same kind of progress then I am sure that we would soon be able to drop the word from our spiritual vocabulary as well.

The prerequisites for this kind of research are great sincerity, spiritual integrity and a sound scientific training. The results of even the most modest initial successes of such a research programme (which would have the added advantage of paving the way for much greater discoveries) would be very far-reaching. They could be the beginning of a solution to the problems of our age, igniting a light of liberation and realisation in the darkness of tragic hardship, fear and hopeless despair in which much of humanity is now languishing, and filling even the most disconsolate among us with inner radiance, confidence and a new sense of meaning.

Notes

1. From the *Majjhima Nikaya*. The version cited here by Ms Ital is from a translation into German by Kurt Schmidt, Berlin, 1963.

2. W. Ostwald, *Grudrisse der Naturphilosophie*, Akademie Verlag, Leipzig, 1914. According to the British Museum Catalogue no English translation of this work exists.

7

Journey to Japan and Stopover in Russia

My second journey to Japan was preceded by many months of uncertainty. In addition to my financial worries – I was going to have to sacrifice everything I had managed to save since my return to Germany four years before in order to make the trip – I was tormented by endless doubts. 'What is your reason for wanting to return to Japan?' I asked myself again and again. 'What is the purpose of making such a sacrifice, why do you want to inflict such terrible hardships and deprivations on yourself again? Haven't you had enough? What is your real motivation?'

I examined my conscience minutely. My love for my Master, Rōshi Mumon, and my desire to see him again were something I could set aside in the course of this examination, for our heart-to-heart connection with one another had never been broken, and there was no need for us to meet physically. What was it then, what was this restless desire to return to Japan? Was it the hope that I might be able to experience new heights of enlightenment there? That could not be, for I was perfectly well aware of the fact that there are limits to what is possible so long as one is still in a human body, and I had already seen the ultimate. Did I long to return to the strict discipline and seclusion of the monastery in order to deepen the *satori* I had already experienced? Perhaps, but at the same time there was no getting around the fact that there was no pressing need to travel all the way to Japan to do that; if one rigorously eliminates all sources of disturbance one can meditate anywhere, no matter where one is.

I meditated on this problem every day for a long time, and although I received replies they were inconclusive, neither yea nor nay. After a while I realised that this was Heaven's way of telling me that it was up to me to decide what I was going to do on my own. I was free to choose, but at the same time there was a small, still voice in my heart which would not be silent.

'If you decide that the risks involved in this journey are too great, especially the risks to your health, then stay at home in Berlin. Nobody will think the worse of you. But remember, you will never ever be able to get rid of the tormenting suspicion that you have missed something, no matter whether there really is something there to be missed or not.'

Finally I wrote a letter to Rōshi Mumon, asking him if he would be willing to allow me to return to his monastery for a few months. If he says yes, I told myself, then I shall go, come what may. It was a completely incomprehensible, irrational decision, considering the state of my health and my finances at the time, but deep in my heart I knew that it was the only choice open to me. His reply, which I received on 3 May 1967, was as follows:

Dear Sister,

I have received your letter. It is good, our Sister. We look forward to the day upon which we shall be able to welcome you.

This letter made me very happy.

During all the months of indecision before my final departure I subjected myself to a very strict meditative discipline, which was much more rigorous than my usual daily meditations. I wasn't sure whether I would ultimately decide to return to the Zen monastery or not, but even so I wanted to be able to give my very best when I was there if I did go.

All of the grosser impurities in my being had long since been eliminated, of course, but there was still the possibility that some tiny shreds of old *karma* might be hidden somewhere deep in my unconscious. I knew that *karma* on this level couldn't cause me any trouble on the earthly plane, but I suspected that it might create obstacles on the mental level, hindering spiritual progress.

I meditated for many long hours every day, mercilessly

destroying even the slightest hint of desire or emotion in all of my *chakras*. In the weeks before I was due to leave I went about this with such relentless intensity that I finally collapsed. Exhausted and feverish, I was forced to delay my departure for another two weeks. I knew that this meant that I would probably arrive when the weather was at its most trying (although the beginning and end of the Japanese seasons can vary by several weeks in either direction) but despite this I felt cheerful and relaxed, as though the trials which lay before me had nothing to do with me personally.

However, just as I was unable to feel worried about what the future might have in store for me, I was also unable to feel any sense of joyful expectation. This profound equanimity, which I myself found astonishing under the circumstances, was the direct result of the strict meditative discipline to which I had subjected myself, and also of the loving instructions from the beyond which I had received every night during this difficult time. These divine messages gave me the inner certainty that I was on the right path, showing me that it was Heaven's express wish that I should continue with the rigorous process of self-dissolution, even to the point of actual physical collapse. The following is the text of one of these messages, taken from a note I wrote in my diary on 23 December 1966:

> Only those who destroy themselves as individuals are able to teach and help others. You have almost completed this process. Continue with your work, do not falter. Even the last small residues must be obliterated utterly.

Sri Aurobindo used to refer to this phenomenon as 'inner speaking'. The instructions I received were often accompanied by wonderful revelations, many of which were repeated many times, but these are things which I shall not describe here as they have nothing to do with my earthly existence.

This time I decided that I would fly via Russia. This was partly because it was the shortest and cheapest route, but mainly because I wanted to see some more of the world. After all, I thought, now that I have decided to embark upon this long journey for a second time I may as well make the best of it. I planned to make an eight-day stopover in Moscow. My primary objective in choosing the Moscow route was not Russia, however, but China. Strange though it may seem I had never really been particularly interested in Japan; it has always been China, and especially Peking, which has inspired a real feeling of longing within me, ever since my childhood.

At first it looked as though the Chinese embassy was going to give me a visa without any trouble, but then the Cultural Revolution broke out and the people at the embassy informed me that a visit to China was out of the question. I was bitterly disappointed, but there was nothing at all which I could do about it.

To me the fact that it is possible to board a plane in Berlin and get off in Moscow two hours later always seems like a miracle. There was nothing miraculous about Moscow airport itself, however. I was more surprised than disappointed really: a country's main airport is the first thing which the visitor from abroad sees, its calling card so to speak, and for the life of me I couldn't understand how the Russians, who are so technologically advanced, could bear to present the outside world with such a shabby and primitive calling card. There were no restaurants, no waiting rooms, no lounges – in short, no amenities of any sort whatsoever. The main airport building consisted of nothing more than a huge, bleak hall, rather like a hangar without any aeroplanes in it. The counters of the customs, passport and currency control authorities were along one side in front of the exit. The passengers' luggage was simply stacked haphazardly in huge piles in the middle of the floor. I suspected that finding my suitcases was going to be a Herculean task.

Most of the other passengers on my flight were travelling in organised groups and they didn't have to worry about such things, as their experienced tour guides took care of everything. I was on my own, however, and the fact that I didn't speak a word of Russian made everything doubly difficult. The Intourist office in Berlin had promised that a car would be waiting for me when I arrived and that the driver would meet me at the airport and help me through the customs and passport formalities, but there was no sign of him anywhere. I waited for a long time, feeling more and more helpless, but nothing happened. Finally I went and spoke to the official at the passport control desk, asking him where I could check up on the whereabouts of the promised driver. He made a long telephone call in Russian, after which he informed me that the driver was coming and that I would have to be patient. There were no seats anywhere. After what seemed like an eternity a man came rushing up to me, apologising for his late arrival in excellent German.

It was the driver of the Intourist car. He got me through passport control at record speed and bundled me into the car, and then he went off in search of my luggage. It took him a very long time, and when he finally appeared again with my two suitcases I breathed a great sigh of relief. I don't know what I would have done if they had gone missing: they contained everything I needed for a year's stay in Japan.

The airport in Leningrad, which I visited a few days later, was no different. The normal comforts and amenities which one finds in airports all over the world, even in the most out-of-the-way places, are as yet completely unknown in the Soviet Union. In Leningrad the tiny airport waiting room also served as the office of one of the airport officials, and the full extent of the amenities provided for the passengers there consisted of a small table on which there was a carafe of water, a few glasses and some technical magazines in Russian. Even so, the helpfulness and friendliness of the airport employees, almost all of whom spoke at least one foreign language, made up for a great deal.

The drive into the city from Moscow airport took around three-quarters of an hour. The driver dropped me off in front of the hotel where I was to stay, the Hotel Minsk. It was in the city centre, on the main road leading to the Red Square and the Kremlin. The hotel reception was large and spotless, and after completing a few brief formalities I took the huge lift up to the third floor. The housekeeper showed me to my room, but when I saw it I was so horrified that I went straight back down to reception to complain. In Berlin I had booked a first-class room, for which I had been charged 68 marks a night, and I made it clear to the lady at the desk that I expected to get what I had paid for and that I had no intention of staying in a shabby little third class cubbyhole. She told me to go and talk to the interpreters in the office next door.

In the office sat three young ladies, interpreters for German, French and English, each with her own desk and a telephone. All the large tourist hotels in Russia have an office like this, a service which makes things much easier for visitors who don't speak Russian. The three interpreters in the Hotel Minsk all spoke their respective languages perfectly, and they were very friendly and helpful.

I told the German interpreter that I wanted another room, explaining that Intourist in Berlin had promised me a private bathroom, and that they had also assured me that the bathroom would have a bath. The room I had been given only had a tiny shower cubicle, and what was even worse than this was the fact that the room's only window, which was very large, had no curtains.

'The hotel management may be of the opinion that the thick layer of dirt and dead flies on the glass is sufficient protection against prying eyes,' I said forcefully, 'but I am not. I have paid for a first-class room and I want to have one.'

The young lady smiled understandingly and picked up the telephone. After making several calls she told me that there was nothing to be done, and that the room which I had been given was the only one which was available. I asked her to give me the address of Intourist's head office, as I knew that it was in Moscow.

'I am afraid that I am not permitted to divulge such information,' she replied politely. This is a wonderful start, I thought to myself. I decided that I would find out where the office was on my own, as I didn't want to make any unnecessary trouble for the interpreter, who really was very charming. She spoke perfect German without the slightest trace of an accent, and looking at her I couldn't help thinking of the many aristocratic young ladies described in the great Russian novels written around the turn of the century. I could imagine her as a delicate young countess, living a quiet, secluded life on her estate in the countryside. She was angelically beautiful, with a slightly wistful, melancholy expression, her face framed by thick, golden, corkscrew curls. She looked like something straight out of a romantic nineteenth-century painting. The enchanting effect was rounded off by her natural charm and her gentle, melodious voice. I can imagine that Heinrich Heine[1] would have fallen in love with her on the spot, just as I did. Russia has many faces, I thought to myself in astonishment.

When I left for Leningrad two days later I gave her all the little trinkets I had brought with me for just such an eventuality: lipstick, powder, perfume and so on. She was overcome with gratitude, and after thanking me profusely she disappeared into the cubicle behind her desk for a few moments, emerging with an envelope full of lovely children's greeting cards. She went through the cards with me one by one, explaining what the text of each one meant and the occasion for which it was meant to be used. I still have these cards now, and whenever I think of

Moscow I think first of this captivating young woman, who made a much deeper impression on me than the Kremlin or any of the other great sights.

The Kremlin! By the time I had finished dealing with all my problems in the hotel it was four in the afternoon, but the sun was still shining brightly and so I set off on foot to have a first look at its golden spires and onion-shaped cupolas. It was quite a long way away from the hotel, but it was very easy to find as the main street on which the hotel was located led directly to it. This street was also the main shopping street, and as was to be expected from the descriptions in our newspapers at home, the displays in the shop windows were rather limited and drab. But it is none of our business to criticise the Russians for this if they are satisfied with their way of doing things. It is true that I didn't see any elegance, but I didn't see any poverty either, and that is something which should give one pause for thought.

To reach the Kremlin, which is probably the most well-known building in Moscow as far as the outside world is concerned, one has to cross the Red Square, the sheer size of which is overwhelming. All the pedestrian traffic in the Red Square and in and around the Kremlin itself is directed by ubiquitous policemen who make sure that no one leaves the permitted paths and walkways, making no distinction between Soviets and foreign tourists.

On my first brief visit I just looked around a little, obtaining an overall impression and orientating myself so that I would be able to take a more systematic approach the next day. I visited the Kremlin three times in all, and every time I was there the feeling that I had been transported into the middle of an oriental fairy-tale became stronger. At the same time, however, I couldn't get rid of the feeling that something was missing. Despite my admiration for the splendour and beauty of its architecture I found it impossible work up any real warmth for the Kremlin; it didn't touch my heart as the temples of Bangkok had done. There is something about its atmosphere which prevents one from loving it, even if one is willing to, as I was. Stones speak, in their own way, even if they seem to be silent.

Despite the fact that it is difficult to love, the Kremlin is nonetheless a magnificent work of art. I was lucky enough to be able to see it at its very best, as the sun was shining on all of my three visits. In the brilliant sunlight the countless golden spires and onion-shaped cupolas of the churches and palaces seemed to take on a life of their own, soaring up into the air like the flickering, luminous flames of huge torches against the deep azure blue of the sky. It is a breathtaking, magical sight, as anyone who has seen it themselves will agree.

Only a very few of the many buildings in the Kremlin are open to visitors, and no services are celebrated in its churches. I was able to visit two of these churches, and it was obvious that they have lost none of their attraction for the Russians, despite the fact that religious services are no longer allowed. It was plain to see that the vast majority of the many visitors were not foreign tourists but locals, simple people from the provinces. One of these churches contained the costly sarcophagi of some of the old Russian rulers from the time of the Czars, and to my great amazement the country folk filed past these relics in solemn silence, with every sign of reverent respect, and none of the officials objected. Both here in this church in the Kremlin and later in Leningrad I was to learn, to my surprise, that the Soviets respect the feelings of their citizens towards the past of their country, even though they have reason enough for vilifying that past, at least as far as the ruling class is concerned.

As everyone knows, the Red Square is also the home of the Lenin Mausoleum. It is an amazing, unique sight, and when I say that I am not talking about the mausoleum itself – what is really impressive is the endless queue of men and woman, two abreast, waiting patiently for their turn to pay their respects to Lenin in his sarcophagus. No matter what time of day it is the queue is always endlessly long. There are some things which cannot be commanded by any power on earth, and this silent procession, which has been going on for many years now without showing any signs of abating, is definitely one of them.

On my way home from my first visit to the Kremlin and the Red Square I suddenly started feeling terribly weak and dizzy, and I realised that I hadn't eaten anything since my arrival. I knew that it was still a long walk to the Hotel Minsk, and so I stopped the first likely-looking woman coming my way and asked her if there were any good restaurants in the vicinity. It was my lucky day. Answering in good French the woman pointed towards a hotel on the other side of the street, explaining that it was popular with foreigners, but that it was very expensive. Since I had my tourist food coupons with me I was certain that the prices wouldn't present any problems, and I crossed the road by way of a covered footbridge. Next to the bridge on the other side of the road was a sign which indicated that the main office of Intourist's head office was just around the corner. I was delighted by this unexpected piece of additional good luck, and I resolved that I would drop by there on my way to the Kremlin the next day.

I left my hat and coat in the hotel cloakroom on the ground floor (the attendant actually locked them away in a cupboard) and then I walked upstairs to the restaurant, which was on the first floor. It was a magnificent sight. Before it had been turned into a hotel the building had been the private residence of a Russian aristocrat, and whoever had planned the conversion and restoration work had been wise enough to leave everything exactly as it had been before, only altering those things which were absolutely necessary for the functioning of the hotel. In the rooms in which the restaurant was located, for instance, the only changes which had been made had been the removal of a few doors. The rooms were all filled with small tables, set with beautiful glass and silverware. Needless to say, all of the places at these tables were already taken when I arrived, but one of the waitresses took me by the arm and led me to a somewhat larger oval table in a room at the back where there was still one free place.

I shared the table with a group of German and Swiss executives who were in Moscow on business, accompanied by their wives. It was a delightful evening. The food was excellent and very varied. The china and silverware of the restaurant was of the very best quality, each item emblazoned with a coat of arms, and the drinks were served in the most exquisite cut crystal glasses I have ever seen. (All the other guests drank a great deal.) I decided that I would eat all of my meals in Moscow here, and at the same time I couldn't help wondering what had become of the original owners of all the wonderful things in these rooms.

The terrible breakfast in the Hotel Minsk the next morning was just what I needed to put me in the right frame of mind for my visit to the Intourist office. The women behind the counter at Intourist obviously didn't have any experience in dealing with complaints. They all simply shrugged their shoulders in unison, saying that there was nothing they could do. I asked to see the manager, and they replied that he wouldn't be in until later. 'Fine,' I said coolly, 'I shall go and visit the Kremlin to pass the time, and then I shall come back at twelve o'clock. In the meantime you can tell your boss everything I have told you, and that I insist on being moved to a first class hotel.'

To my great surprise the manager was actually there when I came back at twelve. He spoke excellent German, and his eloquent dismay at my description of the room I had been given would have done credit to a talented Italian.

'You really don't have a bathroom?' He shook his head sadly, as though he were unable to believe that such a thing were possible.

'The solution to the problem is very simple,' I replied lightly, and told him about the hotel in which I had eaten dinner the evening before. One of the Swiss businessmen had told me what he was paying for his room there; it was somewhat less than what I had been charged for my terrible little cubbyhole at the Minsk. 'All you have to do is give me a room there.'

'I am terribly sorry,' he assured me with a great show of sincerity, 'I have tried everything. There is no room free anywhere.'

'But I am not prepared to remain at the Minsk.'

'Please be reasonable,' he protested, 'you are flying to Leningrad tomorrow morning. I promise you, when you return to Moscow in a few days' time you will be completely satisfied.'

'That may be, but what about tonight?'

'The windows have been cleaned, and the housekeeper in charge of your floor is going to make sure that curtains are installed on the windows before you return tonight. I have taken care of everything.'

I went straight to the housekeeper's office as soon as I got back to the Minsk, and she received me with peals of hearty, friendly laughter. I don't think there is anyone on this earth who can laugh quite as heartily as these earthy Russian working women, when they have a mind to. She accompanied me to my room, unlocked the door for me and pointed at the window, which was spotlessly clean. Then she picked up two grey military blankets which were lying on a chair in the corner and presented them to me with a flourish, indicating in sign language that she was going to hang them over the window as soon as it got dark, at which she broke out into more peals of uproarious laughter, shaking her head and patting my shoulder admiringly. Her laughter was both refreshing and infectious, and I was soon laughing just as loudly as she was. Even though neither of us could understand a word of what the other was saying we understood one another perfectly.

The next morning I boarded a small plane, and a little more than an hour later I was in Leningrad, which is a truly enchanting city, compared to Moscow. Before leaving Berlin I had made myself a fairly detailed map of Leningrad, including all of the streets, squares and important buildings which I wanted to see. I had also worked out a plan of all the tours I wanted to make on each of my days in the city, leaving myself plenty of time for everything and marking the routes of each tour on the map. Even if I did manage to cover everything, I knew that I wouldn't over-exert myself so long as I kept to my plan. This map turned out to be a great blessing, for it made it possible for me to relax and concentrate my attention on the sights of the city, rather than wasting my time worrying about where I was going to go and what I was going to do next.

To my dismay my hotel was on the outskirts of the city, a little way away from the suburban terminus of the Leningrad underground. It was a ten-minute walk from the hotel to the terminus and the journey to Nevsky Prospekt in the centre of the city took a good forty minutes. This was very irritating, as it meant that I had to spend between two and four hours every day simply travelling to and fro between the city centre and the hotel. But this was the only disagreeable point; the hotel itself was modern, clean and very comfortable, and there was a large and very beautiful park next door. An Intourist car had been sent to pick me up at the airport, and when I checked in at the hotel reception I was given a little booklet of meal coupons, just as I had been in Moscow, and a voucher for a guided tour of my choice in the company of an interpreter.

My stay in Leningrad got off to a propitious start, with a delightful and very informative chance acquaintance in the dining room of the hotel. After depositing my things in my room and freshening up a bit I went downstairs directly to see if I could get a snack before I set off to explore the city. It wasn't yet time for lunch, but I felt in need of a little something to revive my spirits.

The dining room was almost completely empty, apart from a lone woman eating a sandwich at a table in the corner. The waitress was just presenting her with the bill as I arrived, which made it easy for me to join her at her table. I ordered toast and a pot of tea. The woman was from England, she told me as we got talking, but she lived in Australia.

'I suppose you have just arrived from Moscow,' she asked. I replied that I had. 'Ah,' she said with interest, 'did you stay at the Minsk while you were there?'

It soon became clear that we were in total agreement as far as our opinion of the Minsk was concerned. She had spent an entire week there, and she described it in very scathing terms. However, when I told her the story of my visit to the Intourist office and how I had complained to the manager there she gazed at me in total astonishment, as though something like that would never have occurred to her.

'I would never have dared to do something like that,' she said after a short pause.

This was an attitude which I encountered several times during my stay. I realised with surprise that many foreign tourists in Russia feel too afraid to complain about anything or make demands of any sort. The staff of Russian restaurants and hotels are often extremely rude and impertinent, and I can't imagine that my English friend in Leningrad or any of the other tourists I met would have been willing to put up with such behaviour at home in their own countries. In Russia, however, they seemed to be afraid of being 'punished' by some authority or other if they didn't knuckle under and do as they were told. This is rubbish, of course. So long as one brings forward one's demands clearly and politely the Russians are just as willing to do their best to try to rectify matters as anyone else is. Like any other country the Soviet Union needs its tourist trade, and if the visitor's complaints are justified they will at least be listened to. Nor is one spied upon – in my experience one can move around in Russian cities with the same freedom as in Paris or Rome.

Everything is always much easier for people travelling in organised groups. Then the tour guide is responsible for dealing with any complaints, and it is much easier for him to get things done than it is for a lone traveller. From a strictly objective point of view I suppose that this way of travelling does have a number of advantages, and it is certainly cheaper, but it is not something which I would ever do myself, especially not in Russia. When one travels alone one is free to plan one's own daily itinerary; one can take one's meals where and when one pleases and go where one pleases, without being restricted by the confines of a rigid timetable.

'I can't tell you how much I envy you,' continued the Englishwoman. 'This is a wonderful city, and I should love to be able to spend a few more days here, but I have to be at the airport to catch my plane back to Australia in an hour. I tried to rebook my flight but it wasn't possible. Mark my words, when the time comes for you to go you're going to feel exactly the same way, you wait and see.' She went on to describe the beauty of the city and the hospitality and friendliness of its inhabitants in the most glowing terms possible.

'It's totally different from Moscow,' she said, 'I didn't like it there at all. The people there, even the ordinary people on the streets, they all seemed so bad-tempered and unfriendly and, well, somehow dull. It's totally different here, it's . . . I can't find the right words to describe it. You just wait and see.'

I was soon to find out what she meant. Half an hour later I walked to the underground terminus and boarded the next best train, assuming that all of them would go to the city centre. Even so, I wanted to be sure, and so I asked one of the men standing next to me (the carriage was very crowded) if the train stopped at Nevsky Prospekt. He replied in good German, saying that it did. Then he tapped a young man sitting in one of the seats on the shoulder and pointed at me. Without a moment's hesitation, the young man leapt up and offered me his seat. I wouldn't mention this if it had been a single isolated incident, but it is something which I experienced again and again. The same scene was repeated on every single one of my many journeys on the Leningrad underground: one of the older men in the carriage would draw the attention of a young man sitting in one of the seats to the fact that a foreign woman was standing up, and the young man would always stand up immediately and offer me his seat, with every sign of good will. Young people in Germany do sometimes stand up and offer older people their seats of their own accord (this is something which never ever happens in Japan), but this was something completely different. In Leningrad the older men obviously felt that it was perfectly natural to remind their younger countrymen of a simple act of politeness, and rather than ignoring the request or complying unwillingly the younger men were always spontaneously obliging and friendly. It was a delightful expression of good manners, and of mutual trust between the generations.

As I have already indicated, St Petersburg (however hard I try I can't get used to calling it Leningrad, everywhere one goes one is reminded that this is the city of Peter the Great and his successors) really is an enchanting city. It is one of the few remaining examples of what Europe was like in its heyday. It has lost nothing of its former glory, for everything which was destroyed during the Second World War has been beautifully and accurately restored, at great expense and with great skill: the Neva embankment, complete with the Winter Palace, the Admiralty buildings and the Hermitage (which now houses the world-famous State Hermitage Museum), the palaces of the Grand Dukes in Khalturin Street, which runs parallel to the Neva embankment, connecting the Neva with the smaller Moyka river, the Marble Palace at the end of Khalturin Street, given to Count Orlov as a present by Catherine the Great, with its majestic gardens and its breathtaking frontage of pink and blue marble, and the old stately homes of the aristocracy along the banks of the Fontaka canal – everything is exactly as it was when it was first built, and not a single detail is missing, not even the golden coats of arms topped by royal crowns on the wrought-iron gates of the palaces. The restoration work which has been carried out is a truly remarkable achievement, and the overall impression which one is left with is one of completeness and perfection. Peter the Great is still there, gazing out to sea from his horse on the Neva embankment, and from her pedestal in Ostrovsky Square, a lovely little patch of greenery next to Nevsky Prospekt, Catherine the Great still smiles down at the modern Russian comrades sunning themselves on the benches, an expression of gracious majesty on her face.

St Petersburg has often been described as the 'Venice of the North', and there is some truth in this. The view across the Neva from in front of the Winter Palace really is magnificent, and just as breathtaking as anything in Venice: to one's right, on the other side of the river, is the Peter-Paul Fortress, containing the Peter-Paul Cathedral and the mausoleum in which the Romanovs are laid to rest in their costly sarcophagi. To one's left, at the bifurcation of the Neva on the easternmost tip of Vasilyevsky Island, is the magnificent and unique architectural complex of the Strelka. But there is also an important difference between Venice and St Petersburg: one cannot help but notice that Venice is crumbling and dying, and whenever I am there I always offer up a silent, spontaneous prayer that God may preserve it, somehow, for just a little longer. St Petersburg, on the other hand, is a city which is literally radiant with health, and there is no sign of decay anywhere.

Both in St Petersburg and Moscow the perfect weather made my stay even more pleasant than it would otherwise have been. The sun shone down brightly from a deep blue, cloudless sky, it was pleasantly warm and summery without being hot, and the bracing breeze which blew in from the Baltic in St Petersburg was enough to enliven the spirits of even the most weary traveller.

I was standing on the Neva embankment one morning, enjoying the wonderful view, when my attention was attracted by a group of young Russian students engaged in cheerful conversation. They were tall and blonde, as Russians often are, and at first I couldn't make out what it was that was unusual about them. Then, to my astonishment, I suddenly realised that they were conversing in Japanese. It sounded so strange in these surroundings that I couldn't help laughing, and I called out a Japanese greeting to them. They all laughed uproariously, and after we had talked for a while they took me over to meet their *sensei* (Japanese for professor or teacher), a charming old Japanese gentleman who was sunning himself on one of the marble benches. We spent a delightful half hour in pleasant conversation. I asked the *sensei* if he intended to return to Japan some day, and he shook his head, opening out his arms in a sweeping gesture and pointing at all the wonders of the city around us.

'*Mō kaerimasen*,' he replied. 'I shall not go back.' The students cheered and applauded enthusiastically. I nodded.

'*Wakarimasu*,' I said. 'I understand.' And it really was easy to understand his reticence to leave. In comparison to Leningrad, with its broad avenues and spacious parks and squares, Japanese cities are crowded and overpopulated, and with the exception of a few main thoroughfares their streets are cramped and narrow, many of them barely wide enough for a single car to pass. I suppose that the *sensei* was a communist – he would hardly have been there if he wasn't – and that gave him another reason for staying. But that is hardly something to make a fuss about in a country like Russia, where everyone is a communist. It simply goes without saying, and so the subject didn't come up.

As soon as the students heard that I came from Germany (all of them spoke excellent English, in addition to Japanese) they asked me the standard question: 'East Germany or West

Germany?' I replied that I was from the West, but this didn't make the slightest difference to their relaxed friendliness. This was something which I experienced again and again during my stay in Russia. No one ever became less helpful or friendly when they heard that I was from a capitalist country. The question was simply a matter of interest, and once the questioner's curiosity was satisfied that was that.

The next day I paid a visit to the Great Palace in Petrodvorets (formerly known as Petergof), which used to be one of the favourite summer residences of the Czars. The interpreter who was to be my guide came and picked me up at my hotel in a taxi. The drive to the palace took about three quarters of an hour, and for part of the way we had a lovely view of the Baltic Sea.

It was marvellously beautiful. Of all the wonders which I saw there I was most impressed by the Grand Cascade, a grandiose artificial waterway running down into the sea from the Great Palace. It begins at the top of the hill with a riot of fountains and cascading staircases and flows into the sea as a gracefully peaceful, deep blue canal. The view out over the endless blue expanse of the Baltic from the top of the Grand Cascade is truly unforgettable.

As usual my interpreter was extremely competent, and tireless in her determination to show me everything worth seeing. Our tour around the many parks and gardens and the smaller palace buildings in the grounds took several hours, in the course of which she told me much more than I wished to know in perfect German. She also took me for a walk along the coast, along a delightful little terraced path paved with white marble.

I never ceased to be amazed by the Russian interpreters. All the ones I encountered during my stay spoke their foreign languages flawlessly, frequently using rare and unusual words, and using them correctly.

The last excursion I made while I was in Leningrad turned out to be a bit of an adventure: I had set my heart on visiting the palace of Catherine the Great in Tsarskoye Selo, which was started by Quarenghi and completed by Rastrelli between 1752 and 1757.

After going for a last walk in the city and eating a relaxed lunch, I returned to my hotel and asked the interpreters there to tell me how to get to Tsarskoye Selo. The response which this seemingly innocent question evoked from the group of young ladies sitting in the office was truly remarkable. They all leapt to their feet and started objecting at once, in several different languages. 'That's impossible,' they cried in horror. 'You can't do that. It's much too far away. It's much too difficult to get there. And anyway, you'd never find it.' Once they had calmed down enough for me to be able to get a word in edgeways I asked them to explain what the problem was.

'You would have to change trains several times in the underground,' said the German interpreter, 'then you would have to continue with the normal train, and after that you have to continue by bus. It's much too complicated for you, you wouldn't be able to manage it.'

When I heard her say that I decided that I most certainly *would* manage it, and I set off at once. The account which follows is a tribute of my gratitude to the Russian people, for it is a particularly touching example of their selfless willingness to help perfect strangers, something which I encountered again and again throughout the entire length of my stay.

I met my first friend in need at the terminus of the Leningrad underground near the hotel. I didn't have the slightest idea which train I had to take or where I had to change trains, and I walked up to a conservatively-dressed man and asked him how to get to Tsarskoye Selo. Actually, I didn't really ask him, I simply said 'Tsarskoye Selo?' in an inquiring tone of voice. He laughed.

'German?'

'Yes.'

'I good German speaking. Prisoner of war.' He took me by the arm. 'I show you change train,' he said as he bustled me on to a train which had just pulled into the station. 'When reach end, then train to city Pushkin. Then bus to castle.' We got off again several stops later and he led me to another platform. When the next train arrived we boarded it together. My guardian angel said a few quick words to the comrade who happened to be standing nearest to me, pointing at me and saying the name of a station, and before I realised what was going on he leapt off the train again just as the doors were closing. Everything happened so quickly that I didn't even have time to thank him, all I could do was wave. The same process was repeated twice again before I finally arrived at the station where I had to leave the underground, each comrade handing me over to another when he had to get off.

I looked at my watch. It had already taken me an hour to get this far. I wrote down the name of the underground station on a slip of paper. The 'railway station', which consisted of a narrow platform under the open sky with railway tracks on either side of it, was on the other side of the road. I bought a ticket to Pushkin from the tiny ticket office on the platform. The official behind the counter explained which station I had to get off at by counting the number of stations off on his fingers. I think it was the eleventh. The train journey to Pushkin, which is a charming little country town on the outskirts of Leningrad, took another hour. After a few trying minutes I managed to find the bus stop I had been told about, and as luck would have it the next bus which came along was going in the right direction. Twenty-five minutes later the bus deposited me at the gates of Catherine's palace.

It took quite a while to walk through the huge park surrounding the palace proper, past several magnificent buildings, but when I finally arrived I knew that all my efforts had been worthwhile. Built by Quarenghi in the classical style, the palace looks like something out of a fairy tale, and despite its great size the main impression which it makes on the visitor is one of delicacy and elegance. In addition to this it blends in so well with its surroundings that it seems almost unobtrusive; in fact, I would even go so far as to say that its presence actually enhances the surrounding landscape.

Next to the palace was a lovely deep-blue lake (when I arrived it was dotted with rowing boats full of cheerful Russians having a day out), with a well-kept path running around its circumference. Wonderful, thick woods stretched out into the distance to the left and right of the lake. It was an indescribably beautiful sight.

Unfortunately I didn't have time to take a tour of the palace itself. One needs a good two days to see everything, and in any case I was more than happy to walk about in the woods and on the banks of the lake, enjoying the beautiful scenery and the glorious weather. Needless to say, I completely forgot to look at my watch, and when the sun suddenly disappeared behind the treetops I came back down to earth with a bump, remembering that I had a long journey before me, and that I had no idea when the next train from Pushkin to Leningrad went.

I rushed back through the park to the bus stop. I had to wait half an hour for the next bus, and when I finally got off at the railway station it was completely dark. The station building and the ticket office were closed, and seemed completely deserted. A terrible thought arose in my mind: was it possible that the last train had already gone? I walked around the side of the station building, and to my great relief I saw that there were a few people standing on the uncovered platform. Perhaps I hadn't missed the last train after all.

There were only two tracks, so at least I could be sure that I would be getting on a train going in the right direction. After an agonising, seemingly endless wait, a train finally did come. I offered up a prayer of thanks to Heaven and got on. I didn't like the idea of travelling without a ticket, but it was the only choice open to me. I spent the entire long journey wondering what on earth I would do if a ticket inspector turned up, and I wasn't able to relax completely until I had got off the train again at my station. It was nightmarish. Quite apart from the fact that I didn't have a ticket, which would have been bad enough on its own, I was also a foreigner in the Soviet Union and I didn't speak a single word of Russian. And to top it all I lost count of the stations, as the train made several unplanned stops in the middle of nowhere.

Opposite me was a well-dressed, middle-aged couple accompanied by their adult daughter, who looked as if she was around twenty. I am sure that they had noticed the worried way in which I looked out of the window every time the train stopped at a station. I finally plucked up my courage and spoke to the mother, showing her the slip of paper on which I had copied the name of the station I had to get off at. As it turned out her daughter spoke very good English. I explained my situation to her, telling her where I was staying, and she assured me that they would tell me where I had to get off in good time.

Father, mother and daughter then started talking agitatedly, and in the course of the conversation I happened to notice the mother give her daughter some money, but I didn't think anything of it at the time. We finally arrived at my station, and all three members of the family pointed to the sign on the platform, indicating that I should get off. I thanked them for their help and then, to my surprise, the daughter got off the train with me and accompanied me to the underground station. In response to my rather astonished question she replied that she happened to be going to the same station as I was, the terminus near my hotel. I was delighted, as this meant that I wouldn't have to trouble anyone else with my questions.

The journey on the underground took over an hour, and we had to change trains twice on the way. As we emerged from the station I asked my companion if she was going to take the road leading off to the left, as I knew that there was a large group of university halls of residence in that direction, where a large number of students lived. I had to turn right to get back to my hotel, and I assumed that our ways were now going to part.

'No,' she replied, 'I shall bring you to your hotel.'

'That's very sweet of you, thank you, but I won't have any trouble finding the way on my own.'

'All right,' she said, and to my amazement she walked back to the counter and bought herself a ticket.

'What,' I asked, speechless, 'don't you live here in the neighbourhood?'

'No,' she replied with a laugh, 'I just wanted to make sure that you got back to your hotel all right.'

I suddenly understood what the agitated conversation in the train had been about. Despite the fact that it meant that the young lady would get home at least two hours late the family had decided that she should accompany me, a foreigner who didn't speak their language, simply to make sure that I didn't run into any further difficulties. And the money the girl's mother had given her had been for the extra tickets she would have to buy.

I wish it were possible for me to let these three wonderful people know how deeply grateful I am to them. Not because I was in any danger of losing my way once I had found the underground, but because it warms my heart to realise that such wonderful, selfless helpfulness really does still exist. One encounters it so seldom nowadays, and that makes it all the more precious.

At midday the next day I flew back to Moscow, full of gratitude that I had been able to enjoy five such unforgettably wonderful days.

I also visited the State Hermitage Museum while I was in Leningrad, but it is so huge that it would take several weeks to do it any real justice. And in any case I went about it in the wrong way. Instead of going directly to the rooms containing the early Russian collections (I was especially interested in seeing the famous Scythian exhibits), which would have been by far the better choice considering how little time I had, I made the mistake of starting off in the Italian and French departments. This was a complete waste of time, as the real masterpieces of Italian and French art are all in Europe, not in Moscow; the collection in the Hermitage is relatively limited. In addition to this initial mistake I was also much too overwhelmed by the matchless splendour of the rooms and the interior decoration of the museum itself, which were more sumptuous than anything else I had ever seen before, to be able to give the exhibits on the walls and in the glass cases my undivided attention. The galleries connecting the exhibition halls were also hung with countless sumptuous tapestries, and they alone would have been worth many visits. I can only repeat: to do justice to the Hermitage one needs a great deal of time. Without it all one is left with is a fleeting impression, overwhelming though it may be.

Back in Moscow I was delighted to find that Intourist really had found me another room. The newly renovated Hotel Metropol was directly opposite the Bolshoi Theatre, whose delightful, white classical façade is as beautiful as it is famous. It was a great improvement on the Minsk.

That afternoon I strolled down to the Red Square to pay one more visit to the Kremlin. For the last time I saw its nineteen golden, onion-shaped cupolas (no less than nine of these cupolas belong to the Cathedral of Vasily the Blessed) reflecting the sunlight in doubled glory, and after gazing my fill for a short while I took my leave, before the shadows of evening could dispel the magical radiance of the scene.

That evening I went to see the Bolshoi Ballet; the tourist office at the hotel had managed to obtain a ticket for me, even though the notice was rather short. I was a little disappointed at first, but I received a pleasant surprise after the intermission. The second half of the performance really was an overwhelmingly beautiful spectacle, and the dancing was brilliant. It was an unforgettable experience.

The next day was my last day in Russia. In the morning I went on a guided bus tour of the city, the high point of which was the wonderful view of Moscow from the Moscow State University, which is housed in beautiful stately buildings up on the Lenin Hills.

At half past three in the afternoon an Intourist taxi came and picked me up at the hotel and took me to the airport. My non-stop flight to Tokyo was due to leave at five p.m., arriving in Tokyo at midday the next day. Apart from the fact that I have always disliked travelling at night I was feeling quite cheerful and confident, and I wasn't in the least bit worried about the flight itself, taking it for granted that the equipment and aircraft of the Russian airline would be the best available.

There were four stewardesses: two Russians and two Japanese. With the exception of myself all of the passengers on board were Japanese, which was hardly surprising, considering that this was the cheapest route to Japan from Europe. The route hadn't been in operation for very long, and every seat in the tourist-class cabin was taken.

We fastened our seatbelts, the pilot started the engines, and the plane started moving. The vibration and noise were unbelievable. Half an hour later, as the terrible vibration and violent jolting (it was worse than anything I had ever experienced on any of my previous flights) showed no sign of abating, I asked the Japanese psychology professor sitting next to me if we were still on the runway.

'No,' he replied, 'we're flying at an altitude of well over fifteen thousand feet.'

It was unbelievable, more like being on a tiny (and ancient) boat at the mercy of an ocean storm than in a modern airliner flying through a clear, cloudless and windless sky. Worse than anything else, however, was the endless, thunderous roar of the propellers. But I don't think any words can possibly describe just how awful it really was.

Later, when I asked the man in the Lufthansa office how something like that was possible, all he could say was that it probably had something to do with the fact that it hadn't been a jet-propelled plane.

After another hour of torment I had a sudden attack of angina, for the first time in my life. I got up out of my seat, intending to walk up and down in the aisle a little, and that is the last thing I remember. When I woke up I was lying in the first class cabin wrapped up in blankets. One of the stewardesses was bending over me with a concerned expression on her face. I had fainted and collapsed in the aisle a few moments after standing up. The vibration and sickening lurching of the plane was just as bad in the first-class cabin, of course, but at least I could lie down, which was a small improvement. I should add that I wasn't the only victim: before the stewardess left my side a Japanese man was carried in and laid out a few seats away from me, and a little later they brought in a Japanese woman who was feeling so ill that she had to be carried off the plane on a stretcher when we arrived in Tokyo. Finally, after an endless night of torment and suffering, we landed at Haneda Airport in Tokyo and staggered down the gangway, green in the face and completely exhausted.

I owe a great debt of gratitude to the staff of Lufthansa in Japan, who sent one of their employees to meet me on the runway in Tokyo (this had been arranged in advance when I booked my tickets at the office in Berlin), despite the fact that I had flown with another airline. This charming young lady helped me with all the passport and customs formalities and then she drove me to the Dai-ichi Hotel in downtown Tokyo, where I had reserved a room. Seven months later, when I flew back home by way of Honolulu, San Francisco, Mexico City, Yucatan and New York, there was a Lufthansa employee waiting to meet me at every single airport, even though they didn't even fly to some of these cities at the time. In the exhausted state I was in when I returned from Japan this amazing service gave me a wonderful feeling of security and being looked after, and I appreciated it tremendously.

I only stayed a single night in Tokyo. The next day I checked out of the hotel and made my way to the railway station to board the train which was going to take me to my true destination, the temple of Shofuku-ji.

On the platforms of Japanese railway stations there is always a series of small signs indicating where each carriage is going to be when the train arrives. The carriage numbers marked on the signs are also marked on the tickets, together with the seat numbers. This is an extremely practical system which saves a great deal of searching and walking to and fro. All one has to do is wait by the right sign, and then one can walk directly to one's seat as soon as the train has pulled into the station.

There were only two other people waiting by the sign indicating where the single first-class carriage was going to stop, a Japanese man and his wife. The man was dressed in a dark business suit, his wife in an exquisite kimono. Judging by the number of Japanese in their very best clothes who came to pay their respects to the man while we were waiting for the train, he must have been an important government official or a company director. He formally introduced his wife to each of the well-wishers who had come to see him off, and the lady bowed deeply three times before every single one of them. How on earth does she manage it? I asked myself in amazement, and started counting the bows. I stopped counting when I reached a hundred, for there was still no end in sight.

There was no doubt about it. I was back in Japan.

Note

1. German poet and essayist (1787–1856), whose chief poetic work is *Das Buch der Lieder* (1827). Many of his poems have been set to music, notably by Schubert and Schumann.

8

A Heart-warming Reception – First Disappointments

I watched my reactions carefully as I slowly climbed the huge, beautiful stairway leading up to the temple, fully alert and centred. To my great surprise my heart did not start beating faster, nor could I feel any particular sense of joy arising within me. I felt nothing at all.

'That's odd,' I thought to myself. It is something which I was to think many times in the days which followed.

It was early afternoon, and as was to be expected at this time of day there were no monks to be seen anywhere in the temple forecourt. I made my way directly to the small house where the Rōshi lived, which was set apart from the rest of the temple buildings. I didn't recognise the attendant monk on duty at the door, who smiled at me through his little window. I greeted him and told him my name. He nodded in reply and went to announce my arrival to the Rōshi. I removed my shoes and waited.

What happened next was completely unexpected, and as it turned out it was to be the most beautiful and blissful experience I was to have during the entire length of my stay in the temple: the sliding doors opened and Rōshi Mumon Yamada strode through the antechamber and came out on to the portico to greet me, holding both hands out in a gesture of welcome. I took his hands in mine, kissed them, and pressed them against my heart. It was a profoundly moving moment, in which two hearts beat as one in the eternal realm of the One. After a few seconds the Rōshi led me into his private study.

Some readers may be asking themselves what it was that was so unusual about this little scene. Normally, a Zen Master, or Rōshi, never ever goes out to meet his visitors. He sits on a huge cushion on the floor of his room, silent and motionless, and the visitors must come to him. And no matter who they are, no matter what their status, anyone who comes in to see a Rōshi must first make a series of very deep bows in the antechamber of the Master's room (the Japanese must bow all the way down to the ground) before they are allowed to sit down before him, on a thin cushion about six feet away from the Master's seat. The gulf which separates Master and disciple is further emphasised by a recess in the floor between them. No movement is allowed once one has taken one's seat on the cushion. In addition to this I should also point out that shaking hands, or any form of physical contact for that matter, is virtually unknown as a form of greeting in Japan, and is usually frowned upon. One bows, and that is all. I was thus completely overwhelmed by the Rōshi's unusual greeting.

'Welcome, dear Sister,' he said, his voice moved, 'welcome to our temple.' A little later, when we were sitting in his room taking tea and cakes, I thanked him for being willing to accept me back in his monastery. I paused for a moment, and then I spoke again, unable to hold back the words:

'My Rōshi, the only reason I have returned is to see you again, and to be close to you.' He nodded silently, and turned away to face the window for a moment to hide his emotion.

I gazed in surprise at the face I knew and loved so well. It had changed.

'Yes,' he replied smilingly, in response to my astonished question, 'I have decided to grow a beard.' A long, thin beard hung down from his chin, and his head was no longer completely cleanshaven as it had been before: there were tufts of greyish-white hair growing above his ears.

The beard and the fact that he had allowed his hair to grow changed his appearance, making him look older, but it wasn't this which had really surprised me. A mere four years before (he had been sixty-four then) I had always been amazed at how young he looked and how smooth and unwrinkled the skin of his face and neck were. Now, however, his face was lined with sorrow, and I knew the reason why. Mrs M., a wonderful woman whom I have already described at length in my first book, the Rōshi's devoted friend and the greatest benefactress of Shofuku-ji, had departed from our planet on 26 December 1965, after more than six months of terrible suffering. I was sure that it was this which had placed such a great strain on the Rōshi, making him age so quickly: having to see a great friend afflicted by such terrible suffering and wasting away slowly before his eyes. Mrs M. was one of the most radiant, cheerful, intelligent, lively and warm women I have ever met.

I first heard that she was ill in the summer of 1965. The letter said that she was in hospital, and that she probably had cancer. I was terribly shocked, and I sent money for flowers several times and wrote to the Rōshi asking him to send her my love and good wishes for a speedy recovery. In October of the same year I received a letter from him which raised my hopes again. I should like to quote a passage from this letter here, for it is a beautiful expression of the love of a great heart:

October 1965

. . . Now I am glad to hear that you will come back to our monastery after eighteen months. And I am feeling more gladness to see your hearty love for our Mrs M. Once she was in a critical condition, but now she became a little well, then we are at ease a little too. Last night I visited her and I read your kind, kind letter to her and told her of your warm, warm heart and we saw her gentle smile and tears of joy. Dear sister, please be free from care, she will be well gradually and you can see healthy her when you come back to me. I have received your money again and Mr Yamamoto will buy some beautiful flowers for her and we can see new tears of joy again.

Please be careful for your health and come back soonerly.

This letter is a wonderful example of the endless love and compassion of the Rōshi's heart. In the West many people still believe that the path of Zen Buddhism demands that aspirants seeking enlightenment or satori must completely annihilate their own personality and free themselves of all human feelings, more or less as an absolute *conditio sine qua non*, in order to make it possible for the Beyond to act within them. In fact, the opposite is the case. However, one should avoid making the common Western mistake of thinking that seekers who are still on the path – who must battle with themselves, denying everything which life has to offer in order to free themselves of attachment – are representative of the ultimate objective of Zen. The only people who are in any way representative of this objective are those who have already attained enlightenment, for only they have transcended the limitations of that which we refer to as 'human character'. A person who returns from the state known as Great Satori – and the Rōshi entered into this state of utter unity and returned from it again many many times – is both Man and Buddha. In Christian terms one would say that God has been realised within such a person, or that they have become divine. Once this has happened they become a vehicle, and God (the great 'It') acts in them and through them.

Nonetheless, the original individuality of the enlightened one remains unchanged. Rōshi Mumon's individuality within the great whole expressed itself in the form of love. And, in accordance with his high calling, his love was a great, self-sacrificing love.

It would be a grave mistake to try to compare such great enlightened beings with one another in order to decide who is 'better'; each of them is utterly individual, without ever becoming dogmatic, and it is this individuality which forms the basis of their spiritual work. Each enlightened Master guides and instructs the monks in his care in accordance with both the absolute Buddha Unity in which they live and also with their own individual nature.

This great love is demonstrated in the Rōshi's letter, where he expresses his enormous gratitude for a simple smile on the face of someone who has not been able to smile for a long time. Our dear friend succumbed to her illness a mere two months after I had received this encouraging letter. And from everything I was told about what she suffered, not by the Rōshi but by his secretary and by the director of the hospital, all I can say is, thank God that it did not take longer.

Mrs M., who had been an extremely elegant and cultivated Japanese *grande dame* of the old school, had been unfortunate enough to come down with a horrible skin disease. If it had been treated in its early stages she probably would have been able to recover from it without any trouble. But in her usual manner she had kept quiet about her illness, saying nothing about it to the Rōshi for fear of troubling him. Not only this, she had also continued to visit him and to take part in *zazen* in the temple so long as it was humanly possible, and then it was much too late.

Money was no problem, and the doctors did everything in the power of modern medicine to help her, but there was nothing to be done. In the final stages of her illness her entire body was covered with ulcers, so that it was no longer possible to give her injections, and her ample figure was reduced to a heap of skin and bones. The doctor also told me that the disease had afflicted the inside of her mouth and throat, making it impossible for her to eat at all in the time shortly before her death. The torments she went through must have been literally hellish. And it can hardly have been any easier for the few people close to her, especially Rōshi Mumon, who had to stand by and watch helplessly as her body disintegrated before their very eyes. That too must have been torture.

If it wasn't for the law of karma a case like Mrs M.'s would be more than enough to make one despair at the absurdity of 'blind fate'. It seems so unjust, on the face of it. She was intelligent and witty and an excellent judge of human character; she had always made use of her great wealth to help others (it was thanks to her that the temple of which Rōshi Mumon was the Master had been able to enjoy many years of healthy development without any financial worries); she was a deeply religious woman who never made any show of her religiosity; and despite her many troubles and worries she always retained her warmth and cheerfulness – she was one of those people who make those around them feel good just by their simple presence. Of all people, no one deserved to have been tortured to death in the cruel and repulsive way that she had.

There is only one explanation for this seemingly inexplicable act of fate: this woman, who had never striven for enlightenment, and who had never gone to the private *sanzen* sessions with the Rōshi because she was convinced that she was not mature enough (this is something that she had told me herself), must have reached such a high level of spiritual and mental development in this life that it had become necessary to eliminate some residual karma as quickly as possible, in order to clear the way for further progress.

From a simply human point of view faith in the law of karma makes it possible for one to accept the suffering which is one's lot with a glad heart. For those who know, however, there is no doubt whatsoever that such drastic decisions are actually made by the Divine Self of the individual concerned, when that Self has recognised that faster progress is possible and feels that the risks are acceptable.

'I have had a small temple built in M. san's memory,' said

the Rōshi. 'You shall live there, and you shall have your own private room there.' I bowed down in thanks. I wondered where the temple could be located, for our monastery was high up on the top of a mountain, and we didn't have large open grounds like the temple in Kyoto. The only land we had consisted of a large portion of the forested slopes of the mountain and I decided, or rather I hoped, that that was where it must be.

'Ah, and here is Sakamoto san,' said the Rōshi with a smile as his secretary asked for permission to enter the study. 'He will help you with your shopping, just as you requested.'

It had been a joyful half hour, and I knew that the Rōshi was happy that I had returned. Even so, I had an uneasy feeling in my heart which I could not explain. I shrugged it off, telling myself that it was only my tiredness, and set off with Sakamoto san to do my shopping. It turned out to be an exhausting outing, for we had to visit several department stores before we had everything I needed. I bought a mattress and bedding, as I knew from experience that they would not be provided in the monastery, and Sakamoto san insisted that I buy a large, sturdy electric torch. I also bought some kitchen utensils and some other things which I would need for preparing my breakfast.

We loaded everything into the taxi and drove back to the temple, and when we arrived Sakamoto san called two monks and asked them to carry my purchases to Myokan-ji, which was the name of the new temple where I was to stay (ji means temple). Sakamoto san and I went on ahead.

I was now treated to my first great shock: I had assumed that the new temple would be somewhere on the monastery grounds, but this was not the case. We left the grounds through a small side entrance and made our way along a complex series of narrow, dirt tracks running this way and that along the mountainside, changing direction several times. I wondered how on earth I was going to find my way here on my own. As it turned out it wasn't quite as bad as I had feared. I did often lose my way, but when I didn't it was a mere seven minutes' walk from Myokan-ji to the main temple.

Even though the front garden was still almost completely empty, the building itself looked more like a pretty Japanese villa than a temple, an impression which was intensified as we entered. The antechamber, with its stone floor and generously proportioned shelves for shoes and umbrellas, was much larger and more comfortable than that in the Rōshi's own residence.

But there was more to come. The ground floor consisted of five very large rooms, all beautifully laid out with *tatami* matting. The actual shrine, which was the reason for building the house in the first place (I find it difficult to refer to the building as a temple) lay between the elegantly appointed reception room and a large living room with built-in wall cupboards. Against one of the walls was a beautiful altar, somewhat larger than the altars one usually finds in well-to-do Japanese homes. I recognised the costly candelabras and other objects with which it was decorated, for they had previously stood on the altar in Mrs M.'s house. In front of the altar stood the ceremonial musical instruments which one usually finds in such household shrines: a kind of gong, shaped like a deep bowl, and a bass drum. On the wall on the left, between the altar and the doorway to the reception room, hung a large and particularly beautiful picture of Mrs M.

There were two more rooms on the other side of the building, to the right of the main entrance. One of them was particularly large, and served as a dining room for the nuns who sometimes came to visit from other monasteries on special feast days or for the special communal *zazen* sessions which took place roughly twice a year. To the right of this dining room was a smaller room containing a telephone, and behind it was the room of the housekeeper and guardian of the entire complex, which was beautifully fitted out with many wall cupboards, a sewing machine and so on.

The identity of the guardian of Myokan-ji was the second shock: it was my old enemy, who had caused me so much trouble in the course of my first visit, the nun E. san. In order to prevent me from being taken unawares Sakamoto san, who was also no friend of hers, had already warned me about this on our way from the monastery.

'But do not worry,' he said firmly, 'she has no authority at all. Only the First Monk has any say in anything.'

Needless to say E. san had been informed that I was coming, and had been given instructions to get everything ready for me. She received us at the entrance with the mandatory formal politeness and showed me around the main rooms of the house, the last of which was a huge kitchen. There was a small dining room to the left of the kitchen, and to the right were a wash-room and a bathroom. At the other end of a short corridor behind the kitchen were four separate toilets.

Everything was there. Not a single comfort was missing. It

was very obvious that the interior decoration of the house had been designed by a woman.

The staircase leading up to the first floor was actually more of a steep ladder than a staircase, apart from the fact that it was permanently installed. Even so, it was extremely dangerous.

We went upstairs, and E. san told me that I should choose myself a place for my things, as this was where I was going to be living. The entire storey consisted of two huge rooms designed to serve as dormitories when nuns came to visit. They were completely bare and empty, with bare wooden floors without any *tatami* matting and no cupboards anywhere. One entire wall of the room was taken up by windows, which looked out over the front garden. There were no curtains, which meant that it would be impossible for me to darken the room. There were no curtains downstairs either but outside the house there were sliding wooden screens a good inch and a half thick fitted in front of all the doors and windows. These screens were closed at night, and in addition to keeping out the morning and evening sunlight they also provided protection against storms and intruders.

I sat down on my mattress, which we had dumped down in a corner together with the rest of my things, completely shattered. It wasn't a European mattress, of course, it was a simple mat covered with pretty material, designed for use on the standard *tatami* matting to be found everywhere. Not even the poorest Japanese sleep on the naked wooden floor.

It was already getting dark, however, and after my journey from Tokyo, the strenuous afternoon in the city, the terrible flight from Moscow (which I still hadn't completely recovered from) and above all my bitter disappointment at what I had found here, I was much too tired even to despair. I resolved that I would go into town again the next day and buy dark curtains for the windows. For the moment I would simply have to rest as well as I could and to try to sleep.

Sleeping turned out to be even more of a problem than I had feared. With nostalgia I thought back on my first visit to Shofuku-ji four years before, when I had lived in the temple proper. There at least the floor had been covered with *tatamis*, and that, combined with the wonderful bedding that Mrs M. had lent me, had made everything more or less bearable. Here the only thing which separated me from the bare wooden floor was my thin mattress. The pain in my joints soon became almost unbearable. I took a painkiller which I had brought with me from Germany, and while I was waiting for it to take effect the neighbourhood dogs started up their cacophonous chorus. It seemed that my hard bed was not to be the only problem.

The small temple in which I was to live from now on was in the middle of a square of residential houses, which were packed very close together, and it seemed that there were dogs in every single house. Since we were completely surrounded there was no way of escaping the noise by going to another part of the house. It would usually start at about eleven in the evening. One young whelp would start whining, and that would be the signal that the dogs in all the surrounding houses had been waiting for. Once they got started there was no stopping them, and their agitated barking and howling would get louder and louder, not dying down for so much as a single moment until the early morning. Earplugs were of no use whatsoever. In European countries this kind of nocturnal disturbance would be a breach of the peace, and the police would be called at once. Here in Japan, however, it wasn't in the least bit out of the ordinary, and locals weren't at all bothered by it – partly because they were used to it, and partly because their houses were all fitted with the sliding wooden screens which I described above, which kept out most of the noise. During the day the dogs all slept soundly in the sun in front of their homes, completely unperturbed by anything going on around them (which is hardly surprising considering how hard they worked all night), preparing for their next night of strenuous activity.

And that was only the beginning. This was followed by ten terrible days, in which I had one physical collapse after another. I shall only provide a rough outline of the events of these days, as simply writing the account means that I must relive that time all over again, and it is so painful to me that I cannot write more than a few lines at a time without having to put down my pen and rest.

I couldn't help thinking that I must have been mad to sacrifice every penny I had to come here again, simply for the sake of a vague spiritual notion, at a time when I had finally been able to afford a little more comfort at home, for the first time in many years. There wasn't even the smallest indication that the hopes with which I had left Germany might possibly be realised, nor did it look as if there were anything to be done about the terrible conditions under which I had to live. After the first three days

I simply broke down. I couldn't sleep at all, there was no hot food (E. san had suddenly gone off on a journey, without any warning and without saying anything), and it seemed that I was surrounded by nothing but animosity on all sides. There is only one entry in my diary: 'I am a total wreck. I cried terribly on Sakamoto san's shoulder today.' This shows just how despairing I must have been at the time, for I almost never cry.

After I had finished crying, I informed the Rōshi's secretary about a strange disturbance to which I was being subjected every day, as I couldn't imagine that it was something that he knew about: every morning at half past five, every evening, and also at other times during the day a young Japanese woman dressed in normal secular clothes would suddenly appear in the room in which I was living and disappear through a door in one of the walls without saying a word. I hadn't noticed the door at first, because it had been papered over with the same wallpaper which was on the walls. The Rōshi had promised me that I would be staying in a room in which I would be completely undisturbed, I told Sakamoto san, but now it seemed that I was living on a public thoroughfare where anyone who felt like it could disturb me at any time of the day or night.

Since all doors in a temple are always unlocked I had taken the liberty of having a look at the room behind the concealed door, and I had been speechless at what I had seen. It was the only room on the upper floor which had been properly completed and furnished. The floor was beautifully laid out with *tatamis*, there were built-in cupboards in one of the walls, and the windows were fitted with the standard sliding wooden screens. All four sides of the room were very well protected against the noise at night: on the street side were the wooden screens in front of the windows, and the other three sides were insulated by the built-in cupboards, an unused prayer room and the huge empty dormitory in which I was living.

As I had expected, Sakamoto san was very surprised to hear this, and he took me straight to the First Monk, whom I already knew very well from my first stay in the temple, to discuss the matter.

Why had this room been kept a secret, and who was this woman who was living there? As it turned out it was E. san's younger sister, a young woman of twenty-five who had nothing at all to do with Zen Buddhism. She worked in an office in Osaka, and E. san had simply allowed her to move in there without telling or asking anyone. This was the way it had come about: a long time before, E. san, who was very much older than her sister, had asked the Rōshi if it would be all right for her younger sister to spend the weekend in Myokan-ji, and he had given her his permission. But instead of leaving when the weekend was up the sister had moved in permanently, and the arrangement would probably have remained a secret for much longer if it hadn't been for the irritating fact of Ital san's arrival.

Sakamoto san went and told the entire story to the Rōshi, who was very upset, and E. san was called in to the First Monk's office to explain. She protested vociferously, but it didn't do her any good, as there was no getting around the facts. Nonetheless, it wasn't until a week later that the First Monk got around to coming to Myokan-ji Temple and inspecting everything for himself, and it was a week which was anything but easy for me.

The following is an excerpt from my diary:

June 6th 1967

Everything is much, much harder that I ever could have imagined. The loneliness of this house, the animosity, my inability to sleep, the fact that I don't have anywhere to put my things – I am forced to spread everything out on the floor, which means that it looks terribly disorderly, and I have to bend down every time I need something – and the climate. This terrible, damp, sticky heat! I've brought a number of good remedies with me from Germany, and they make bearing the climate a little easier, but nonetheless it is still a constant battle against the limitations of my body.

I spent several hours sitting in meditation in my makeshift quarters today, allowing the question which is plaguing me to sink deep within me: Despite everything, is it really the will of God which has brought me here? After sitting for a long time I slipped into samadhi without even noticing it, and while I was still in this state the answer arose within me like a great shout: 'Yes!'

This answer is my only comfort.

I really was close to despair, for on top of everything else I was also faced with other, totally unexpected problems, and the combination of all these troubles very nearly broke me.

Those readers who are familiar with my first book may remember that in Zen Buddhist temples the monastic year is divided into two semesters, a summer semester and a winter semester. At the beginning of each semester a different senior monk, known as the First Monk, is appointed to oversee the worldly affairs of the monastery, and the other monks are all subject to his absolute authority so long as he holds this position. The First Monk who was in charge upon my return wasn't happy about my presence in the monastery, and he made use of his power to prevent me from sitting in the *zendō* with the other monks for *zazen*, insisting that I should sit apart from them in the *hōndō*. Far worse than this, however, was the fact that he informed me that I would not be permitted to go to the Rōshi for *sanzen*. This was the greatest blow of all, far worse than anything else, for these private instruction sessions with the Rōshi had been my main reason for coming to Japan.

The *hōndō* is the largest meditation room in the temple. It is here that the Rōshi conducts the early services between four and five every morning, and all the important celebrations and ceremonies on special feast days also take place here. The lay disciples of the Rōshi who wish to take part in the Great *Zazen*, a particularly intensive period of meditation which takes place once a month, are permitted to 'sit' in the *hōndō* between 6 and 9 p.m. every evening.

The *zendō,* on the other hand, is exclusively reserved for the monks living in the monastery, only they are allowed to sit in *zazen* there. It is located a little distance away from the temple proper, and it is taboo for everyone else. Four years before, the Rōshi had given me his express permission to join the monks in the *zendō* for *zazen*. I was the only woman who had ever been granted such permission. The new First Monk was of course well aware of this state of affairs, but this knowledge didn't intimidate him in the least. The final blow was his refusal even to consider allowing me to take part in *sanzen*.

'That is completely impossible,' he snapped angrily in response to my chagrined question, indicating that nothing I could possibly say would be of any use. The effect couldn't have been more shocking if he had hit me over the head with a club. I was completely shattered.

I had embarked on a risky pilgrimage from one side of the Earth to the other, sacrificing everything I had and placing all my trust in the Rōshi. And now this! Even now, as I sit here and write these words, I find it difficult to understand how I managed to live through that terrible time of both physical and spiritual defeat, but live through it I did. And despite everything

I sat in *zazen* all on my own in the *hōndō* from six to nine every night.

This was the point at which I realised that I would have to go to the Rōshi and speak to him about the matter. Even though I hated to trouble him with my little problems, I knew that he was the only person who could possibly help. And so I went and spoke to Nan san, one of the Rōshi's two attendant monks, about the matter. Nan san, who had previously been known as Hō san, was a delightful, warm-hearted man, and he had been one of the many monks who had been my friends during my last stay. He arranged an appointment for me at eight a.m. the very next day. The account which I wrote of this meeting with Rōshi Mumon in my diary opens with the following words:

> The Rōshi looked terribly tired, and not well at all. Seeing him like that was like having a knife driven into my heart. He was very kind to me – he had probably already heard the entire story from his secretary – and before I could say anything he told me that I would be able to take part in *zazen* in the *zendō* from now on, and that I could start coming to him for *sanzen*, saying that I should start that very evening. I felt very happy when the time came to leave, for the first time since my arrival.

I naturally felt that it was my duty to inform the First Monk of the Rōshi's decision, and I went straight off in search of him as soon as I had left the Rōshi's room.

'No!' he shouted emphatically, before I had even finished speaking. Completely astonished that he could dare to defy the Rōshi's wish I turned on my heel and walked straight back to the Rōshi's residence. It was not possible for him to receive me when I arrived, and so I informed Nan san of the First Monk's reaction, and he went in to speak to the Rōshi. He was smiling happily when he came out again a few minutes later.

'Rōshi Mumon will speak with Shika san,' he said. Shika san was the First Monk.

I felt very nervous for the rest of the day, but my suffering was somewhat alleviated by the fact that I went into the city and treated myself to the first hot meal I had had since leaving Moscow, in order to fortify myself for the coming encounter with Shika san. When I returned at five in the afternoon I went to Sakamoto san and asked him to accompany me to my meeting with the First Monk, as I needed an interpreter. My Japanese wasn't nearly good enough for this kind of argument, and I wanted to know exactly what had been decided.

Shika san was extremely bad-tempered.

'So,' he said angrily, 'you may join the monks in the *zendō* for *zazen*. But that is all. You may not go to the Rōshi for *sanzen*. That is out of the question.'

'But the Rōshi himself gave me permission to come,' I replied, shocked.

'The Rōshi does not have the right to decide anything,' he retorted furiously. 'When I came here years ago, seeking acceptance as a monk, I had to wait in front of the gates for four days and four nights on my knees, without any food or drink. Only then was I permitted to enter.'

'I know,' I said, 'that is the rule for monks. But as you yourself very well know, when I was here four years ago I took part in every single *sanzen* session with the Rōshi during the entire course of my stay, and this proves that I was also accepted as a member of the community here. I would never have presumed to come here from Germany if the Rōshi himself had not assured me that I could return and that I would be admitted to the monastery again.' I showed him the two letters which the Rōshi had sent me, which I had brought with me in case such a situation should arise. Shika san didn't even deign to look at them.

'What the Rōshi has written to you in his letters is no concern of mine. Perhaps he will give you private *sanzen*. But you will *not* come to *sanzen* with the other monks.' He turned on his heel and left. I was crushed.

'I can't believe it,' I said to Sakamoto san, 'how is it that he can take such liberties and simply ignore the Rōshi's express directions? How on earth can he dare to say that the Rōshi has no right to decide anything?'

Sakamoto san explained the situation to me, and his explanation was the biggest shock yet. It was incomprehensible.

'Shika san is right,' he said, 'the Rōshi really doesn't have the right to make any decisions. The First Monk of each semester has supreme authority over the other monks and the affairs of the temple. The Rōshi's position is only higher from a spiritual point of view, he is nothing more than the spiritual heart of the monastery community, so to speak, the Buddha Being of the temple.' I was flabbergasted.

'Then E. san really was telling the truth,' I replied. 'I went to her and told her politely that I wasn't willing to continue camping on the floor and that the Rōshi had promised me a room of my own, and she was very contemptuous. She too told me that the Rōshi had no right to decide anything. At the time I thought that what she had said was unbelievably arrogant and presumptuous.'

'It *was* arrogant and presumptuous,' said Sakamoto san, and then he left the room as well.

At quarter to six I arrived in the *zendō* with my cushion and was shown to my place. I knew that the First Monk would be watching me like a hawk, ready to throw me out at the first indication that I was not sitting properly. But I didn't have any problems. I sat in *hanka*, straight as a ramrod, maintaining the position much better than many of the younger monks.

One and a half hours later the Rōshi's little bell rang and all the monks rushed out into the gallery outside the Rōshi's room, where they knelt down in the *suwari* position, awaiting their turns to go in for *sanzen*. I continued meditating – I was the only person remaining in the empty *zendō*.

The sequence of events during these *zazen* sessions was the same every day. Once all the monks had finally returned to their places – this usually took between half an hour and forty-five minutes or even more – the signal would then be given for a short break, during which we had to go outside and walk around the *zendō* hall several times, very quickly, in order to bring the life back to our limbs. In some temples the monks have to walk more slowly, in some so slowly that it looks as though they are moving in slow motion, but these differences of detail are not important.

There were two large entrances to the meditation hall of the *zendō*, one to the west and one to the east, and next to one of these entrances hung a large gong. A loud blow on this gong was the signal to return to our places, and as soon as it came everyone would rush back into the meditation hall as quickly as possible and sit down again on the two long, raised, built-in benches along the long sides of the hall, adjusting their positions as they did so. This all had to be done very quickly, as there were only a few seconds before the bell signalling that *zazen* had started and no further movement was permitted, and anyone who was not ready in time was punished immediately. The monk in charge of discipline in the *zendō* always sat at the head of the row, and of course for him this process of getting seated was no problem; he was always ready almost as soon as he had entered the hall again. It was quite another kettle of fish for me, however, as I sat right at the back at the other end of the row, and these few seconds between the ringing of the gong to enter the *zendō* and the beginning of the next *zazen* session were always very strenuous and hectic.

In the last hour of this first *zazen* in which I was allowed to take part in the *zendō*, after *sanzen* with the Rōshi was over, something happened which had never happened to me once during the entire eight months of my last sojourn in the monastery: I was hit with the Zen stick.

Most readers have probably heard something about this Zen practice of hitting the meditator with a special stick known as the Zen stick, and I should like to say a few explanatory words about it. What is the reason for this practice? A great Chinese Zen master who lived in the first century AD (he died in 867), known as Rinzai by the Japanese, is said to have been the first to introduce the use of the Zen stick. Its use was seen as a gesture of compassion towards the monks under his tutelage, as a way of awakening them and bringing them back to the heart of the matter quickly when they started to wander off or doze during *zazen*, and it has been a standard part of the tradition of Zen practice ever since.

It is important to understand that rebuke and assistance are understood to form an integrated whole in this practice, inseparably interwoven within each blow. And even today both the monks and the lay disciples accept the blows with the Zen stick with gratitude and respect, for in reality the use of the stick is an act of compassion, not of violence.

But I was neither wandering off nor dozing. On the contrary, I was sitting there as straight as a ramrod, absolutely aware and completely motionless. Even so, after handing out blows to a number of other monks in the hall, the monk doing his rounds with the Zen stick came to a stop in front of me and bowed deeply. I was deathly afraid, for I knew exactly what was going to happen. The ritual is always exactly the same. I bowed down deeply and waited for him to begin, knowing that I was not permitted to sit up again until he had finished. After a brief pause he struck a single light blow to each shoulder, then he stepped back, raised the flattened end of the long stick high into the air, and struck three more blows to each shoulder, very vigorously this time. These were followed by one more blow, the hardest of all, to the middle of the back. Then he bowed down again and I sat up slowly. I must have looked at him with an expression of utter confusion on my face, for in response he pointed at my straw sandals on the floor in front of me with the stick. I looked down. The sandal on the right was not quite straight.

The use of the Zen stick for such a petty reason is not permitted, and with this gesture the monk who had struck me demonstrated that the venerable old monastic tradition was now giving way to a much more arbitrary rule. At the same time this incident also made it very clear that the monks in charge of the monastery had no intention of welcoming the intruder in their midst; on the contrary, they were obviously determined to treat me with the utmost severity.

It was very difficult to suppress the tears of pain which sprang to my eyes. It was very hot, and all I had on was broad, black silk trousers and a thin half-kimono, which offered no protection against the blows of the stick. There were nasty red welts on my shoulders and back.

I should point out, however, that my crooked sandal really was an infringement of the rules, although it was a minor one: one is normally required to be barefoot, but on the stone floor of the *zendō* the Japanese straw sandals known as *zoris* must be worn. (These are the sandals which consist merely of a sole and two straps running from the sides of the sole to meet between the big toe and the second toe.) When one sits down at one's place on the long, raised wooden meditation bench one must slip these sandals off very quickly while one is in the process of sitting down, taking great care that one's feet touch neither the stone floor nor the wooden platform. This is something which requires a certain amount of practice. Nor is one allowed to use one's own sandals. In our temple there were always two baskets full of sandals standing next to the entrance of the *zendō*, and we had to grab a pair from the basket and put them on as we entered. Needless to say, one often ended up with sandals which didn't match, or which had broken straps. Europeans, whose feet are usually much longer than those of the Japanese, have additional problems to deal with. My heels always hung out over the ends of the sandals, and since one is not allowed to touch the floor with one's feet I had to walk on tiptoe, which slowed me down a great deal. On my last visit to the monastery four years before I had been allowed to use my own sandals.

There was no question of that now, of course. Everything had changed.

What troubled me more deeply than anything else was the fact that I was not, after all, to be permitted to go to the Rōshi for *sanzen*, the private dialogue in which the Master gives the disciple individual instruction. What am I to do now, I asked myself. What am I here for?

At half past nine I slowly made my way back to my room in Myokan-ji, my back still smarting. I resolved that I would write a letter to the Rōshi before I went to bed. It was my only hope.

Now I understood why Sakamoto san had insisted that I buy a sturdy electric torch, for finding my way home at night without it would have been an extremely dangerous undertaking. After walking down the steep mountain path I had to cut off to the left along a complex series of small dirt roads, which were really no more than alleyways about six feet wide. There were no streetlamps, of course, and there were potholes, rocks and rubble everywhere. Even if one walked very slowly and carefully, feeling one's way, it was still very dangerous at night. There was an unwalled cemetery to the right of the road just before Myokan-ji, and I always breathed a sigh of relief when I had left it behind me, for then I knew that I was almost home.

After a while I got fairly good at finding my way home in the dark. I knew where most of the larger potholes and rocks were, and I didn't need to worry that the position of the rocks would ever change. No Japanese would ever dream of bothering to move them out of the way, not to speak of removing them completely.

When I got home I kneeled down on my mattress and composed my letter to the Rōshi. This is what I wrote:

My beloved, most esteemed Rōshi,

Please forgive the way in which this letter is written, which is unworthy of you, but I am forced to write it on my knees as I have neither a table nor a chair.

It saddens me deeply that I must trouble you with this letter, but I am plagued by the most terrible doubts, doubts which are greater than any I have ever had before. Yesterday morning when I spoke with you you said, 'Of course you shall come to me for *sanzen.*' Nonetheless, the First Monk still refuses to permit this.

I do not know what to think. I cannot imagine that anyone other than you is in a position to decide who is worthy to come to you for *sanzen* and who is not worthy. How is it possible that the First Monk of a holy man like yourself can set himself above you in this manner?

I can practise *zazen* at home in my own country, there is no difficulty in that. But my holy work with you, my Rōshi, is something which I cannot do anywhere else, and it is in order to continue with this work that I have returned to the monastery. You know that this is so. Whom on this earth can I trust, if not you?

The First Monk also said the following words to me: 'The Rōshi has no right to decide anything here. Perhaps he will be willing to give you a private *sanzen* session, but for you to take part in the monks' *sanzen* is absolutely out of the question.'

If it is not permitted now, why was it permitted four years ago? I do not understand. What has changed?

My beloved Rōshi, I am sure that you will understand that I am unable to understand these things. With all my heart I beg you to help me.

Your deeply sorrowful

Sister Gerta

The next morning I brought this letter to Nan san and asked him to pass it on to the Rōshi. I only wrote a single line in my diary that day: 'I feel utterly broken.'

I took my place in the *zendō* a quarter of an hour before the *zazen* session was due to begin. The monks who were living in the seclusion of the *zendō* complex during that semester were already there. Those who were responsible for running the monastery (and who would exchange places with the *zendō* monks in the next semester) started coming in after I had sat down, carrying the thick, folded quilts which they used as cushions on their heads. From now on this was the way it was to be every day.

Then a monk outside started striking the huge bell out in the courtyard, reciting a sutra as he did so. This was the signal for us to get into the correct sitting position. Everyone always made a few movements at this point, rolling their heads or stretching their shoulders, for once the *zazen* began no movement whatsoever was permitted for the next hour and a quarter.

The great wooden doors at either end of the long, rectangular meditation hall always remained closed until the arrival of the

Jikihitsu ('the sun in the hall'), the monk in charge of the *zendō*. The monks coming to take part in the *zazen* session were only allowed to enter through the door on the left, and they were not permitted to open it any wider than was absolutely necessary to be able to pass through, closing it directly afterwards. After bowing deeply the monks would then go to their places and put down their mats on the raised bench, bowing again before taking their places.

At precisely six o'clock the entrance door would fly open and the *Jikihitsu* would stride into the meditation hall, accompanied by the monk who assisted him, and take his place at the head of the row of monks on the right hand side of the hall. His assistant would then go and open the door at the other end of the hall, through which one had to pass to go to the Rōshi for *sanzen*. Both doors remain open for the entire duration of the *zazen* session, no matter what the weather is like. The *Jikiuhitsu* would then light a stick of incense and ring a small bell, signalling that the session had begun and that no one was permitted to enter or leave the hall.

It is a strange fact that people who are capable of practising *zazen* properly forget everything which is going on around them. This is something I have experienced myself time and time again. Even physical suffering simply ceases to exist after the first few minutes. It was the same with my worries now: everything which had been troubling my heart so deeply simply disappeared. I sat in total inner silence, and not a single thought of what was to be troubled my mind.

After an hour and a half the Rōshi's bell rang, signalling the beginning of *sanzen*, and the monks all rushed out of the hall as usual, as if they were taking part in a race. I stayed behind obediently. One of the monks returned to the hall, but I was in such deep meditation that I didn't notice this until he actually bowed down in front of me. I looked up, and he pointed to the door through which the monks had just disappeared on their way to *sanzen*, indicating that I should follow them. The time had finally come.

I lay awake in bed for a long time after my first *sanzen* with the Rōshi, for he had asked me a question which puzzled me.

When I finally reached the front of the queue the Rōshi's silver bell rang once again, indicating that it was my turn. I got up, and as I did so the First Monk sitting at the end of the gallery struck the great bell twice, indicating to the Rōshi that I was coming. I walked slowly along the gallery towards the door of the *sanzen* room for the first time in four years. The shattering, exhausting events of the last few days had left me in a strange state of mind. I felt as though I were in a kind of physical and spiritual vacuum. It was hard to tell whether I was walking or floating, for I had no conscious sense of my body at all. In the anteroom I passed by the monk who had just come out of the *sanzen* room without even noticing him, as though I were in a trance. I bowed down to the ground on the threshold of the *sanzen* room, my arms stretched out in front of me, my palms turned upwards in the gesture of receiving. After standing up and completing the ritual of greeting which the Zen disciple must perform when he approaches his Master I cowered down in the lotus position before the Rōshi Buddha, who was enthroned in front of me and above me on a huge cushion.

After a long silence the Rōshi inhaled deeply, allowing the breath to sink down deep into his belly with a sound with which I was very familiar. Only then did he speak. I snapped out of my trance very suddenly at his words, for what he said threw me into a state of utter confusion:

'Have you mastered Jōshū's Mu completely? Have you known it in its totality?'

The reason that this question was so confusing for me was this: I knew that the Rōshi was perfectly well aware of the fact that I had already worked on Jōshū's Mu with Master Osaka, and that the amazing results which I had attained had even been described in Zen periodicals. Master Osaka's own words to me at the time had been, 'You have attained the Buddha Unity.'

In *sanzen* the disciple must answer the Rōshi's questions without any hesitation. Fortunately, as soon as the question had been asked I immediately realised (something which I was very glad about later) that 'yes' and 'no' have no meaning whatsoever in the realm of the Original Source. The sole objective of Zen is attaining to the state of unity with the Original Source, nothing else matters.

'I don't know,' I replied. The Rōshi rang his bell, indicating that the session was over.

So be it, I thought, Jōshū's Mu it is.

9

Outward and Inward Changes in the Temple

Before describing my second long struggle with Jōshū's famous kōan I should like to say a few words about a few events which had taken place in the temple during the four years I had been absent, and which resulted in significant changes, both for me personally and for the monastic community as a whole.

The effects of my letter to the Rōshi were immediate and overwhelming, despite the fact that those in charge of the affairs of the monastery had announced several times that he had 'no right to make any decisions'. I suspect that these effects were even more overwhelming for those who claimed to be the rulers of the monastery than for me.

The first major change was that I was called in to take part in *sanzen* that evening, as I have already mentioned. The next surprise came in the early morning of the next day. The First Monk suddenly appeared at the door of Myokan-ji, the little temple in which I was living. This may not sound particularly surprising to the reader, but in fact it was something completely unheard-of. With a very surprised but nonetheless assiduously devoted E. san in tow he climbed the rickety ladder up to the first floor of the building in order to inspect my 'quarters'. The long and short of it all was that I was 'ordered' to move into the only really habitable room on the first floor, the room which E. san had fitted out for her younger sister. Space was also made for my things – which I had been forced to keep on the floor of the huge attic in which I had been living – in the wall cupboards in this room. In order to save face the First Monk acted as though he were telling me to do things which he knew would be unpleasant for me.

'You shall be given a chair and a small desk,' he snapped, 'and a rod for hanging up your clothes will be installed.' I knew perfectly well that these were all orders which came directly from the Rōshi, but the First Monk didn't mention this at all.

Shika san really wasn't a particularly pleasant person. Even so, in the course of the semester we got to know each other better and we ended up getting on quite well with one another, once our great confrontation was over. Needless to say, I took great care not to act as though I had in any way scored a victory over him, and a little while after his visit I visited him in his quarters and brought him a small present, thanking him for the way in which he had helped me. He accepted the present gratefully, for my gesture had prevented him from losing face.

The arrangement also turned out to be advantageous for E. san's sister. She had only been living in the little upstairs room because she and E. san had been afraid of what might happen if it was discovered that she was living in Myokan-ji; now she could live in the spacious quarters downstairs, which was an excellent trade from her point of view.

Life became much more bearable. I was able to put my things away in the cupboards, and once the clothes rail was installed it became possible to live in a tidy room again. One disadvantage was the fact that the room was quite dark, as it only had one small window, but I alleviated this problem somewhat by buying a large desk lamp which I installed next to my bed. A monk named Katsu san, who was an old and dear friend of mine, made me a 'desk' out of two large wooden planks and installed it in the small alcove in front of the window. The chair which was brought from the storeroom was a great surprise: it was a brand new and very modern office chair. I suppose it must have been a present to the temple from some well-wisher, and, since no one had any use for it, it had simply been lying around in the storeroom ever since.

The greatest blessing of all, however, was the fact that I was no longer troubled by the howling and barking of the dogs at night, and that I was finally able to get a few hours' sleep, for the first time since my arrival. In the bare, open dormitory I had also been completely at the mercy of the many different noises downstairs, and in this respect too my new room was a great improvement.

With the exception of services and celebrations in the *hōndō* absolute silence is the rule in Zen temples, as everyone in the community is expected to meditate alone in their cells after the communal *zazen* sessions are over. Any speaking above and beyond that which is absolutely necessary is also forbidden. It was painfully apparent that E. san, the housekeeper of Myokan-ji, thought very little of these rules. This is a subject to which I shall return again later on.

I am certain that the Rōshi was convinced that life would be much more pleasant for me in Myokan-ji than it had been during my last stay in the monastery, and as far as physical comforts were concerned this was certainly the case. After all, the new temple had running water, a modern washroom with a beautiful big sink and a bathroom (even though a fire had to be lit outside to heat the water in the boiler). On the other hand I would have been more than happy to give up all of these amenities in exchange for my old room in the temple, where I had lived under the same primitive conditions as the rest of the monks. But that was not to be, not now that the memorial temple had been built for Mrs M. Allowing a woman to live in the same temple as the monks had been a great, unheard-of exception to an ancient rule, and it would never be repeated again, this is something which I was assured of time and time again in the course of the next months. Even so, if Myokan-ji had not been built I am sure that Rōshi Mumon would have once again insisted that I be allowed to live in the temple, but now, unfortunately, there was no longer a pressing reason to do so.

I must admit that I never really got over the shock I felt at no longer being able to live in 'my' temple, even though Myokan-ji was really a part of the main temple of Shofuku-ji. But the simple fact that Myokan-ji was away from the main temple complex made it feel separate, and in effect it had turned into a kind of private villa for the nun who had been put in charge of it, E. san. I only made one very brief entry in my diary the day after Shika san's visit: 'Life in this house is unbearable.'

E. san was furious that I had been given permission to live in Myokan-ji, for it meant that I was able to observe her and how she lived. In addition to being as unfriendly and impolite as she could, she also did everything she could to make life as unpleasant for me as possible.

In the first two weeks of my stay absolutely everything had gone wrong at once: no proper room to live in, my set-to with the First Monk, no *sanzen*, no peace at night, the exhausting climate, no food apart from breakfast, and on top of everything my overall feeling of utter disappointment. Considering all this, and everything else which was to follow, my final collapse was hardly surprising.

E. san received money from the main temple to pay for the food for the residents of Myokan-ji. She knew that I was allowed to make my own breakfast, just as I had been four years before. This meant she didn't have to make breakfast for me, but she was officially required to prepare the other two meals of the day, which consisted of the standard monastic fare: boiled rice. To make a long story short, she didn't give me any food at all. The first three days weren't so bad as there was no *zazen*, and I was thus able to go into the city and eat my meals in a restaurant. Even so, this too was something that I only managed with a very great effort, for I really was at the very end of my inner resources.

These three free days only came once a month though, and I had no idea what I was going to do when *zazen* started again, for then I wouldn't be able to get away. Before I could come to any kind of conclusion E. san came up with a new and extremely effective way of making life difficult for me, taking advantage of the fact that the Rōshi was away at Myōshin-ji temple in Kyoto for the duration of the three free days.

A while before, E. san had been forced to put up a young nun from another city in one of the downstairs rooms. This nun had been involved in a car accident in which she had suffered severe head injuries and brain damage, and she had come to stay in Myokan-ji while she was awaiting further treatment. The poor thing's injuries caused her terrible pain, and even though she was under extremely powerful medication all the time, she moaned and groaned in agony ceaselessly. The noise was very loud, but it created no disturbance for E. san unless she was working in the kitchen, as she had given the young nun a room which was right over on the other side of the house, well away from her own quarters.

On the evening of our second 'day off' I went out to dinner at the home of the director of the University Hospital in Kobe, Professor Imachi, who was an old friend of mine. Before I went I informed E. san that I would be returning later than usual.

I came back home at around ten, and as I entered my room I thought for a moment that everything I had been through had finally succeeded in driving me out of my mind, and that I had started to hallucinate. I was quite certain that I could hear someone groaning. I looked around carefully. The room was empty.

The groans continued. A terrible possibility suddenly started to dawn on me. I walked over to the paper screen which separated my room from the small prayer room next door (which could only be reached by passing through my room, as it had no entrance of its own) and pushed it aside. It was just as I had feared: E. san had moved our poor sick guest into the prayer room. I could hardly believe my eyes. I hadn't been in the room for more than twenty-four hours, and now this! It meant that I wouldn't have a single moment's peace from now on, and that both sleep and *zazen* would be impossible.

In my diary I wrote, 'No sleep. No *zazen*. I can't stop thinking that perhaps I should go back home to Germany.' That I had reached such a point a mere two weeks after returning to the monastery gives some small indication of my state of physical exhaustion and of the mental suffering I had been through. It is not a subject I wish to say anything more about.

I had no other choice but to go and talk to the Rōshi's secretary again. First I asked him if it would be possible for me to prepare my own meals in the kitchen of Myokan-ji, since I was being excluded from taking part in the meals there, and then I went on to describe the new state of affairs in the little temple. Here is what I wrote in my diary the next day:

> I told Sakamoto san about the new situation and the difficulties which it has created for me, saying that as I saw it the young nun's transfer to the room next to mine could only be an act of malice. After all, I said, almost all of the other rooms in the house are unused, and Rōshi Mumon had made a point of insisting that I was to have a room of my own. I also said that if there really were no way of changing this, and that if the Rōshi really did have no authority to intervene, as E. san had assured me, then I would prefer to return to Germany.
>
> Sakamoto san asked me to write everything down. He must have taken the letter to the Rōshi this morning, for when I returned home today a miracle had taken place. The sick nun had been moved out of the little prayer room and she was back in her own room downstairs. I am terribly relieved.
>
> I have had a bunch of roses sent to the Rōshi.

Ever since the first day of my arrival one of the sayings of

Heraclitus had been welling up into my consciousness: 'You cannot step into the same river twice.' It came a little hesitantly at first, and I tried to push it aside, unwilling to listen, but the voice soon became so loud that I was forced to pay attention to it and to take stock of my present situation.

I knew that in order to attain a state of clarity regarding myself and the river into which I had now stepped for a second time I would have to meditate on the inner meaning of Heraclitus' saying. Both I and the river were no longer that which we had been. There were two possibilities open to me: either I could work to attain a state of reasonable harmony between myself and the river – both of us in our present, new states – or I could simply step out of the river again and go home.

The transformation which had taken place in me in relation to the temple was plain to see: I was not coming here as a novice this time, I was coming as an initiate, as one who had attained to knowledge. Knowledge of the temple and everything connected with it, knowledge of the Rōshi, knowledge of Zen and the goal of enlightenment, knowledge of my own inner nature.

What I did not know, for the time being at least, was *why* I had returned to the temple. In this context my love for the Rōshi was an emotional distraction, and thus had to be eliminated from my meditations.

I had longed to get away from the outside world and return to the strict seclusion and discipline of the monastery, where I would be able to concentrate on the tasks which would be given to me and enter once more into the realm of Ultimate Truth. I knew that this desire was in full accordance with the wishes of the Rōshi. In my letters to him I had said that I was returning to my second home, and that is exactly how I felt about the temple, until I actually did return.

What was it that had changed? The change was so radical, so far-reaching, that I was aware of it all the time, right from the very first day. The atmosphere of the temple was completely different.

I had known that I would miss Mrs M. very much, but I hadn't imagined that her passing would create such a deep and apparent change in the spirit of the temple community. I wouldn't have believed that it was possible if I had not seen it for myself, and I must admit that it is a phenomenon which still preoccupies me today.

Four years ago, in my first book, I wrote that Mrs M. had been known as 'the mistress of the temple'. With her the 'female principle' had departed from our midst, a principle which had filled the entire temple with warmth, good humour and a feeling of joy. Now the atmosphere had become chilly, and sometimes I even had the feeling that the general attitude had become one of indifference, as though life in the temple had been reduced to a mere routine.

I can imagine that some of the older monks had always been opposed to the natural, matter-of-course way in which Mrs M. had been treated as a member of the monastic community. The old, traditional point of view is that women's only function is to serve, and it is likely that these monks had only tolerated Mrs M. at all because all of them had profited greatly from her work as the temple's patron. Mrs M.'s passing had brought about a very profound change in the structure of the entire community. It was a change which, in subtle ways, also involved opposition to the Rōshi himself.

Even the Rōshi had changed. It wasn't only his Bodhidharma beard; he had become tired and weary. Four years ago his wonderful good humour, which had always made him seem so young and full of life, had been like a constant aura of light shining from the innermost depths of his being. Now it was gone. It was as though this light had been buried together with Mrs M., as though having to watch the terrible suffering and death of this wonderful woman and friend of the temple had simply been too much. Something human in the Rōshi had been broken.

Many people believe that the total extinguishing of the 'personality' which is an integral part of the practice of Zen means that the seeker's 'humanity' must of necessity also be destroyed. The Rōshi's moving example is a perfect demonstration that this is not so. Nothing which is a part of one's true being is ever lost, not even the ability to suffer. It is transcended, and it becomes universal, but it is not lost. Rōshi Mumon's true nature was universal love. This is something which is predestined to run into trouble on our planet, and the Rōshi is by no means the first person who has experienced this fact. Again and again during the months of my second sojourn in the temple I saw how deeply he was wounded by the inability of those around him to understand (to phrase it kindly), and how shamelessly his endlessly kind and trusting heart, which would never dream of thinking ill of anyone, was exploited by their egotism.

In addition to this the temple had also been faced with financial difficulties since the death of Mrs M. I could hardly believe my ears when I heard this, but the fact of the matter was that no will had been found, and thus, even though she had supported the temple almost single-handedly while she had been alive, it was now suddenly forced to get along without her help. Perhaps, I told myself, the will had gone missing somehow – after all, she had been in hospital for more than six months when she died, and she hadn't been able to attend to her affairs . . .

We had all simply assumed that her beautiful estate would one day become a part of the temple's property, and that she would write a will making sure that the financial support she had given the temple would continue after her death. It seemed unlikely that Mrs M., who was the very soul of prudence and good sense, could have failed to write a single line indicating what she wished to have done with her property. Nonetheless, no matter how incredible it seemed to those involved, the fact of the matter was that there was no will, and there was no getting around it. It was a reality which had to be accepted and digested.

In the course of a number of long conversations about this matter with the Rōshi's secretary I slowly managed to put together a fairly clear picture of the shocking events connected with this case and the astounding behaviour of Mrs M.'s legal heirs; but after everything which Mrs M. herself had previously told me about these people I was not at all surprised at what I heard.

What this admirable Japanese woman had told me about her own life was as follows: she and her husband, had been very happy together, even though their marriage was childless. Upon realising that they were unable to have children of their own they had decided to adopt two, a boy and a girl. They were both so young when they were adopted that Mr and Mrs M. were to all intents and purposes really their parents, and they showered the children with love and care. The boy received an education designed to prepare him to take over his father's company, and the daughter was educated in all the famous Japanese arts. They grew up in a wonderful and wealthy home.

And then something amazing happened: the two children got married. If this had been a marriage of love it would have been the crowning event of the entire adoption, but as it was it was clear that the match seemed simply to be a financial calculation, in order to prevent the family fortune from being divided.

The newly-wedded pair moved to Tokyo, where the son managed the business affairs of the company there. When I came to the monastery for the first time in 1963 Mrs M.'s husband had been dead for around two years. In his will, according to what I was told, he had made his wife his sole heir with control over his entire fortune and had at the same time appointed his son to be director of the company. Those close to the family felt that he had arranged matters in this way in order to protect his wife from his son.

The son acted quickly, and set to work to convince his mother that she should hand control of the family fortune over to him. 'We are all members of the same family,' he told her sweetly, 'how could you possibly think that I would do anything which would reduce your financial freedom? In any case, it is only fitting and proper for the person who is in charge of the family business to have control of the fortune as well. It is nothing more than a formality, and it will spare you a great deal of work and trouble.' Mrs M. was overwhelmed by his unaccustomed display of love and concern, and allowed herself to be convinced.

From the financial point of view everything went quite well at first, but now that they had got what they wanted the children's 'love' for their adoptive mother was reduced to nothing more than formal gestures of politeness. Once a year Mrs M. travelled to Tokyo to see her grandchild, and the couple refused to allow her to stay in their house. She had to take a room in a hotel. I happened to be staying at Mrs M.'s house at the time of one of her daughter's visits to Kobe (which were by no means solely for the purpose of visiting her mother). Her daughter also stayed in a hotel, and didn't once set foot on the grounds of the house in which she had grown up. Mrs M. had lunch with her twice at the hotel in the course of her visit, but that was all – apart from that they didn't see one another.

Mrs M. was a very motherly woman, and her warmth was always a joy to everyone who got to know her better. I hate to imagine what she must have suffered. She was too much of a lady to let her sorrow show, and her natural sense of humour helped to ward off the pain from her heart.

Her husband had not been averse to her efforts on the path

of Zen Buddhism, even though he himself had no religious tendencies; his had been the mind of a businessman. He simply let her have her way. After his death she was left completely alone in the world, which made it possible for her to devote all her energy to the practice of Zen, thus fulfilling her most heartfelt desire. Although she was totally dedicated to her spiritual work there was never anything of the dogmatic religious fanatic about her.

She became the greatest benefactor of Shofuku-ji and a close and devoted friend of the Rōshi's. She was always there to help whenever the temple was in difficulties, and she gave her help as a matter of course, making it possible for the Rōshi to carry out the functions of his difficult office without needing to worry about material matters. I was lucky enough to have been able to stay in the monastery during one of these happy years in which the Rōshi had been completely free to devote all of his energy to his spiritual work. Even though he was already quite old at the time the impression he made on me was one of glowing youth, and he mastered his enormous workload with seeming effortlessness. These are all things which are described in detail in my first book.

According to Sakamoto san it seems that Mrs M.'s son had already drastically reduced her income even before she became ill. She was a multimillionaire in her own right, but he cut her allowance back drastically, and made it impossible for her to use money from the family company for charitable purposes.

During all the terrible months in which she was lying in hospital, in incredible pain and suffering, the only time her children showed any interest in their adoptive mother was when they called to enquire how long her death was likely to take. About a week before she died her son sold her wonderful house and estate, which were her own private property, behind her back, without either informing her or asking her permission.

'That was the final blow,' Sakamoto san told me, 'to be told that news by someone else. That is what killed her.' Son and daughter, who were also man and wife, were now the sole owners of a huge company.

After Mrs M.'s death some of her friends tried to tell her son that her most heartfelt wish had been to make sure that the temple should want for nothing materially. He is reported to have said that that would be a waste of money.

'That is modern Japan,' said Sakamoto san. I wasn't satisfied, and I argued that Mrs M. must have known her own adoptive son, and that it would have been perfectly possible for her to make a will during her many months in hospital, in order to make sure that the temple was taken care of. Sakamoto san's reply was beautiful: 'Her spirit was no longer attached to material things,' he said. It was a very decent statement, and I am sure that he was only repeating the Rōshi's own words, but even so I think that there were a number of sides to the affair which remained troublesomely unclear, for everyone concerned.

I asked Sakamoto san if a memorial service had been held for her in the temple. He replied that it hadn't.

'Memorial services are very expensive,' he replied, 'every monk who takes part receives 3,000 Yen. That alone would have cost 90,000 Yen. Then there are other necessary expenses. In all it would have cost between 150,000 and 200,000 Yen. Her son was not willing to pay that much.'

I remembered how many of these unique services had been held at the temple during my first visit in 1963. My recollections of the service in memory of Mrs M.'s own husband were particularly vivid. As can be imagined, they were one of the temple's main sources of income. I now realised that Mrs M. must have been the driving force behind these events, most of which had been organised for or by wealthy friends of hers or the directors of associated companies, for in the entire seven months of my second stay there were only two memorial services held in the temple.

The first result of all of these radical changes was that the Rōshi now had to bear the entire financial burden of supporting the temple on his own again, without being able to neglect any of his other duties. He was responsible for the training and guidance of both the thirty monks of our temple and of those at Myōshin-ji in Kyoto, where he also had to officiate at the ceremonies on all the great feast days. In addition to this he was also president and head teacher of the Zen University in Kyoto, which he had founded with Mrs M.'s assistance. And then there were the countless lectures he delivered in Kobe and Kyoto and the surrounding area: Since he was paid for these lectures he was now forced to deliver many more than before, and in addition to this he also started delivering lectures on the radio and on television. He never slept more than three hours a night. How he managed it is a mystery of truly transcendent proportions. To crown it all he was also required to write a new book every year, on top of all his other obligations. He worked on his books in the early mornings, after the early service in the *hōndō*, which began at four and ended at five, as he could be fairly sure that he would not be disturbed by visitors before eight.

With a sad heart I soon realised that it was hardly surprising that the man had changed. He didn't have a single moment for himself, let alone for a quiet hour drinking tea and chatting with someone else. Even smiling now cost him a great deal of effort. A mere four years before his smile had been wonderfully natural, and a delight to behold.

And what about the monks? Even on my very first walk around my beloved temple upon returning I had sensed that they too were not the same as before, and as it turned out these changes were not changes for the better. The process had probably taken place quite slowly, beginning with the new poverty of the temple, but for me it was as if the transformation had taken place overnight. The negative impression which I received shocked me so deeply that I really did feel like a stranger in the temple which I loved so much.

Now that the Rōshi was forced to work day and night in a superhuman effort to make the money which the temple and his monks needed in order to survive he had been forced to withdraw more and more from the life of the community, and he was frequently away. As a result of this the monastic discipline had slipped and become lax, and a certain air of disrespect towards the Rōshi himself had also become apparent, even though it was still very subtle most of the time. Before, none of the monks would have dreamed of saying something like 'The Rōshi does not have the right to decide anything', especially not in such a brutal and arrogant manner.

One of the most painful things from my point of view, however, was that many of the monks I had loved most were now gone. Of my close friends only Katsu san and Nan san were still living in the temple.

It is not unusual for young monks to move from one temple to another, and these moves are often made on the instigation of the Rōshi in charge of their temple. It is also normal practice for a Rōshi to appoint particularly capable and qualified monks to high positions in associated temples. However, it is very important that a group of monks who are to be trained to become Masters themselves should remain. And two members of this inner circle in Shofuku-ji were now missing. I had been looking forward to seeing them again very much. They had been close friends of mine, and both of them were men who would have immediately objected to any attempts to harass or intimidate me on the part of the others. At first I comforted myself by telling myself that they must be away attending to some business or other for the Rōshi, but when I saw that they were not there for *zazen* in the *zendō* I could contain myself no longer and I went to see Sakamoto san.

'Where is K. san?' I asked him, coming straight to the point. 'We were such good friends. I hope he is only away on a short trip. And where is X. san?' In view of what Sakamoto san told me I have chosen not to mention the names of these two monks here. He answered my question about X. san first.

X. san was a very fat and endlessly cheerful man who had been in the monastery for very many years. He had been one of the most advanced monks in the community, and we had been on particularly cordial terms with one another.

'He no longer belongs to the monastery,' replied Sakamoto san, his voice hard. 'Do you remember that he was friends with Mrs N.?' I remembered very well, for X. san himself had introduced me to this extremely pretty young divorcee and her little daughter. After her divorce from her unfaithful husband she had managed to build up a new life for herself. This is no mean feat for a woman in Japan, as alimony is completely unknown. She had become a seamstress, and when I met her she already had two employees and was completely independent. Her home had been tiny, but adequate, and it had contained everything she needed for a pleasant existence.

At the time I hadn't felt that there was anything unseemly about X. san's friendship with Mrs N. The two of them were such an unlikely couple that it never would have occurred to me to think that their relationship might be anything other than platonic. Mrs N. was charming, intelligent and very beautiful, and X. san was hulking and ungainly, and he had a waddling gait which made him seem rather ludicrous sometimes.

'They lived together as man and wife,' continued the secretary. 'Everything went well for several years, but then one of the Rōshi's lay disciples brought the matter to the Rōshi's attention. X. san had just been made First Monk when the Rōshi returned from Kyoto unexpectedly and caught him *in flagrante* with Mrs N. There was a terrible scene, and then X. san revolted against the Rōshi's authority, something I never would have expected of him.' What happened next was even more shameful. Sakamoto san told me that it had all taken place shortly before my return to the temple.

Mrs N. was no longer permitted to enter the temple and she moved to Okayama. X. san then announced that he intended to enter into another temple there. Before he left, however, he gave vent to his anger at the Rōshi, knowing full well that he did not need to fear retribution, as the temple could not afford the scandal which the dismissal of the First Monk would have caused.

'He accused the Rōshi of being a "propaganda Rōshi", who neglected his temple duties and appeared on television and on the radio purely for the sake of his own aggrandisement,' said Sakamoto san.

Whether they admitted it or not the other monks in the temple were perfectly well aware that statements like that were nothing but the purest malice, for they all knew the real reason why the Rōshi had been forced to take on these unpleasant extra chores: so that *they* could pursue their holy vocation. Even so, it is hardly surprising that the frequent repetition of statements like these did have some effect on the other monks, especially as they were usually made at times when the Rōshi was forced to be away from the temple for several days at a time, attending to his teaching duties at the Zen University in Kyoto.

But then something truly shocking happened which brought all the other monks back down to earth with a bump: One fine day X. san went out for a walk from which he never returned. Investigations were made, and it was discovered that he had boarded a merchant ship in Kobe, bound for America, and the money which he had needed for the journey was missing from the temple cash box. In his position as First Monk it had been his duty to adminstrate the finances, and he had had free access to the cash box. I could hardly believe my ears.

'But he doesn't speak a single word of English,' I said.

'No,' confirmed Sakamoto san, 'not a word.'

'What on earth does he think he is going to do in America then?'

'I have no idea.'

As it happened I was able to find out X. san's reason for wanting to go to America a few days later, and I was able to pass on this information to Sakamoto san. But more of that later. For the moment there was only one question burning in my heart.

'And where is K. san?' I asked in trepidation.

Before I write an account of Sakamoto's answer to this question I should like to say a few words about K. san himself, who was a very close and dear friend of mine. He was very different from all of the other monks in the monastery, and also from all other Japanese I had ever met. He was unique; he did not fit into any category.

Let me begin with his outward appearance: He was the most handsome Japanese whom I have ever encountered, and his physical beauty was enhanced by a kind of luminous aura which seemed to surround him; or perhaps it was the aura which gave him his beauty in the first place. In addition to this natural radiance he also possessed an alertness of mind which, in comparison with the other twenty-nine monks, made him seem like a lion among sheep. His lively temperament was very un-Japanese, and in his passionate enthusiasm he would sometimes overshoot the mark by quite a long way, but when his attention was drawn to his mistakes he always devoted the same innocent and energetic enthusiasm to clearing matters up again.

Because of his strength and the ecstatic joy and totality with which he lived for the great goal of Zen, sacrificing everything for it, I had always regarded him as the only monk in the monastery with the potential to become the Rōshi's successor someday. I only had one great fear, which I was unable to banish from my mind: What would happen if this passionate, radiant young man, who was one of those people whose very presence fills one with joy, were to be struck by the lightning bolt of carnal love? Would his spiritual passion be strong enough to tame his earthly desires?

I knew that he had no trouble dealing with his more minor emotions, for he himself had told me of the strict discipline to which he subjected himself. He had also been thirty-two when he had entered the monastery, and he had lived a great deal in those thirty-two years, which made leaving the world behind him easier. I had hoped that he really would be one of those very rare cases: a man overflowing with the energy of life and yet so deeply enthralled by the spirit that he is capable of bending his budding, outward-driving energies to the wheel of renouncement and to cleanse them and purify them and, ultimately, to raise them up transcendentally to the level of the One, the Creative Spirit Being.

Apart from the Rōshi himself K. san was the person I had been looking forward to seeing most. Four years are a long time if one devotes all one's efforts to unstinting spiritual work, and K. san had already been very far advanced on the path when I had left. I was eager to hear what new levels of realisation and spiritual joy he had reached.

'And where is K. san?' I asked in trepidation.

The Rōshi's secretary hesitated before he answered. After all, only a moment before he had told me the almost incredible story of the flight of a trusted and respected monk who had been a devoted disciple of the Rōshi for very many years. Sakamoto san must have sensed the fear which underlay my question, and he could not hide his own sadness when he finally did answer.

'K. san has been away on leave from the monastery for some time now.'

'On leave? What does that mean?'

Precisely what I had feared most had happened. This monk, whose greatest passion had been the search for the One, had 'fallen' in love, and as was his nature he had done so totally, accepting all the consequences. He hadn't tried to keep anything a secret; on the contrary, he had gone directly to the Rōshi, who had given him a dispensation to go on leave 'temporarily'.

However, this arrangement did not solve the problem. K. san was still a monk in his heart, and it was his most ardent wish to continue to belong to the monastic community of Shofukuji. More specifically, he wanted to marry his sweetheart and, at the same time, to continue to live in the monastery and to be the Rōshi's disciple. Such an arrangement was completely unheard-of, of course, and permission was refused. But K. san, who had moved to his mother's house in Gifu by this time, had been adamant. He refused to stop wearing his monk's robes, and he came to see the Rōshi again and again to ask him to change his mind. The Rōshi actually received him every time he came, but his hands were bound: monastery rules required him to refer K. san's request to the First Monk. As was to be expected, the First Monk brushed him off in no uncertain terms. Sakamoto san gave me a very dramatic rendering of Shika san's furious reply to K. san's humble petition:

'*You* have no right to so much as enter the *zendō* any more!

If you wish to take part in *zazen* then you must do so as a lay disciple, in the *hōndō*! And you must wear secular clothes, you are no longer permitted to enter the temple in your monk's robes!'

To me it seemed as though such total insensitivity to K. san's situation could only be the result of mindless hatred, and when I said this to Sakamoto san he confirmed my suspicions, his voice sad. Envy and jealousy which had been hidden for years, and which had never been plucked out by the roots as they should have been, had suddenly sprouted up within Shika san's heart and burst into ugly flower. Now that K. san had fallen from his former heights it wasn't enough for Shika san to give him a kick, he had to shame him in front of everyone else as well.

Shattered, I returned to my room in Myokan-ji and sat down in *zazen*. My heart was heavy with sorrow and grief. The root of the problem was the fact that, for years now, misdemeanours committed by the monks in the monastery had been covered up and kept quiet rather than being punished immediately, so that the Rōshi never came to know of any of these infringements of monastic discipline. If the Rōshi had been present in the temple all the time he might have been able to prevent things from taking such a turn, but the circumstances had made it impossible. Things had got especially bad after Mrs M.'s death and the financial difficulties which this caused for the monastery, which had forced the Rōshi to be away from the temple even more than usual, and the monks' bad conscience had then turned into opposition against the Rōshi.

The last events of which Sakamoto san had informed me had taken place between one and two months before my return. Now I knew why I had felt like a stranger in the Shofuku-ji – the aura of holiness was gone, it had been driven out. The outward appearance of monastic order was still there, but doubts and mistrust were seething beneath the seemingly peaceful surface, and the monks' hearts were taken up with arguments about the rectitude of what had happened, displacing the spirit of Zen.

Once again the thought came to me that it would be by no means a bad idea if the monks were to be required to give the Rōshi an honest account of their own state of mind and feelings at regular intervals. Not a confession in the Catholic sense, but a simple opportunity for an open dialogue outside of the *sanzen* room, in the course of which the monk in question would be able to unburden his heart and which would also show the Master the direction which the instructions given in *sanzen* should take.

Such a practice would be impossible, however, for it would not be in accordance with the tradition of Zen. The Masters of the past never countenanced any discussion of anything. The only thing which had any validity for them was that which contained everything and which eliminated all opposites, the Universal One, and in the face of that everything else was completely irrelevant and without substance. The old Masters were hard men, who were very strict with their disciples. Their own stony and unbelievably painful journey to the peak of enlightenment had taught them that there was only one way of winning this battle. Even so, according to the accounts which have been handed down to us none of these Masters ever had more than one or perhaps (at the most) two disciples, out of hundreds, who managed to attain to the truth of cosmic Buddhahood, despite their iron discipline.

In the past Zen temples were in secluded, undisturbed places where not a single 'civilised' sound disturbed their meditative peace. In those days the monks had to steel themselves with extreme physical exertion in addition to their spiritual exercises, often marching on foot over hill and dale for days on end and sleeping under the open sky. In ancient China, and later on in Japan, the conditions for retreat and meditation were truly ideal, but even then enlightenment was regarded as a rare and wonderful event. Nowadays, in our modern world, the conditions are very far from ideal. So much so, in fact, that one is tempted to believe that the attainment of the ultimate has become completely impossible.

The inconstant spirit of our age is opposed to that spirit whose essence and substance is nothing but simple, undivided Truth. It is no longer possible to see the stars from the night-time streets of our cities. In their blazing sea of light neon signs in all the different colours of the rainbow create an artificial day, eliminating the ancient magic of the night. This high-speed, noisy, elbowing spirit is like a hungry plague of weeds sucking the life out of everything, and it has made the kind of quiet retreat which was once possible almost completely unthinkable.

And quite apart from that, very few of the temples which were out-of-the-way in the past can lay any claim to that pleasant epithet today. And those temples which are unfortunate enough to be classified as national monuments, with parks and gardens famous for their aesthetic beauty, are overrun by daily busloads full of hoards of foreign and Japanese tourists, and additional busloads full of schoolchildren during the school holidays.

Our own temple, which is situated high up on a mountain a long way outside the city of Kobe, also used to be a place of peace and quiet and silent meditation. Now there was a busy main road a mere five minutes' walk away, and the temple was surrounded by little residential houses, some of them directly in front of the temple gates.

The result of this was that the monks were unable to avoid coming into contact with the neighbours whenever they went outside the temple, and since the men were usually away at work during the day the majority of people they encountered were women.

When a monk is asked to come to a private house to conduct a ritual he has to travel by public bus to get there. Japanese buses are always crowded, and no matter whether the monk wishes to or not he is forced to be in the company of a large number of other people and to come into physical contact with some of them. There is no way around it. The spirit of our age is opposed to the Spirit, its very essence consists in the total suppression and denial of the Spirit. Even now, everything on our planet is already out of balance, and what the final result of it all is going to be is no great mystery – all one has to do is look at any one of the many little everyday tragedies taking place all around us and extrapolate a little. Nothing can remain stable long when the inner balance of life has been destroyed, and despite all the artificial supports and crutches we have created to try to prevent it the collapse is bound to come sooner or later.

In our temple too the inner balance had been disturbed. Of course, there have always been disobedient monks, in every monastery, there is no denying that, but in the past their disobedience was born of their inner spiritual struggle, a battle which continued until they finally attained to the realisation of the true Self. In those days there was virtually no possibility of their being 'tempted' by the world outside, and it is not something which is ever mentioned in the records which have been handed down to us.

Now, however, things had changed, and the monks in Shofuku-ji were being ceaselessly bombarded on all sides by influences from the outside world. The monks best equipped to deal with this challenge were those who had entered into the monastery in middle life, for a man who has already lived and experienced 'life' in the outside world and has decided that he would like to leave it behind him is less likely to succumb to the temptations of that world.

Naturally, none of these temptations and disturbances creates any problems for religious geniuses like Rōshi Mumon. He is a being of the utmost and most total purity, and he attained to full enlightenment at a very early age. He is an exception to every rule, and can be regarded as a saint by any standards. It is the young monks and nuns who are just embarking on the great path who have the greatest difficulties with the distractions of the modern world.

Of the thirty monks in our temple there were only three, at most, who were over thirty years of age, and all of these young men were in constant contact with the outside world. For instance, the monks who did the shopping often secretly brought newspapers back to the monastery with them, newspapers which contained material which had an explosive effect on the monks' minds. And that is but one example among many.

Before they could make the transition from the noise and bustle of the outside world to the silence of *zazen* these monks first had to eliminate a wide range of inner and outer distractions which were completely unknown to the monks of the past. As late as the turn of the century the conditions in Zen monasteries were still more or less as they had been hundreds of years ago.

It was this constant and omnipresent threat which made me think that it might be of great value if these young monks were to be given the opportunity to unburden themselves of their troubles and worries in a regular open dialogue with their Rōshi, rather than ignoring them completely in accordance with the traditions of Zen. But the more I thought about the idea the clearer it became to me that it could not be put into practice. It would be impossible for the monks to go to the Rōshi with their earthly confusions. He was a being of pure spirit, living in an exalted and rarefied plane, and the only response which he would be able to give to the problems and questions of their plane, no matter whether they were impertinent or merely despairing, would be silence.

The only alternative was the old, traditional method which Zen monks have always used: self-discipline. The monks of the past only had to contend with the inner enemy, and even though this task is infinitely more difficult than building a rocket to fly to the moon it has become more difficult still for modern monks, for in addition to this inner battle they must also overcome the entire outside world as well.

The only effective way of saving the great work of enlightenment from this burgeoning spirit of laxity would be to reintroduce the iron discipline of the past, the kind of discipline which was prevalent in Zen monasteries a hundred years ago. But many experts contend that this too would be impossible, saying that the only result would be that the monks would simply leave and enter into other, more liberal monasteries.

For my own part I had to ask myself what it was that had brought me here at this time. In returning I had hoped to be able to get away from the mundane world and its distractions and duties, to find the peace and silence in which I would be able to enter again and again in the indescribable joy of samadhi. Instead, I had landed in the middle of a crisis. From my very first day back in the monastery onwards I had sensed the effects of this crisis so intensely that I had not been able to be really happy for a single moment, and the many practical difficulties which had been created for me only went to make everything worse. The one great exception to all this had been the Rōshi's wonderful reception upon my arrival.

Why? This question was to turn into a second kōan for me, one which was to preoccupy me very deeply.

Shortly after my conversation with Sakamoto san that morning I was allowed to go in to see the Rōshi, who had just returned from Kyoto. First of all I thanked him for the way in which he had helped me. Then I plucked up my courage and told him how deeply saddened I was at what Sakamoto san had told me about K. san, whom I had loved so dearly. An expression of pain appeared on the Rōshi's silent face.

'He will return,' I said, 'I do not have the slightest doubt about it. He has a passionate heart, and such a heart is always in greater danger than one which is lukewarm. But it is precisely that passionate heart which will not rest until it has brought him back to the place which he knows is his true home: to the One, in Zen. And my Rōshi, he loves you. He loves you more than anything else on this earth. He once said to me, "He is my father and my mother. He is my all in one, and my love for him knows no boundaries." And those words were the truth.

That monk is so deeply imbued with the spirit of Zen that there is no turning away from the path for him. He will return.'

My words were a spontaneous reaction to the pain in the Rōshi's eyes, and I was completely certain of the truth of what I was saying, without knowing why. I spoke up for his beloved disciple from the conviction of my heart, not from my intellect, and I know that my words were very different from the arrogant condemnation of K. san's spiritual 'illness' which the Rōshi must have heard all too often from others. What I said seemed to please him, and his spirits revived a little. 'Perhaps he will return when he hears that Ital san has returned . . . ' he replied after a short pause, smiling an endlessly loving smile.

At six o'clock that evening the three-day break came to an end and the seven-day Little *Zazen* began. Of course, *zazen* is always practised every day in the monastery, but this Little *Zazen* is a period of more intense meditation than usual, during which the monks are required to sit for longer periods, both in the *zendō* and in their cells. All the monks taking part also went to the Rōshi for *sanzen* on each of the seven days, something which was not always possible the rest of the time, as he was often away from the temple.

In my first *sanzen* session after my return, which I have already described in the previous chapter, the Rōshi's question had been:

'Have you mastered Jōshū's Mu completely? Have you known it in its totality?'

Today too Jōshū's Mu was the subject of his question.

'The monk asked Jōshū whether a dog has the Buddha Nature,' said the Rōshi. 'In reply Jōshū said, "No." What did he mean with this "No"?'

'Nothing,' I replied.

'Yes,' said the Rōshi. 'This Nothing is what you must realise.'

There was nothing for it. I was going to have to set to work on Jōshū's Mu all over again!

Obediently I returned to the peace and quiet of my room in Myokan-ji (which really was peaceful and quiet now) and started to meditate on Mu. I spent many hours in *zazen*, allowing this powerful, creative word to sink down into the very depths of my being. I started by using the method I had learned four years before from Master Osaka, the 'lay Master' under whose tutelage I had been before I came to Rōshi Mumon, and for whom I still have a very deep respect. It had been while I was practising this method that I had experienced my first great breakthrough into Cosmic Unity.

Even before I had started I had sensed that my experience with Jōshū's Mu was going to be different this time, and this feeling was very soon confirmed.

Everything was different, for everything took place on a different level. I must hasten to add that this statement is incorrect in strict Zen terms, for 'levels' do not really exist in any real sense. Even so, since I am not writing for Zen Masters but for the lay reader who is trying to grasp the method of Zen and what it is about I must sometimes use terms which may not be exactly accurate in order to get an idea across. Let me put it this way: after 'overcoming' or 'attaining' something one must again and again penetrate into ever deeper depths of realisation, and the experience becomes ever more profound and differentiated. In this context it can be helpful to speak of 'different levels', so long as one remembers that these levels do not really have any concrete reality. They are a kind of intellectual crutch.

One of the next questions which the Rōshi put to me in *sanzen* will help to illustrate how different things had now become:

'How is your Buddha Nature?'

Before, it had been my task to attain Buddha Nature. Now the Rōshi was asking me a test question, a question which had to be answered as quick as a flash. If one tries to use one's intellect to answer such a question one simply demonstrates that one does not have Zen.

The Rōshi accepted my answer. He nodded affirmatively and rang his little bell.

It seems that the way I had answered (what I said is irrelevant, what is important in situations like this is *how* the disciple answers) demonstrated something crucial to the Rōshi, for in the months which followed he did not ask me a single question. Instead, whenever I came in for *sanzen* he would simply make some brief statement. My task was then to realise the essence of the statement in my meditation. On the seventh day of the Little *Zazen*, for example, after his usual profound silence, he repeated the little anecdote of Jōshū's Mu once again. The usual closing line of this story is, 'Jōshū said, "Mu".' But instead of this the Rōshi said, 'Jōshū said, "No".' And then, after a short pause, and with a wonderfully humorous smile, he added, 'A very wonderful answer!' Then he rang his bell.

And so this 'wonderful answer', 'Mu' or 'No', became an

integral part of my being from now on, dogging me like an inner shadow day and night. It was as though everything in existence apart from myself and the kōan had simply ceased to be. And I was completely alone with it, for the Rōshi did not give me any help whatsoever in *sanzen*, nor did he give me any hints as to 'how' I was to carry out the task which he had given me. Even in the course of my meditation on the kōan of 'one hand clapping' four years before, the extreme exertion of which had resulted in a total physical collapse, he had at least guided me with admonitions and corrections. This time he did nothing of the sort. At first I went into each new *sanzen* session with high hopes, thinking that he would at least give me a hint, some fine thread of a direction which I would be able to follow, but that was not to be. Nor did he ask me any questions, as was the usual practice in *sanzen*, thus making it impossible for me to give any replies which he would have been forced to respond to.

The Rōshi left me completely alone with Jōshū's 'Nothing' (one of several translations of the word 'Mu'), adrift in the huge expanse of the Void. That wonderful, superlative Master! Again and again when I think back to the 'cruelty' with which he pushed me out into the boundless open sea I am overcome with a feeling of tremendous gratitude. It was as though he were saying to me, 'All right, you have learned how to swim. Now save your own life, or drown. And don't waste your time looking for something to hang on to, there is nothing.'

The events of the next months were so terrible that I hesitate to even write about them. This is partly because I do not think that I have the necessary gift of expression to be able to do them justice, and partly because the process of reliving these events, both physically and spiritually (which is necessary if the reader is not to be fobbed off with a mere account of 'results achieved') is so overwhelming and painful that I am often unable to write more than a few sentences at a time. This is something which I have experienced again and again in the course of writing this book. But write I must, for what transpired is very important: Everything, literally everything, seemed to be conspiring against me in order to drive me to the very brink of utter catastrophe. Finally, physically helpless and ill, Heaven brought me to a point at which I could not move in any direction. I was almost literally nailed to the spot, and forced to endure.

It is never until after the fact that one is able to see that circumstances such as these, which drive one on until one is within a hair's breadth of being destroyed completely, are actually a wonderful blessing, if one only has the strength to persevere and come out on the other side. So long as one is actually in the middle of the situation itself all one knows is that one is fighting for one's very survival.

At the end of the Little *Zazen* the Rōshi returned to Kyoto, and that very evening, when I returned home to Myokan-ji from *zazen* in the *zendo*, I found that the poor little nun with the head injuries had been moved into the prayer room next to my bedroom again. I felt terribly shocked, and, of course, I wasn't able to sleep a wink the whole night long. The next morning I went and objected to E. san.

'She stays there!' she snapped angrily. I protested, telling her what the Rōshi himself had said about the matter, but she cut me off in mid-sentence, repeating what she had already said several times before: 'The Rōshi has no right to make any decisions here!'

It was completely impossible for me to meditate under these circumstances, and the combination of this and my inability to sleep was more than I could bear. I was in a terrible state. The Rōshi's secretary wasn't there when I went to see him, and by the time I finally managed to find him the next day I was feeling so low that I had made up my mind that I would either fly back to Germany or rent myself a room somewhere in the neighbourhood.

When I told him what had happened Sakamoto san was so incensed that he took me straight in to see the First Monk. Shika san was now on our side, as he knew perfectly well that all the rooms in Myokan-ji were empty. He sent a messenger to tell E. san to come to see him. I never found out what he said to her, or what she replied.

As it turned out, however, the Rōshi had returned from Kyoto unexpectedly, and he called E. san in to see him in his chambers that evening. Sakamoto san had informed the Rōshi's attendant of what was afoot, and he was in the room next door when the nun arrived. Afterwards he told Sakamoto san what the Rōshi had said, and Sakamoto san passed it on to me.

'The Rōshi was very angry,' said Sakamoto san. 'He told E. san that you had been a friend of Mrs M.'s (in whose memory Myokan-ji had been built) and that you need peace and quiet to practise *zazen*, and then he ordered her to leave you alone and not to trouble you. And before telling her to go he said, "I built Myokan-ji with my own money, and I decide what happens there, no one else." '

The little nun was moved back downstairs again.

10

The Great Zazen

The Great *Zazen*, a seven-day period of even more intense meditation than the Little *Zazen*, began on the first of July. Our daily programme was as follows:

4.00– 5.00 a.m.	Service in the *hōndō*
8.00–10.30 a.m.	*zazen* in the *zendō*
1.00– 3.30 p.m.	*zazen* in the *zendō*
6.00– 9.30 p.m.	*zazen* in the *zendō*

In my diary I wrote, 'I can only pray that I manage to find the strength to see it through to the end.' Of course, the Great *Zazen* is an enormous exertion for everyone who takes part, but nonetheless it was still easier for the other monks than it was for me, and not only because of their youth. Their cells were a mere thirty seconds' walk away from the meditation hall, so it was possible for them to go there and rest after every *zazen* session, and their meals were also prepared for them by the monastery kitchen. On my last visit I too had had the benefit of these advantages, but now I had to be up and dressed before half past three in the morning in order to be able to get to the *hōndō* in time for the early morning service. It was still pitch dark at that early hour, and it usually took me at least ten minutes to grope my way to the temple, even if the weather was good. On top of all this I also had to make my own meals, walking back and forth between Myokan-ji and the main temple between the *zazen* sessions.

A few minutes before four o'clock in the morning the monk

on duty would make his rounds of the monks' cells with a torch and a little bell in his hands, stopping in front of each cell and ringing the bell gently to wake the monks and call them to the morning service. They slept in their grey under-robes, and all they had to do after getting up was to wrap their belts around their waists, pull their thin, dark blue robes over their heads and rinse their faces with a little cold water at the well. My morning toilet was unbelievably complicated in comparison.

Traditionally the Great *Zazen* began with the Saturday evening *zazen* session. The next morning, the first official day of the Great *Zazen*, I was waiting in front of the entrance to the *hōndō* even before the monk on duty had set out on his rounds to wake his brothers. He gave me an astonished and rather unfriendly look as he walked past.

The first day of the Great *Zazen* was particularly taxing. It was Sunday, and in addition to the usual programme the Rōshi also delivered a one-hour lecture for the residents of the monastery and his lay disciples, starting at seven a.m. This meant that it was impossible for me to rest at all between the morning service and the beginning of the lecture, as I had to return to Myokan-ji to wash, change my clothes and do my hair. I had only been able to wash perfunctorily in the darkness of the early morning, and I knew that it was important for me to make a good impression, as it was the first time that I was going to be seen in public since my return and I was bound to be the centre of curious attention.

I have to admit that the Rōshi's lecture was a terrible ordeal for me. I was completely exhausted, and I wasn't able to understand a single word of what he said. I had to gather all my inner resources to keep my head from dropping forward on to my chest. (This was a battle which some of the monks sitting around me lost, incidentally.) When the lecture was over I and all the other monks returned directly to the *zendō* for the next *zazen* session, which lasted from eight until ten thirty. As soon as I sat down in the *zendō* and began to meditate, however, my tiredness disappeared completely, as though it had never been there.

During the seven days of the Great *Zazen* the monks went in to the Rōshi for *sanzen* during every single *zazen* session, which meant that they saw him four times a day. The Rōshi thus had to give a total of 120 *sanzen* sessions a day, and in every session he had to be completely concentrated and alert, giving each individual monk precisely the instructions he needed.

I only went in for *sanzen* twice a day, which meant that I was treated to two wonderful periods of particularly profound silence every day, after the Rōshi had rung his bell and the monks had rushed out to wait in the gallery outside the *sanzen* room.

'You must be oneness with the "Muuuu . . . ",' said the Rōshi again and again as I kneeled down before him in *sanzen*, making the sound of the 'Mu' particularly long and resonant. Then he would ring his bell, indicating that the session was over.

I always felt envious of the other monks while I was kneeling in the silence of the gallery outside the *sanzen* room, waiting for my turn to go in to see the Rōshi. All of them, without exception, were in the room with him for longer than I was, some of them several minutes longer. This meant that they had to answer questions, and I knew that no matter how unsatisfactory their answers were the responses which the Rōshi gave them, even if it were severe criticism, would give them an indication of the direction in which they needed to go. The only help he gave me was the endless repetition of that same cryptic command, 'You must be oneness with the "Mu".' There was nothing I could say in response, nor could I ask any questions. It was up to me to attain it, that was all. I was on my own.

Diary, July 4 1967

I have a fever. Today is the fourth day of the Great *Zazen*, and although I did manage to drag myself to the *zendō* this morning I had to turn back at the entrance. I was simply too weak. The fever has been brought on by the extreme weather, which is making the strain of the Great *Zazen* even worse than usual. The rainy season started unusually late this year. The first rains came on the second of July, which was the day before yesterday. Even though I had an umbrella with me that morning I was soaked through when I arrived at the *zendō*, and I sat in *zazen* for three and a half hours in my wet things. It didn't rain the next day (that was yesterday), but the air was hot and sticky, like the air in a greenhouse, and my temperature started going up. Even so, I went to the *zendō* and took part in *zazen*. If only I was able to live in the temple as I did before! Then I wouldn't have got wet at all.

Diary, July 5 1967

I was forced to stay in my room again today. I felt so deathly weak this morning that I couldn't even leave the house, I had to lie down again a few moments after getting up. Why is all this happening to me? I can't make head or tail of it. I don't understand myself, and I don't understand what is going on. It must be the climate. The awful changeability of the weather in the rainy season is literally breaking me. But what is the spiritual implication of my failure in the Great *Zazen*? It can only mean that I am supposed to continue with my work here in peace and quiet, away from the pressure and the terrible overexertion. I haven't said anything about this to the Rōshi yet. The certainty which I feel is so profound and overwhelming that I do not want to say a single word. I want to allow the truth of it to bear witness to itself, in silence.

Diary, July 8 1967

Yesterday was the last day of the Great *Zazen*. I didn't feel at all well. The weather was terrible. Everything was damp and wet and steamy. It was impossible to see clearly, the entire world was shrouded in wet, white steam. Breathing was torture, and for the first time since my arrival I felt a terrible sense of constriction in my chest, as though it were being crushed inwards by an iron band. Nonetheless, I still managed to make it to the temple early this morning for *zazen*.

In *sanzen* today the Rōshi said, 'Be oneness with the kōan "Mu".' That was all, as usual. The Buddha within him is driving me deeper and deeper into the state of total detachment.

The realisation which I have already attained must be deepened, it must become a complete and utter reality. And to do that I must destroy myself, willingly, knowingly, using 'Mu' as my tool.

Diary, July 9 1967

The rain is pouring down in buckets. The world has disappeared. There is only rain, a leaden, wet curtain hiding everything. Nonetheless, I feel cheerful and buoyant within. The work of destruction with 'Mu' has started to bring results. Yesterday I started to come out of the state of depression I was in, in which I was simply 'enduring'. I have also become free of the desire to escape that feeling of depression. I am going to destroy myself, come what may. Mu!

I have also received the inner instruction that I should work more, and more intensely. I shall obey. The period of adjustment with my concomitant inner resistance to my situation must now come to an end. I *shall* destroy myself.

And what is the outcome of this incredibly intense meditation? Relaxed cheerfulness. It is incredible.

Two hours later:
It is impossible to imagine what these Japanese typhoons are like until one has experienced one oneself. E. san and I were able to close and bar all the downstairs windows of our little nunnery before the storm struck, as we had been warned that it was coming, but it was already upon us by the time we started on the upstairs windows, and one of them was blown open by the wind before we could close it properly. The opening was no wider than the palm of my hand (the catch which prevents the window from opening any wider than that held), and it was only open for a couple of seconds, but that was enough to knock us both over and soak us through and through. Once we had cleaned everything up again (we were alone in the house) we stood by the window in silence for a long time and watched the storm. It was as if a cosmic ocean were crashing down on us out of the sky. All we could see were storm-tossed, blue-grey masses of water.

Will our little nunnery be able to withstand this terrible onslaught? And what about the main temple, perched precariously on the mountainside? What if there is a landslide and it is completely buried? To try to go there now would be certain death, all I can do is accept the situation as it is. One is simply helpless in the face of these gigantic, elemental forces.

Diary, July 11 1967

We have survived the storm, but there have been many terrible tragedies. On the radio they said that there hasn't been a typhoon like this one in Japan for more than thirty years. It swept across the whole country, all the way from Osaka to Hiroshima, but the main centre of destruction is here. In Kobe and the surrounding area the death toll has already reached 354, not counting all the people who have been buried by rubble and landslides and who haven't been found yet. The scale of the destruction is unbelievable. The city centre of Kobe has been closed off completely by the authorities.

An air raid is destruction by fire. This is destruction by water. Some of our little mountain paths and alleyways have been turned into streams and rivers, others into stinking mud slicks. Either way they are impassable. Nonetheless, this morning I donned my rubber boots and managed to make my way to the main temple, by a very roundabout route. I am not quite sure how I managed it. The temple is still there, thank God, but the front garden is knee-deep in a sea of mud, and the gate at the top of the broad flight of thirty-two steps leading up to the Rōshi's residence has collapsed. (This is the gate which remains closed when the Rōshi is not in the temple.) It is an incredible sight. The steps themselves are completely gone, and where they used to be is a raging torrent of water flowing down from the mountain. Some of the obstacles in its way it buries beneath a layer of mud and rubble, others are swept along with it into the valley.

Luckily, the Rōshi was away in Kyoto during the storm, and he is not going to be back until tomorrow morning as the trains have all been cancelled. All the monks in the monastery are completely exhausted. They have been working outside in their tall fisherman's rubber boots and their working trousers ever since the storm began.

Diary, July 13 1967

We have had no bread since the morning of the tenth. Our flour supplies were all washed away in the storm. There is no milk, no vegetables . . . in fact we have nothing at all. It is terrible.

Diary, July 14 1967

What the monks have managed to achieve in a few short days is truly incredible. This tragedy has shown that the spirit of Zen is alive in them, the spirit which demands that one should do that which is most important now, in this very moment, and do it totally. They have been working day and night in two shifts to repair the worst of the damage. They have cleared a great deal of the mud from the front courtyard, piling it up into two huge piles, one on the left and one on the right, and they have laid out wooden planks on the ground so that we can at least make our way through to the *zendō*. We had our first *zazen* since the storm today, but it only lasted for two hours because the monks were all so tired. Nonetheless, we still went in to the Rōshi for *sanzen*.

This afternoon – at last – a police contigent was sent to help clear the little mountain roads of the mountains of mud and debris. Even if any food were available no one here would be able to get down to the main street to go shopping.

Diary, July 15 1967

Today I put my rubber boots on and made my way down through the mud to the main street. The people living a little further down the mountainside have been circulating the rumour that food has become available again.

The sight which met my eyes was both terrible and impressive. Terrible because of the sheer scale of the disaster, and impressive because of the way in which the work of cleaning up is being carried out. There are mountains of cloying mud everywhere, and the streets are still full of water because all the drains are blocked. Tractors and bulldozers were shifting all the mud out of the way, mud which was full of dead animals (mainly snakes) and rubbish. Planks had been laid over several huge holes in the tarmac and the pavements, and there were policemen standing at either end of these planks helping the pedestrians across. Needless to say, no buses and taxis are running yet.

We don't have a refrigerator here in Myokan-ji and so I only had supplies for a single day when the storm struck, because of the heat. All I have had to eat since then has been one cup of coffee for breakfast in the mornings and one piece of crispbread later in the day. The crispbread is a present from Germany which a friend sent me a while ago.

Despite my leaden tiredness I managed to make my way to the shops at the end of the main street, step by step, where I was able to do a little shopping. On the left hand side of the road, on the same side as the shops, was another sight which I shall never forget. There were a large number of makeshift beds on the pavement near to the road, and in the beds lay the children and the wounded. The bedrooms at the back of the little shops, on the side facing towards the sea, had been completely washed away. But everyone was already hard at work rebuilding the light structures, and the air was full of the noise of hammers, saws and shovels.

Again and again on my way home, I have no idea how often, I had to fight back attacks of weakness. I have no idea how I managed it, but I knew that my legs were the only means of transport available, and that I simply had to manage it. Even so, I don't think I would have made it if I hadn't be able to stop at one of the little roadside cafüs. Luckily, the air-conditioning was actually working, which was a godsend considering the state I was in.

I had an extremely interesting conversation with a chance acquaintance in this café, in the course of which I learned a great deal about the reasons for X. san's disappearance from the monastery and about a number of other things as well. I only wrote a few, very telegraphic words about this encounter in my diary. What follows is a much fuller account written from memory, with the help of my notes.

I sat down at one of the tables and ordered a glass of iced coffee to revive my flagging spirits. The waiter came with the coffee, and after drinking it I started to feel better almost at once. A moment later a young American – he must have been about thirty or so – came and sat down at my table. I had seen him at evening *zazen* in the temple a couple of times. After exchanging a few polite phrases about the storm and the destruction which it had caused – in response to my question he replied that he hadn't been able to come and help the monks in the temple because the road had been 'too bad' – he finally came to the point. He knew all about my first visit to the temple four years before, and that I had published a book on the subject. I got the impression that the monks had painted him a rather exaggerated picture of the success which my book had had at home in Germany. To put it in a nutshell, he found me 'interesting'.

'I've heard that you've got students of your own in Germany,' he said with brazen directness, 'I'd sure be interested to hear how you teach them Zen.'

I replied very cautiously, as there was something about his cheeky arrogance and the way he talked about Japan in general and the temple in particular which I did not like at all. I began by asking him, as politely as I could, how it was that he was able to participate in evening *zazen* in the *zendō*, something which was normally unthinkable for outsiders. He laughed.

'Oh, X. san fixed that up for me.'

That's interesting, I thought, remembering that X. san had been First Monk until his sudden departure four weeks before.

'I was very sad not to find X. san here when I returned,' I replied, 'he was a very good friend of mine. I miss him very much.'

'Oh, that's great, X. san is my best buddy,' said the American with great enthusiasm.

'Unfortunately, the circumstances under which he left the monastery were anything but pleasant,' I added sadly. It was as though I had given him a signal. He immediately launched into a long tirade about X. san, whom he referred to as an 'enlightened monk', and the monastery, informing me that everything I had been told about what had happened was nothing but a pack of lies. X. san had been a wonderful monk, he said, and greatly loved by everybody, and he asserted vociferously that these lies had all been fabricated and circulated merely to cover up the real reason for his sudden departure, which was that he had no longer been able to tolerate the state of affairs at the temple.

'But what on earth is he going to do in America?' I countered. 'He can't speak a word of English.'

'No problem there,' replied the clever *zazen* participant with a cynical laugh, 'I gave him lessons for several months before he left. And as soon as he arrives in the States he's gonna learn a whole lot more.'

'And what is he going to live on there?'

'Don't you worry about that, it's all fixed up. He's gonna live at my parents' place. He's really gonna make it big over there.'

'That won't be easy,' I said, 'there is no short supply of Eastern gurus in America.'

'If it doesn't work in the States then we can go to Mexico and pull off the trip there. I speak Spanish and I love Mexico.'

'Oh, I see, you are going to be his partner . . . ' My voice trailed off in astonishment.

'Yeah, of course. Why else do you think I'm getting into all this mumbo-jumbo here?'

I felt sick. It was about at this point that he realised that he had said more than he should have and that I wasn't a potential accomplice. He immediately changed the topic of the conversation, telling me that the little summer house that he and his girlfriend had rented up in the mountains had been destroyed in the storm. They had been planning to spend the next few months there.

'We had laid out a vegetable garden up there. We wanted to find out what kind of stuff grows best in the heat and the dry soil. For Mexico . . . ' He laughed.

After taking my leave of him I made my way back home slowly through the quagmire. I was covered with a crust of dried mud by the time I got back to Myokan-ji, but it didn't bother me in the least. At least mud can be washed off, I thought with a wry grimace.

Now I understood the reason for X. san's seemingly inexplicable flight to America: the American had managed to get a hold on him while he was going through a time of personal crisis, taking advantage of the monk's weakness for his own ends. It had been a coolly calculated ploy. The American had no profession of his own, and with X. san's help he hoped to be able to find his way onto Easy Street. He was only practising Zen in the temple in order to find out how to 'set up the business', so to speak. I was aghast. 'So this is how Zen schools in America get founded,' I thought to myself, 'as a way of making a quick buck!'

The third person in the American's little gang, apart from

himself and X. san, was his girlfriend Miss O. She was from America too, the daughter of a Polish immigrant who had been somewhat less than successful in the New World. She was a dancer by profession, and her teacher in America had suggested that she travel to Japan to study with a famous Kabuki Master in Tokyo. Her studies there were quite successful; at least, I assume that they were, as her boyfriend told me that she had planned to return to the USA to teach Kabuki there. But then, after one and a half years in Japan, she suddenly started having severe trouble with her knees, and her Kabuki Master gave her a letter of introduction to Rōshi Mumon, in which he asked that she be permitted to take part in the open *zazen* sessions in Shofuku-ji. Since Kabuki dance is one of the traditional Zen arts the Rōshi granted his permission. And so she came to Kobe, bringing her boyfriend with her.

Miss O. supported herself in Kobe by teaching English. The little house she lived in was actually the gatekeeper's lodge of Myokan-ji, and in exchange for being permitted to live there she had to help out in the kitchen in Shofuku-ji when the big lecture hall was rented out for large parties and other social gatherings, something which happened quite frequently. This was a welcome source of extra income for the monastic community, for in addition to the rental fee for the hall itself all the food and drink was provided by the temple and prepared in the temple kitchen. Extra help was always welcome, as the work of preparing the food for a hundred people or more often took several days, and washing the dishes and cleaning up afterwards was also no mean task.

When I got back to the temple I went straight to Sakamoto san and told him the whole story. When I reached the part about the gang of three's plan to found a Zen school under the guidance and tutelage of 'Master' X. san, Sakamoto san burst out into peals of laughter and said that it was bound to be a very amusing establishment. I was very surprised at this, but then the reactions of the Japanese are always unpredictable and unexpected.

I then pointed out that it was hardly likely that taking the money from the temple cashbox had been X. san's own idea. I felt that it was much more probable that X. san had been following the 'advice' of his American partner, as I was sure that he had no scruples whatsoever when it came to realising his own objectives. Sakamoto san nodded, and agreed that this was probably the case.

To my great astonishment, however, nothing at all happened. The American continued to come to evening *zazen* whenever he felt like it. This shocked me even more than everything else which had preceded it, and more than that which was to follow as well, for it demonstrated a high degree of shameful opportunism on the part of the monks in charge of the monastery. Their reason for tolerating him was obvious: they were afraid that he would take revenge on the monastery if they were to refuse to allow him to take part in *zazen*, by telling people in the city interesting pieces of gossip about the doings of some of the monks on their days off. It was an open secret that he had access to plenty of information which could have been embarrassing to the temple.

Two months after my conversation with him in the little café this American gentleman simply did a bunk, without saying a word to anyone, and of course without bothering to thank the Rōshi for everything which he had done for him. The hospitality and friendship which he had been shown in the temple didn't seem to have meant anything at all to him.

I learned of his departure from Miss O., almost immediately after he had left. I was just coming out of Myokan-ji early one morning when I saw her walking up the road towards me, looking tearful and distraught. I knew that she hadn't spent the night in the gatekeeper's lodge where she lived, but that was nothing unusual, and in any case it was none of anybody's business as she was not really a member of our little community.

'What on earth is the matter?' I asked her.

'My boyfriend has gone!' she replied miserably. She was so upset that she blurted out the whole story. It seems that her delightful lover had kept his plans to himself until the very last minute. They had left his room together that morning, and after locking the door he had simply handed her his keys, asking her to take care of a few things which he didn't have time to deal with himself. When she had asked what he meant he had explained that he had a boat to catch, a freighter on which he was going to work his passage to New York.

I was flabbergasted. If he was capable of treating his own girlfriend in such a cold, calculating way, then what about X. san? I couldn't help wondering what sort of tricks he had used to get the monk to participate in his plans.

Diary, July 15 1967

Yesterday too we only had a brief *zazen* sitting, and it looks as though these short sessions are going to continue for quite a while. Even clearing up the very worst of the damage and debris is a mammoth task, and the monks are so exhausted from all the physical work which they have to do every day that they are in a state of near-collapse in the evenings. And there is still a huge amount of work yet to be done.

Going back and forth between Shofuku-ji and Myokan-ji has become something of a balancing act. I have to use a very roundabout route, hopping from stone to stone and crossing yawning chasms in the roads on 'bridges' consisting of wooden planks, which are in short supply, like everything else. The city authorities are unable to do anything for us up here on the mountain, of course, as they need every available man down in the city, which is still in a state of total chaos, and also for the search parties which are being sent out to look for people who have gone missing and to dig out the dead bodies from the rubble and mud on the slopes. Everything has to be done very quickly now; the weather has become extremely hot and humid – much hotter than before – and if all the dead animals are not disposed of soon we could well have an epidemic on top of everything else.

The Rōshi is driving me deeper and deeper into 'Mu', into Non-Being. The combination of the overwhelming natural catastrophe which we have been subjected to, in the face of which human intelligence is completely helpless, and all the different shocks and trials which I have had to face since I arrived, has made it much easier for the Void to break down the last crumbling barriers between myself and It.

While I was meditating it dawned upon me, in the form of an inner message, that I must now extend the scope of my work of self-destruction, to include both my wish for a pleasant, agreeable existence and my wish for non-existence. All desires have to go, without exception.

The Rōshi no longer gives me hints or suggestions as to which way I should go. That is no longer necessary at this level of the work with 'Mu'. (Once again I have to use the word 'level' to explain what I mean.) If the seeker meditates properly, without making any allowances for his own humanity and everything connected with it, the instructions come of their own accord, like sudden flashes of illumination from the depths. And one must respond and obey with the same lightning speed. There is no way I can possibly describe this inner process which takes place during *zazen*, for nothing takes place which could be described. One simply 'knows' what is required, and one must then choose whether one is going to follow the directions or not.

At midday today Sakamoto san came to see me unexpectedly, bringing me presents from the Rōshi: a packet of good English tea and an envelope containing 10,000 Yen. Today and tomorrow are days on which one traditionally gives presents in Japan. I couldn't understand why the Rōshi should be sending me money, and when I asked Sakamoto san about it he explained that the Rōshi was very concerned that I should receive my food from the temple just like all the others. Since E. san is still refusing to prepare my food for me he feels that sending me money is the only way of accomplishing this.

'The Rōshi said that Ital san has the same status in the monastery as all the other monks,' said Sakamoto san, refusing adamantly to take the envelope back when I tried to give it to him. He claimed that he was not allowed to.

After Sakamoto san had taken his leave I sat down and wrote the Rōshi a letter of thanks, in which I asked him to take the money back, saying that I know how hard he has to work to make the money needed for the maintenance of the temple and that I don't want him to be burdened by any unnecessary expenses on my account. I also promised to contact him immediately and ask him for his help if I ever do get into dire straits during my stay here.

As I was giving the letter to the Rōshi's attendant in his residence I met Sakamoto san, who whispered in my ear that the Rōshi had decided to order a small refrigerator for me so that I can keep a small supply of food and drink cool during the hot season. I whispered back that there was nothing which could have made me happier.

Despite all his troubles, despite the chaos everything is in at the moment, the loving heart of this holy man still finds time to think about a refrigerator for me. It is unbelievable.

The hot weather has now descended upon us. In its own way the heat is just as violent as last week's typhoon. It is a wet heat, which makes the earth steam and reduces the human beings who must live on that earth to a state of utter helplessness.

Diary, July 18 1967

It was terribly difficult, but on the Rōshi's birthday I managed to make my way through the mud and rubble to his residence. He had given me his permission to visit him, and I was able to spend quarter of an hour in his company. He looked very tired. He had left for Arima at five in the morning, directly after the early morning service, and he had just returned as I arrived at his residence. Arima is about one and a half hour's drive from Shofuku-ji. He had been visiting some of the rich benefactors of the temple to ask them to help finance the repair and restoration work which now has to be done. The most urgent project is the building of a wall to protect the temple buildings against landslides, at least at the most dangerous point. According to the estimate which has been made this alone is going to cost a million Yen, but it must be done very soon. Even though the destruction caused by landslides everywhere in the district is already incalculable it seems that the worst may yet be to come. The newspapers say that the next typhoon, even if it is only of medium intensity, could easily cause entire mountainsides to start moving at once in all the areas where they have already been loosened by the first storm.

I gave the Rōshi the small birthday presents which I brought with me from Germany, and we ate an ice cream together. As soon as we had finished he went directly to the large lecture hall. He delivers public lectures there several times a year, and today was one of the days. His talk had actually been due to start at ten, but because of our little birthday party it was now 10.15, and the lecture hall was already packed with hundreds of people.

His lecture lasted until a little before half past eleven, and few minutes after he had finished speaking he set off to catch a train to Kyoto, where he was due to deliver another lecture at two. His programme for the rest of the day was as follows. Straight after the lecture in Kyoto he received visitors (only those with appointments). Then, between six and seven in the evening, he had to deliver yet another lecture. At nine he boarded the train back to Kobe, arriving here in Shofuku-ji at ten. Sakamoto san was waiting for him when he arrived, and they spent the rest of the evening going through the galleys of the first sections of the Rōshi's new book, which had just come back from the publishers. And that after an eighteen-hour day of ceaseless activity, in this murderous heat!

Diary, July 19 1967

I am afraid that I shan't be able to stand it much longer. The heat is worse than anything I have ever known. I can hardly move at all. Under normal circumstances the location of my room has a number of advantages, but now it is like an oven. Worse. Even the electric fan which I have borrowed is no help, for the air which it moves around is so hot that it feels like air from a heater. Sitting in *zazen* has become impossible. This is driving me to despair, for meditation is my only reason for being here. I am usually only able to 'sit' in the very early morning. I don't have the strength for it later in the day. Luckily, there is no *zazen* at the temple at the moment.

To top everything I have now come down with the same allergy that I had four years ago. I have tiny little white lumps under the surface of my skin all over my hands, arms and neck. I have no idea what it is that causes it, but it itches terribly.

Diary, July 20 1967

Feeling too wretched to write much. Temperature in my room over a hundred during the day, and it only drops by about one degree at night. Nothing cool to drink, as the tap water is warm and the refrigerator hasn't arrived yet. Didn't sleep more than three hours last night, and that with the help of sleeping pills. Then three hours of concentrated *zazen.* Too weak to go on now. How utterly devastating a change in climate can be!

The Rōshi noticed the allergy and sent me to his doctor. He gave me some pills and a little vial of ointment.

Diary, July 23 1967

This is the first entry for two days now. I have managed to keep up with my *zazen*, but only with a desperate effort. Afterwards I am so tired that I am unable to do anything else.

Last night Sakamoto san came and informed me that the Rōshi had no time to attend the annual Zen archery festival, and that he had decided to send me to represent him. This festival, which took place today, is a very important event.

'You must be at the temple before eight o'clock tomorrow morning,' said Sakamoto san. 'The festival president is going to come by to pick you up. He is the greatest living archery Master. I shall accompany you, to interpret.' I thanked him for the honour and asked him how I should dress. 'European. Elegant,' he replied.

The famous Master's car arrived shortly before eight this morning. After we had been introduced we drove to the outlying district where the festival was to take place. It took a little more than half an hour to get there, and I was very glad that the car was air-conditioned. After the wonderful coolness of the drive, which had revived my spirits considerably, stepping out into the murderous heat again was a terrible shock, and for the first few minutes I felt almost paralysed. My Japanese companions fared no better than I, however, so I didn't feel too bad about it.

A huge, horseshoe-shaped marquee had been set up in the middle of the meadow. The stand for the guests of honour was in the middle of the marquee. On the right of the stand was a very long table for the committee of judges, and off to the left was an enclosed space where the archers were to perform.

No spectators were allowed. The sports fans who had come to try to get at least a glimpse of what was going on had to stand a long way back, behind the fence at the other end of the field. The archers, disciples of Zen Masters from all over Japan, sat waiting for their turn behind a curtain to the rear of the tribune.

Before the actual performance started all my time was taken up with a seemingly endless series of introductions, which, in Japan, means bowing again and again and again. I was the only woman among the guests of honour, and of course this unheard-of event had to be explained to all of the gentlemen in the judges' committee, one by one. All of them were dressed in very formal European suits, in black.

'*Doitsu no Mumon Rōshi wa*,' announced Sakamoto san with obvious pleasure to each of them as I was introduced, using the loving nickname given to me by some of the monks in the temple. Translated into English what he said means, roughly, 'Germany's Rōshi Mumon.'

Shortly before half past nine, which was when the performance was due to begin, I was led to the Rōshi's seat of honour, on the president's right. 'The Lady-Rōshi seat,' whispered Sakamoto san in my ear as I sat down. The next two hours were an unforgettable experience.

Diary, July 24 1967

I was unable to write any more yesterday. I had plenty of time, as the president drove me back to Shofuku-ji in the late afternoon, but the heat in my room made it impossible for me to think. It was dreadful. I shall try to finish the story now.

As the first archer made his appearance the president leaned over and informed me that the man was an important Master in his own right. The noble grandeur of his performance was so overwhelming that it made me shiver. He was dressed in the traditional costume of a samurai, and simply to see him striding out slowly to the place where he was to shoot was an impressive sight on its own. Then he 'danced' the movements of the opening ceremony, nocked his arrow and lifted the bow high above his head, very slowly, as if in slow motion, pulling back the arrow as he did so. Then he lowered the bow into the position from which he was going to shoot and waited for a few moments, absolutely motionless.

The moment he made his first steps I emptied myself inwardly, becoming one with archer, bow and arrow. Before the arrow was released I was in the state of Buddha Unity. 'It' carried the arrow to its destination.

After the arrow had struck the target the Master bowed. This bow was not a response to the thunderous applause which swelled up behind him; he was bowing to the event itself, to the suchness of the moment. He released three arrows in all, and every one of them struck the very centre of the target, which was a good two hundred yards away from him.

This unique experience of being both spectator and participant at the same time would never have been possible if I hadn't been aquainted with Eugen Herrigel's famous book, *Zen in the Art of Archery*.[1] Once again I was reminded just what a priceless jewel this enlightened little book of Herrigel's is.

'Do you know where the Master's arrow went?' asked the president. He had been watching me during the Master's performance, probably to see whether I really did live in Zen, as he had been told.

'Yes,' I replied, 'into my heart.' He smiled and said something to Sakamoto san in Japanese, very quickly.

'The president asks me to tell you that you should not do what you have just done too often,' said Sakamoto san. 'It is too taxing.'

Then, one after another, the other archers stepped forward and shot their arrows. All of them were dressed in the same ceremonial costumes, made of dark blue material with long, enormously broad trousers which looked rather like divided skirts. There were many breathtaking shots, but it was not the hits which were important – what mattered was what took place *before* the arrow was released.

Among all the archers who took part there was only one woman. She was a disciple of the president's. She did not score a hit, but her performance was marvellous all the same. After the event was over the president invited me to join him for a simple meal of rice, at which several members of the committee and this young lady were also present. I was told that she conducted archery courses for university students (for women only, of course) and high-school girls.

After we had finished eating the president had a bow brought in. He beckoned me to come over to where he was standing, holding out the bow to me. He guided my hands, helping me to put my fingers in the right position, and then he told me to pull back the bowstring. He repeated this again and again, watching everything I did very attentively and repositioning my fingers almost every time. Of course, my attempts were very far from perfect, and without his help I wouldn't have managed it at all, but throughout it all there was not the slightest tiny desire to achieve anything in my mind. I have no idea how he managed to sense my emptiness (Sakamoto san told me later that the president had spoken to the young lady who was his disciple about this), but the fact is that he did sense it, and he suggested that I should take part in the next course, which is going to begin in September.

'I should be delighted to, with my Rōshi's permission,' I replied. It was a truly unforgettable day.

Today Sakamoto san came to Myokan-ji, accompanied by two men carrying the new refrigerator.

'The main compartments of the refrigerator are for Ital san. Order from the Rōshi,' he said energetically to E. san as he left. He was obviously well aware of what was likely to happen if he hadn't made this statement. Even so, I found the situation very embarrassing.

'I am sure we shall be able to come to some arrangement,' I said to E. san, in an attempt to console her.

I immediately sat down and wrote the Rōshi a letter, thanking him for his spiritual and material presents – the experience of the archery festival and the refrigerator.

Diary, July 25 1967

I went and visited Sakamoto san today, bringing him some fruit I had bought on one of my night-time shopping trips (the shops down on the main street are all open till midnight). He told me that the Rōshi had said that I am like a daughter to him. It is things like this which give me the strength to go on.

Diary, July 29 1967

The heat is merciless. On the 26th I collapsed in a dead faint, and when I finally came to my senses I was lying on the floor downstairs, next to the little ladder leading up to the dormitories and my room. I must have been unconscious for several hours. I went to see Dr Imachi, the director of the University Clinic. He prescribed ice packs, saying that nothing else would be of any help, and so I went and bought two of these rather odd contrivances. They consist of plastic bags, about eight inches wide and twelve inches long, filled with a strange, semi-liquid substance. If one leaves them in the ice compartment of the refrigerator for long enough they freeze solid, and they remain frozen for much longer than ordinary ice. Now I am doubly grateful for the Rōshi's refrigerator, it really is a blessing! When I go to bed at night I place an ice pack at the back of my neck, shifting it onto my heart after a while. Of course, the bed gets damp quite quickly and it is not possible to bear the ice directly on one's body for too long, but it is certainly a help. During the day, when I am sitting in *zazen*, I wrap an one of the packs in a cloth and prop it up on my crossed legs so that it presses against my stomach, and now I am using one to help keep me cool as I write.

The ointment for my skin allergy, which is driving me to distraction, is finished, and in any case it hardly does any good. I can't understand why the doctor is only willing to prescribe such Lilliputian quantities of this ointment, which is manufactured in his own laboratory. I always hesitate to use enough of it, because if I did it would be finished within two days. And so I only apply a very small amount just before I sit down for a *zazen* session here in my room, so that I can at least have a little relief while I am meditating. Even so, the itching is terribly draining. Sometimes I feel like scratching my skin from my body.

The day before yesterday, it was the 27th, we had the last *zazen* session with *sanzen* before the beginning of the vacation between the summer and winter semesters.

After inhaling deeply the Rōshi said, 'Be oneness with the kōan "Mu". Go into deep *samadhi.*'

Diary, July 31 1967

Yesterday was the last day of the semester. There was a great ceremony in the *hōndō*, at which the Rōshi's lay disciples were also present. After the huge bronze bell in the front courtyard had been rung the monks who have been taking care of the worldly affairs of the monastery this semester filed in and took their places. They were then followed by the *zendō* monks, whose entrance was accompanied by hollow drumbeats and the sound of a large, bowl-shaped bronze gong which was struck with a kind of wooden club. Then came the abbots of the Zen temples in the surrounding area (all the other temples here are subordinate to Shofuku-ji) dressed in wonderfully ornate robes. The gongbeats and drumbeats started getting faster and louder. Most of the abbots were very aged, but as far as I could see not a single one of them was missing. I remembered them all from the same ceremony four years ago.

As soon as the abbots were all seated the sound of the instruments rose to a wild crescendo, which felt like a spiritual whirlwind sweeping through my heart and senses, and the Rōshi entered the *hōndō*. The absolute peak of intensity was reached at the very moment of his entrance, and then, as he stepped across the threshold, there was a sudden and utter silence. The contrast to what had gone before was total. I have experienced this ceremony many times before, but this sudden plunge into the Void is always shattering, I never get used to it.

Then the monks recited the *Prajnaparamita Hridayam Sutra* while the Rōshi made his ritual prostrations in front of the altar, lying down on the ground and standing up again a total of thirty times without stopping. I was terribly afraid for him. It was well over a hundred in the shade, and even sitting there without moving at all was strenuous enough. Everyone in the *hōndō* was drenched with sweat. But the Rōshi had to perform his duty. I had the unpleasant feeling that some of the monks from our monastery were watching him with an expression of cold calculation in their eyes, wondering whether he was going to be able to manage to do the full thirty prostrations or not. However, I doubt whether a single one of them would have been able to duplicate his feat under the same circumstances, even though the oldest among them was at least thirty years younger than he.

After finishing his prostrations the Rōshi climbed up the three steps of the little stand in front of the ornate wooden throne, sat down, and delivered a lecture which lasted precisely one hour. This throne was made in China, and it is very ancient. It is always brought in for the Rōshi's lectures.

A meal had been prepared for everyone present, and after the end of the ceremony each of us was given a red laquer tray packed with little bowls, one for each of the many dishes. I didn't eat much, only nibbling a little bit here and there.

The ceremony in the *hōndō* marked the end of the semester and the beginning of the temple vacation. I don't know whether I am sad or happy at the prospect of such a long time without any communal *zazen* sessions in the temple. Perhaps I will be able to delve more deeply into the reasons for my presence here now that I have to meditate on my own for a while, without any outside help.

Note

1. Eugen Herrigel, *Zen in the Art of Archery*, Routledge, 1972.

11

A Tragic Death

Diary, July 31 1967, late in the evening

Something terrible has happened. K. san has taken his own life!

Even though I feel utterly shattered, as though an inner earthquake had racked both my body and my soul, I am nonetheless going to try to write an account of how it happened.

Today was my first free day, and I went into the city to do some shopping. I bought enough supplies for an entire week, so that I would be able to devote all my time and energy to my meditation without being distracted by such mundane matters. I also bought several packets of the American cigarettes which Sakamoto san likes so much, and on my way back to Myokan-ji late this afternoon I stopped off at his home (he doesn't live in the temple itself, of course) to give them to him. Doing so was no trouble, as the bus stops right in front of the simple apartment block where he lives.

He looked very upset when he opened the door. 'K. san has killed himself,' he blurted out, not even greeting me. In his agitation he said 'Sh. san' instead of 'K. san', and at first I didn't understand who he meant.

'Who?' I asked in puzzlement. He repeated his statement, mispronouncing the name yet again. I still didn't understand. 'Who is that?' I asked again. Then he lost his patience.

'Your friend! K. san!' he shouted.

I uttered a shriek of horror, burying my face in my arms against the wall. Sakamoto san remained silent until my sobs had subsided. Finally I managed to stammer a few words and ask him how it had happened.

I must write a very simple, factual account of the story, otherwise I shan't be able to write at all. It is so terrible.

Yesterday afternoon, wearing his monk's robes, K. san threw himself in the path of the 'Super Express'. He died instantly. There is nothing left of him. A newspaper reporter brought Sakamoto san the terrible news at midnight last night. He rushed into the Rōshi's bedroom immediately and woke him up to tell him what had happened.

'What did the Rōshi say?' I asked.

'The same as you. He was silent. And then he turned his face away and wept.' The Rōshi wept! That is something which has never ever happened before in our temple. But I can understand it. K. san was his best, most radiant monk, his most beloved son, and now he is gone.

'Why, Sakamoto san, why?'

'He could not find any way out of the dilemma of his heart. I am told that his mind was confused in the last weeks of his life. I have spent the whole day going from one newspaper office to another, even the offices of the newspapers in Osaka, to ask them not to publish anything more about this case which might be harmful to our temple. The editors have all promised not to do so.'

That is the way of this earth. No sooner has the pain of such a tragedy been felt than it is shrouded and hidden by practical considerations and the fear of 'consequences', even in a Zen monastery.

Still unable to believe the unbelievable, I went to the temple to ask Nan san if the Rōshi would be willing to receive me. I was ushered into his room without a moment's delay. Two monks were there with him, sitting to one side. This was unusual, for the Rōshi rarely receives the monks in his private chambers. One of them was Katsu san. He and K. san were close friends, and they entered the monastery together, many years ago.

The Rōshi turned his face away as I offered him my condolences, unable to control my own sobs. He sat there silently, looking as though he were literally drowning in sorrow.

'He loved you,' I said. 'He was your son.' As I spoke these words the Rōshi turned his head and looked at me directly again, his eyes dark with tears.

'I know,' he replied. 'I thank you for your love.'

On the Rōshi's orders Katsu san and three other monks travelled to Gifu this evening (it is about three hours away on the express train) to conduct the death rites at the household altar in K. san's mother's home, which is where he has been living for the last few months.

After taking my leave of the Rōshi I returned to Myokan-ji.

E. san didn't believe me at first. She thought that she had misunderstood what I had said, as my Japanese is very bad. It was only when she saw my tears that she realised that it really was the truth.

Diary, August 2 1967

The Rōshi went to Gifu yesterday to pray for K. san at his family altar. Sakamoto san told me about it, confidentially. No one apart from Sakamoto san is supposed to know anything about it, but he trusted me enough to let me in on the secret. It is against the monastery rules. A Rōshi is not supposed to have any personal feelings, but the deep sorrow of his loving heart is stronger than any rules.

'The Rōshi had to go to Kyoto yesterday, as he had things to attend to there,' said Sakamoto san, 'and he said to me, as though it were nothing important, "I shall make a brief stop in Gifu on my way to Kyoto." That is typical Rōshi. It is not possible to stop in Gifu on the way to Kyoto. One must change trains in Kyoto, and the journey from Kyoto to Gifu takes two hours.'

Zen monks are usually cremated when they die, but in K. san's case it was impossible. There was nothing left of his once so beautiful body to cremate. Just a few shreds, which had to be buried. He left his home as a man and returned as a little parcel.

No ceremony is going to be conducted for K. san here in Shofuku-ji, but the Rōshi's prayers, offered up into the One from the very depths of his being, are worth more than a thousand ceremonies.

Diary, August 5 1967

I have been unable to write anything here for the last few days, because of the terrible heat. I simply lie here on my ice packs with the fan on. What am I to do? I feel paralysed, and I am finding *zazen* very difficult. I have almost completely lost my appetite.

The Rōshi has gone to Kyoto for a while to get away from all the people here who have been pestering him with their questions. I asked Sakamoto san to take him some fruit, with my good wishes.

'He is in deep melancholy,' Sakamoto san said when he returned. He also told me about an incident which had taken place while he had been in Kyoto.

'While he was talking to the Rōshi one of the monks there said that K. san's suicide had been an act of worthless stupidity,' said Sakamoto san. 'At that the Rōshi became furiously angry, and he shouted at the monk and everyone else who was sitting there. He said, "It is *you* who are stupid, all of you! You don't understand!" '

But it is true. These people do not understand anything. Nothing. It is the same here as everywhere else. Mediocrity is incapable of understanding the extraordinary. The Rōshi is alone. K. san was alone.

My body feels broken but my spirit is awake. I can't sleep. How could something like this happen? How is it possible? This question has been tormenting me ever since I first heard the news of the terrible tragedy. Something must be wrong here in the temple, I am sure of it. I sensed it as soon as I returned. But what is it? What is wrong?

My diary lies before me on the desk now as I write. Basically, this account says everything which needs to be said, but I should nonetheless like to add a few details which I omitted then, in order to make the story of K. san's death more comprehensible to the reader.

The fact that he was determined to remain a Zen monk under such impossible circumstances was not K. san's only problem: his private life was also in a complete shambles, and I am sure that this had a great deal to do with his tragic end.

To start with there was the money problem. When a Japanese man leaves home to become a monk he is required to renounce all claims upon his family's fortune in favour of his brothers and sisters. All that he is allowed to keep is the small pittance which he needs in order to be able to survive as a monk. I have been told that this is an absolute rule, and it seems that K. san's siblings were unwilling to relinquish that which they had gained by his entry into monastic life. Nor did he have any way of earning his living on his own, for he had given up his law studies at the university in order to become the Rōshi's disciple. He was 37 when he left the monastery, and although he was extremely talented he was unable to 'do' anything in the normal sense of the word, as he had none of the necessary qualifications.

The fact that he had been treated as a total outcast had also wounded him very deeply. In all his years in the monastery he had always lived a life of perfect asceticism, never ever breaking the rule of celibacy, and he was all too well aware of the extent of the unpunished activities of many of the other monks. He couldn't understand why he was rejected while they were accepted. Another problem was the fact that the Rōshi never gave K. san any advice on worldly matters, even though he received him and talked to him again and again. The Rōshi was his spiritual Master, not his worldly mentor, however, and K.

san ought to have known that approaching his Master with anything but a clear decision was a waste of time.

K. san's mother, at whose house he was staying, was a weak-willed woman who wasn't up to dealing with the complicated and emotional situation, and the girlfriend for whom he had given up everything also appears to have failed him. It must have seemed as though the entire world was conspiring against him. It is hardly surprising that he felt desperate. In addition to all these other things, however, there was yet another factor, something which only I and a few other people who were directly involved in the affair were aware of: the role of the American, Miss O.'s boyfriend.

In my disconsolate state it wasn't until I started to meditate on the tragedy that I understood the significance of some of the things X. san's seducer had said to me in the course of our conversation in the little café, a mere two weeks before K. san had taken his own life. He had referred to both X. san *and* K. san as his 'buddies', and he had also spoken at length about K. san's departure from the monastery, saying that the affair with the girl hadn't really had anything to do with it. He had also said, in a very cynical tone of voice, that it was ridiculous to even suggest that there had been any kind of real bond between K. san and his girlfriend, and that the real reason for his departure had been, once again, the state of affairs at Shofuku-ji. At the time I hadn't paid any attention to his words, as it was obvious that they were nonsense. I knew how hard K. san had tried to work out a compromise with the Rōshi and the First Monk. Now, however, what he had said appeared in a very different light.

I have no doubt that this Tempter in human form tried to exert his influence on K. san as well, taking advantage of the fact that he was weakened by doubt and uncertainty. He probably told the monk that he wanted to help him to attain his 'freedom', and to 'become happy', just like X. san before him. As a by-product, of course, the American's plan also involved a substantial improvement in his own material fortunes. He always chose victims whose downfall (and it is hard to imagine a more classic 'fall' than K. san's) would be to his own advantage: K. san spoke excellent English, and he was very experienced and advanced in the practice of Zen.

At this point one feels inclined to ask (phrasing the question in Christian terms): what about God? What was His role in all this?

There is only one answer to this question, and it is very important to understand it: K. san himself had allowed his state of unity with the Original Source to become clouded by the thick fog of the so-called 'real world'. It was his own doing and no one else's.

It is a terrible mistake to assume that That which is, of itself and in itself, the unnamable and formless Absolute, which can only be experienced in the lightning flash of sudden enlightenment, is required to 'do' anything. It is up to Man to act, it is his duty and his calling.

For thousands of years seekers after God have known that the risk of going astray increases as one progresses on the path; the more wonderful the revelations, the closer one comes to Eternal Truth, the greater is the danger. It is one's own Divine Self which hunts down one's weaknesses, be they ever so minor, and which leads the seeker – and thus also itself – into temptation, in order to reveal the weaknesses and lay them bare.

When the seeker is confronted with a weakness in this way it is very important that he should not attempt to hide it under the comforting wraps of the bliss which he has already experienced on the way. On the contrary, now is the time to get to work and make use of what one has learned, to go within and look at the weakness from all sides and in all possible contexts, and to attempt to transform it. And the seeker who does this, and perseveres, always receives help from God. What this really means, in actual fact, is that one receives help from one's own Divine Self, the divine spark within.

K. san, envied secretly by all who knew him and loved by many who were able to recognise his profound and luminous heart, was drawn deeper and deeper into the whirlpool of the 'world', and in this life at least he was not able to work his way out again. At the same time, however, he did not allow himself to be drowned completely. It is true that his tortured mind was no longer able to bear the strain of the terrible dilemma in which he found himself, and that some small signs of the mental confusion caused by this situation had begun to become apparent. But seeing this, he donned his monk's robe, the robe which is now his for all eternity, and embarked upon his final journey. He died a true Zen monk: aware, and – who knows? – perhaps enlightened.

But what about the others? What of their responsibility? I don't mean the other members of his family at home – for them he was an outsider, and they never understood him, or his life – no, I am talking about the Zen family in which he had lived for so many years, the other monks in the monastery and, difficult though it may be for me to say so, I am also talking about the Rōshi.

K. san was an experienced monk who was well aware of the fact that his Master could not concern himself with worldly problems, for to have done so would have caused conflict within his monastic community. The Rōshi was simply the Master, the teacher of the Way, and nothing more. But K. san was in search of a father. He wanted someone he could lean on, someone who would throw him a lifeline. The Rōshi, however, was not a father. In a sense he was an eternal child, for he had attained to ultimate enlightenment as a mere lad, and he had had no experience of 'worldly suffering' in the unenlightened sense. As a young monk in his old monastery he had been so spiritually advanced that even if he had been faced with a temptation he simply would have dissolved it in an instant, transforming it into the One. He had already left such confrontations with the 'world' behind him in earlier incarnations, and in this life they simply didn't exist for him. His home was the cosmic Buddha Nature. Can one possibly regard this as a fault?

This aspect of the Rōshi's suchness had already become apparent to me during my first sojourn in the temple, but I can well imagine that his radiant, good-natured cheerfulness may have led others to imagine that he was something which he was not.

What was needed in a monastery with such a transcendent Rōshi was a wise mediator. Officially, this was supposed to be the job of the First Monk, but he was not up to the task. And this fact gives rise to a very knotty question: Is it possible that the Rōshi was unaware of the incapacity of the monk who had been chosen for this job? It seems hardly credible that this could have been so. On the other hand, if the Rōshi *had* been aware of the First Monk's failings – and I am personally convinced that K. san had informed his Master of the First Monk's ugly response to his pleas – then shouldn't he at least have offered his disciple the warmth of his heart, giving him a little comfort and hope?

This unfortunate constellation of events raises so many unanswerable questions. One thing which *is* certain, however, is the fact that K. san felt that the Rōshi had abandoned him to his fate. This was made very clear by a letter which he wrote to his brother shortly before he took his own life. His brother informed Sakamoto san of the contents of this letter, thanking him for his helpfulness and understanding in the whole affair, and Sakamoto san passed the information on to me.

'Don't say anything about this to the Rōshi,' I beseeched him, 'his grief is already deep enough.' Sakamoto san agreed with me. Then a thought occurred to me.

'Sakamoto san, K. san wrote a letter to his brother explaining how he felt,' I said. 'Don't you think that he might have written a similar letter to the Rōshi?'

'No,' explained Sakamoto san, 'that is not done in Japan. It would be against our etiquette. All that would be permissible would be to send a message indirectly. For instance, he could have written a letter to his family, and they could have then brought the message to the Rōshi, in all humbleness and respect. But it would be up to them to decide whether they wanted to bring him the message or not.'

Once again I was forced to realise that feelings which we Westerners regard as natural – in fact, which we *expect*, as a matter of course – are often considered to be unusual, or even improper, by the Japanese. They don't think in straight lines, they think in curves and around corners. 'Do we really understand one another at all?' I asked myself yet again, with a feeling of great sadness in my heart.

Another thing which was manifestly obvious was the Rōshi's tremendous grief at K. san's death. Everything which he did (some of it in secret) was both unusual and unprecedented: he travelled to Gifu to perform the death rites at K. san's family altar, and two days later he sent Sakamoto san to Gifu with a year's supply of the most expensive incense sticks available. He withdrew into his chambers for days on end, refusing to receive anyone in order to avoid having to answer questions. He mercilessly denied himself even the tiniest comforts, as though he were punishing himself for something – for example, a while before K. san's death the Rōshi's doctors had prescribed him the occasional small glass of whisky for his heart (he never ever took medicines), and now he stopped taking it completely. And he refused to allow anyone to criticise K. san; any monk who was foolish enough to do so could be certain of a severe tongue-lashing.

Was he taking the collective guilt (a guilt born of the inability to understand) upon himself? Was the source of his misery the fact that he, as the Master, had not been allowed to be a father?

The Rōshi, the Master whose constant home was the Buddha Unity, was suffering. Everyone who was close to him was aware of it. The death of his most beloved monk had wounded him deeply, and even though it was not possible to know what the final consequences of this event would be the first small indications were already beginning to become apparent . . .

I too felt wounded. The pain had begun on my first day back in the temple, and it had become more intense with each of the many shocks which I had suffered in the months which followed. I knew that the time had come to expose my wounds to the healing effects of the light and the open air. Anything else would have been nothing more than laziness and self-deception.

'Why have I returned? Why have I returned now, at this time, in the middle of this situation?' Before K. san's death I had tried to push these questions out of my mind, feeling that they were somehow improper. Now, however, it was no longer possible to ignore them. They returned with a vengeance, searing their way through my thoughts like red hot irons, and I had to stand up and face them.

My lifelong attempts to live the way of Tao and the experiences I have had on this path have taught me that it is always Life itself which provides the answers to questions such as these. And the answer which Life gave me now was very simple, and unmistakably clear: 'You are here because it is right for you to be here.' There was nothing I could do but accept it.

12

A Holiday in the Solitude of a Mountain Temple

Diary, August 11 1967

I went to see the Rōshi early this morning. I was wet through when I got there, as if I had been swimming in my clothes. He was very kind, and he gave me a copy of his new book, which was published yesterday. He wrote a dedication in the flyleaf: *To my dear Miss Gerta Ital, from Rōshi Mumon Yamada.*

Nan san, one of the Rōshi's attendants, told me that the Rōshi has not had a car at his disposal since Mrs M. died, and that he is now forced to use the overfilled buses and trains of the public transport system whenever he goes anywhere. In this heat! Even the *O-bon* festival days, which are dedicated to the memory of the spirits of the dead, are no exception. (The observances of the *O-bon* festival are described in detail in my first book.) For the entire four days of the *O-bon* season the Rōshi is under way almost non-stop, travelling from temple to temple and from town to town to conduct ceremonies. Even though I have very little money myself at the moment I put some in an envelope and gave it to Nan san secretly – he always accompanies the Rōshi wherever he goes – telling him to order a taxi whenever the Rōshi seems to be exhausted.

I find it absolutely incredible that none of the Rōshi's lay disciples appear to be willing to lend him a car, at least during the *O-bon* festival and at other difficult times.

Diary, August 8 1967

According to the newspapers this part of Japan, the area including Kobe and Osaka (which is about half an hour away from Kobe by express train) has been the hottest place on the entire earth for the last few weeks. Hotter than Singapore, Karachi, Bombay and so on. They write that it is the worst heat wave Japan has experienced in the last eighty years, and, unfortunately, that it is likely to continue.

Diary, August 21 1967

It looks as though I shall be leaving Kobe for cooler climes on the 24th, for a short holiday. The Rōshi sent Sakamoto san to see Dr H. in his temple on Mount Hiei a few days ago, and he has agreed to allow me to come there to stay for a while. It is about one and a half hour's train journey from here, via Kyoto. Dr H. is the Rōshi of the temple, which is very large and belongs to the Tendai sect. Mount Hiei is nearly four thousand feet above sea level, and I am told that it really is pleasantly cool there. Even so, I have great reservations about going, although I am not sure why.

It is very late. I just took a short break to get fresh ice packs from the refrigerator, as I don't want to go to bed yet. First I want to write something about an interesting result of my work on my 'second kōan'. Of course, my main task in my solitary hours of *zazen* is to allow 'nothing' ('Mu') to sink down into the very depths of my being. At the same time, however, the question 'Why am I here?' has also been a constant object of my meditation, which is why I refer to it as my 'second kōan'. In the course of this meditation I recently received a very sudden and completely unexpected answer to this question. It is not something which would have occurred to me at all under normal circumstances: one of the reasons that I have travelled half-way around the world to Japan is because I have to put right my relationship with the housekeeper of Myokan-ji, the nun E. san.

When the Rōshi admitted me to the monastery four years ago, giving me the same status as the other monks (a decision which caused a great sensation), he also ordered E. san to remain in Shofuku-ji to keep me company, instead of returning to her own temple at the end of the Great *Zazen* as she had originally planned.

I opened my heart to her, but she was not willing to accept me, and she regarded me as her enemy from the very start. Her many intrigues against me, all of which were designed to drive me out of the temple, were very nerve-racking, and she succeeded in making life extremely difficult for me. Sakamoto san, who had himself taken several months to get around to accepting my presence in the monastery, referred to her several times as 'an evil woman', an opinion which he still holds today.

At first I couldn't understand why fate had brought us together again. On our own here in Myokan-ji, we are forced to have even more contact with one another than we did four years ago. I knew that nothing ever happened to me without a good reason, but what, I asked myself, was the reason for this?

Then the mists parted, and the reason suddenly became clear: we have a karmic connection with one another, and the time has come for this old karma to be destroyed. I knew that I was the one who had to destroy it, because I am the one who has become aware of the situation.

I worked on this in my meditation with all the energy I could muster, and within two days I felt inwardly free. With a deep feeling of joy I decided that there would be no more strife between us, and that I would respond to all her unfriendly acts with a heart full of peace and love.

I am very grateful for this realization. Now I know that one of my reasons for coming back to the temple was to end an old feud – a feud which was born in a previous incarnation – and to dissolve it in the 'Great Mu'.

Once I had ended the feud within my own being everything suddenly became very easy. I no longer needed to act myself, 'It' acted.

One evening, it was a Monday, I happened to meet E. san's young sister in the kitchen, shortly after she had returned from work in the city. I knew that she had spent the weekend at the seaside, and I asked her if she had enjoyed herself. In reply she pulled up her sleeves and showed me her arms, with tears in her eyes. She had a terrible sunburn. I gasped in astonishment and sympathy. Despite the terrible state she was in (she had sunstroke as well as sunburn) the poor thing had spent the whole day working in the office! I rushed upstairs and a few moments later I returned with everything I needed from my well-equipped first-aid box. E. san stood to one side and watched curiously as I applied ointment to her sister's sunburn. When I was finished I gave her a painkiller and a sleeping pill and told her to go to bed. When she returned home from work the next day she said that she was feeling much better; she had slept deeply and the pain had been reduced to a minimum.

As far as I was concerned what I had done had simply been a matter of course, and I didn't give it a second thought at the time. Not so E. san. The fact that I had been willing, and able, to help her sister seems to have astonished her no end, and from that moment onwards the atmosphere between us started to become progressively more relaxed, of its own accord. More and more opportunities for me to offer my help in little ways started to present themselves, and the feeling of tension which used to fill the air whenever our paths crossed has now given way to a kind of dispassionate mutual tolerance. Of course, that is as far as it goes, but it is all that is necessary. Ever since the episode with her sister's sunburn all of her more extreme ploys have ceased, and that is worth a great deal. She has accepted the fact that there is nothing to be done about my physical presence here in Myokan-ji, and she also seems to understand that I am not a threat or a disturbance to her in any way: I keep myself to myself and the only thing which is of any interest to me is *zazen.* And since I, for my part, am determined to turn that which I have realised in my meditation into a physical reality, I don't think there is likely to be any more unpleasantness between us. I am an eternal optimist.

Diary, August 22 1967

A *zazen* meditation course for lay disciples and teenagers started today. It is only possible to organise these events during the vacations, when most of the monks are away. It is because of this course that I have decided to postpone my departure to the cool heights of Mount Hiei until the 24th, for the Rōshi's sake. Most of the lay disciples know that I have returned to the temple, and they would be bound to ask questions if I were not here. After all the sad events which have taken place here recently I should like to spare him such questions. But I am only going to participate today and tomorrow. I really am going to leave on the 24th, early in the morning.

Twelve young girls are staying here in Myokan-ji (they are taking part in the *zazen* course). Ten of them are in the empty dormitory room upstairs, next door to my room.

E. san put them to work straight away. Their first job was to clean the temple building from top to bottom with water and detergent, and then they had to do the garden. It is very hard work, especially when one is not used to it, as these girls are obviously not. At first they all took to it very cheerfully, with much laughter and giggling, but after a few hours of weeding and hoeing outside in the hot sun their spontaneous outbursts of good humour became more and more infrequent.

They are mere children – the youngest is fourteen and the oldest is seventeen – and after all this backbreaking labour I can't imagine that it is possible for them sit in *zazen* properly for more than five minutes, especially when one considers the oven-like heat in the overcrowded *hondō.* No outsiders are allowed in the *zendō* of course, but some of the more advanced lay disciples who are participating in the course are allowed to go to the Rōshi for *sanzen.*

Diary, August 23 1967, late in the evening

The Rōshi extended the scope of the kōan today. As I was sitting before him in *sanzen* he said:

'Be oneness with the whole world. Be oneness with everything. Be oneness with the kōan "Mu".'

I am looking forward to spending a few days in the cooler mountain air. I hope that I shall be able to meditate better there. What with all the people in Myokan-ji at the moment it has become completely impossible.

Sakamoto san has given me a slip of paper on which he has written the entire itinerary for my trip in Japanese, so that I can get help on my way if I need it. He told me that the Rōshi had laughed, saying, 'Ital san is escaping.'

Diary, August 27 1967

I am already back in Myokan-ji. I arrived yesterday afternoon, it was the 26th. It was terrible. Luckily I have time to write a full account of the entire trip, as the house is still full of the noise of all the young girls, and meditation is out of the question.

I had been so looking forward to the coolness and lonely peace of the mountain temple, up there in the clouds, four thousand feet above sea level. More than anything else I had hoped that my rash would get better, and that the terrible itching would die down a little; the Rōshi's doctor had told me that no improvement would be possible before the weather got cooler.

Before I left the Rōshi's secretary reminded me that there were no shops up there, and that there would be no European breakfast. There would simply be two Japanese meals a day, he said. And so I went into town and bought everything I needed: Nescafé, butter, jam and cheese. I didn't have to buy any bread, as I still had a small supply of German crispbread. I was quite heavily laden when I left, for in addition to all my supplies I also had a suitcase full of my clothes and my other things.

I was feeling so miserable in the heat that I didn't care at all about the huge hole I was knocking in my finances, and I was determined that I was going to have a really good rest, staying for between ten days and a fortnight. I hoped to be able to recover my strength enough to be able to stand the strain of my life down here better when I returned. Even so, I felt that 2,900 Yen was a pretty inflationary price for a simple room in a temple, with only two meals a day. But I had no choice, and so I boarded the train for Kyoto.

I caught the bus to Mount Hiei outside the railway station in Kyoto. It was unbelievably hot in the closed bus, and the freshly asphalted road up the mountain was very steep and winding. If it hadn't been for the oven-like heat I am sure that it would have been a delightful journey, but as it was I and most of the other passengers on the bus simply leant back panting with our eyes closed for the greater part of the trip. At an altitude of a little more than three thousand feet we drove past a wonderfully situated luxury hotel with a large swimming pool. There were a large number of cheerful-looking people cavorting in the water. 'That is probably the right place for me,' I thought to myself. Not because of all the people, but because of the comfort and amenities of the hotel.

We arrived twenty minutes later. The sight which met my eyes was surprising, and the surprise was not a particularly pleasant one. The square in front of the entrances to the Mount Hiei temples was as busy as a country fairground. I plumped my luggage down on the ground – there was no shade, and the sun beat down mercilessly – and waited for the monk who was supposed to come and pick me up, feeling downcast and helpless.

The temple on my right was particularly large and beautiful, and also particularly popular with the endless droves of tourists. I wondered why the bell in this temple was being rung so often, almost incessantly. Later I was told that anyone was allowed to ring it, in return for a fee (in addition to the entrance fee which everyone had to pay at the gate), something which I found rather sobering. To my great relief this temple was not the one where I was going to stay, even though it too belonged to the Tendai sect.

After a while it seemed fairly certain that no one was going to come to pick me up, and I lugged my suitcase and my other things over to one of the many little stands selling fruit and Japanese sweetmeats. I asked one of the ladies tending the stands which way I should go by showing her the piece of paper which Sakamoto san had prepared for me. When she told me that it was at least half an hour's walk away I lost my nerve and asked her when the next bus back down the mountain was due. She shook her head and pointed to one of the gateways, indicating that that was where I should go.

I left my luggage on a bench by the fruit stand. I was feeling so frayed and exhausted by this time that I wasn't in the least bit worried that it might get stolen, at least then I wouldn't have to carry it any more. The gatekeeper said that I couldn't enter without paying an exorbitant entrance fee, at which point I finally lost my patience. With great difficulty I managed to make him understand that I was a registered guest and that it had been promised that I would be picked up and brought to the temple. He picked up the telephone, dialled a number and started a long conversation. When he was finished he let me come and wait in his little booth, which was at least shady, even though it was very cramped. Half an hour later a car pulled up at the gate. Two monks stepped out and piled me and my luggage (which had not been stolen after all) into the car, and we drove off.

After a fast ten-minute drive we stopped in a large square in front of a broad, low building with very extensive wings on either side. To my great astonishment, it wasn't a temple; it was a holiday guest house run by the temple community, with a proper hotel-style reception. It was very much a Japanese institution, designed primarily for Japanese visitors, and no one spoke a word of English. I feared that there would be complications, but for the moment I only had one wish: to lie down. The attendant led me along the endless corridors to my room.

The room was quite pretty, and I began to gather fresh hope. It was very different from what one would expect in a European hotel, of course: the only piece of furniture was a hat and coat stand in the corner, which looked as though it had been purloined from an old Viennese café. At least I shall be able to hang a few things up, instead of leaving them in my suitcase, I thought as I saw it. The room's best feature was a little veranda, which was really an extension of the room itself, as there was no wall between the two. On the veranda stood a small table and two wicker chairs, and it looked as though the view of a deep ravine and the forested slopes of the mountain might be very beautiful. For the moment, however, everything was hidden in steamy white mist.

The attendant, who was a very pleasant and amenable old woman, opened the wall cupboard and pulled out the futons for my bed. There were quite a few of them in the cupboard, and she piled several of them on top of one another. I discussed my programme with her, asking her to bring me my meals in my room. I knew that the guests would all sit packed close together at a long table in the dining room, and I wished to avoid the curious attention that I was bound to attract as the only European in the place. I also asked her to bring me hot water for my coffee in the mornings and the afternoons. She promised that she would see to everything. She was true to her word, bringing the water in a big thermos jug (these jugs are very common in Japan) which kept it boiling hot for hours on end. Finally I gave her my calling card and asked her to give it to Dr H., the Rōshi of the temple. She took it and left. A few moments later a monk from the reception appeared and informed me that Dr H. was not yet there, but that my message had been passed on to his residence by telephone.

It had been Dr H. who had made my visit to Mount Hiei possible (he was the most senior priest of the famous Tendai sect), and I had planned to pay him a visit in the course of the next few days, in order to thank him. It had also been Rōshi Mumon's wish that I should do so. What I had not been prepared for, however, was that it would be he who would pay a visit on me! There was suddenly a swishing of robes, and when I looked up the Tendai Rōshi was standing there before me on the veranda of my room.

'I am very happy that you have come,' he said, his faced wreathed in smiles, 'I have heard much about you.'

After I had expressed my surprise and greeted him in the proper manner we sat down at the table on the veranda. Rōshi H. stayed for almost two hours, and we had a fascinating conversation. It turned out that he really did know a great deal about me – Sakamoto san, who had visited him earlier to arrange my visit, had obviously passed on a great deal of information – which meant that we didn't need to go into my spiritual life story before we started talking about other things. One thing which he didn't know, however, and which he was very pleased to hear, was that I had also spent a length of time under the tutelage of Master Osaka in Tokyo.

'He is a good friend of mine,' Dr H. said happily. 'We studied together under the same Master. He is a very great Zen man. I am very happy to hear that you attained *Mu-Satori* while you were with him. Have you seen him again since then?' I replied that I planned to visit Master Osaka before I returned to Germany, and that I would tell him about our meeting.

After this revelation that we had a mutual aquaintance in Master Osaka the ice seemed to be broken completely, and Dr H. told me some amazing things about himself. He told me that he had been a sick man when he had been made Rōshi of the temple here – one would never think so to look at him now, for he radiates vitality and joy in everything he says and does – his health ruined by many years of ascetic spiritual struggle. Seeing this, he had decided to steel his body by going for long walks in the mountains, just as the ancient Zen Masters had done.

'At first I would get exhausted after a single hour, but a year later I was able to keep going for several hours at a time, and my health returned. For the last twenty years I have gone for an eight-hour walk in the mountains every day, and I feel wonderful.' He looked at me with a merry twinkle in his eyes.

'I can see that,' I replied. He really did convey an impression of unusual strength and good health. 'But how do you manage to take care of the many duties you must have as the Rōshi of this temple if you are out in the mountains for eight or nine hours every day?' He laughed heartily.

'That is no problem. I go for my walks at night.' I stared at him in disbelief.

'At night? Do you walk on the paved road?'

'Of course not.'

I knew what the so-called 'paths' through the mountains in Japan were like. To use the word 'paths' to refer to them is more than euphemistic. They are so covered with rubble and rocks that walking on them for more than a few minutes at a time is torture, and in addition to this they often run precariously along the edges of yawning abysses, into which one can plunge if one puts so much as a single foot wrong.

'Rōshi, please excuse me, but I still don't understand. There is no way that you can see where you are going at night.'

'I carry a lantern, just as the ancient Masters used to do,' he explained cheerfully, holding out his arm to show me how it was done. My God, I thought, not even an electric torch. A simple lantern with a candle in it. It was amazing.

'Most respected Rōshi, you also said that you have gone out for your walks every single day for the last twenty years. But what do you do in winter, in the icy cold up here in the mountains, when the paths are buried in snow . . . ?'

'That makes no difference,' he answered with a sunny smile. 'Look at me. I am sixty-six years old. Last night I spent eight hours walking through the mountains. When I returned I conducted the early morning service, after which I had breakfast and gave instruction to the monks in the learning hall.'

'And when do you rest?'

'At midday. I have just had three and a half hours' sound sleep.'

'If I may say so, it seems that your walks are your private hobby, which has turned you from a sick man into a paragon of health. But when I compare your programme to that of my own Rōshi, who never has a single hour to himself, then one could be tempted to think that your Zen tends to get neglected. Or am I wrong?'

'There is no question of that,' he replied. 'I am always in Zen. And now that I am in the very best health I am able to do more for my monks than I was able to when I was a weak and sick man of forty.'

'Forgive me,' I admitted openly, 'but I know almost nothing about Tendai. I would be very grateful to learn more about it. Tendai is a school of Zen, is that not so?'

'One could also say that Zen is a school of Tendai,' he answered.

'How do you mean that?'

'It is very simple. Tendai includes everything, all the sects: Sōtō sect, Yōdo sect, Nembutsu sect, Rinzai sect, Shintō—'

'What?' I said in amazement, 'Shintō too?'

My amazement was justified, for Shintō[1] (or *Kami no michi*, the 'way of the Gods') is the original religion of Japan, preceding both Buddhism and Zen, to which it is not related in any way. The central deity of Shintō is the sun goddess Amaterasu, who is held to be the ancestor of the Japanese emperors. After the arrival of Buddhism in

Japan Shintō was relegated to second place for hundreds of years. Nonetheless, Shintō retained its popularity among the people, and in 1870 it was declared to be the national religion and the emperor (*Tenno*, the Japanese word for emperor, means 'Heaven King') was made its head and first priest. Then, after the end of the Second World War in 1945, Shintō was banned by the Americans.

No matter what one's personal opinions about this religion are, one cannot deny that it has had a decisive, formative effect on Japanese culture throughout the country's history. And when one takes the law of karma into account (a law which is seminal to all East Asian cultures), I see no reason for objecting to the old Shintō belief, which has persisted since time immemorial, that the emperor is chosen for his office by fate.

And in any case, why on earth should anyone try to ban a religion? Alexander the Great, a man who had conquered most of the known world, is recorded to have said 2,300 years ago that such a move would be both unworthy of him, and unwise. But this is not something which the representatives of the so-called 'culture' of the twentieth century understand. It is not enough for them to defeat their enemies. They are not satisfied until they have humiliated them as well, by smashing that which is most precious to them and which forms the very basis of their existence as an individual people: their religion, their ethics and their love for their country.

Be that as it may, Shintō continues to exist. It is no longer the national religion, but its wonderful temples with their famous red gates are among the most beautiful buildings on this planet.

But let us return to my conversation with Dr H. 'Shintō too?' I had asked him in astonishment, knowing full well that of all the sects he had mentioned it alone had nothing to do with Buddhism.

'Yes,' he said emphatically. 'Our founder, Dengyō Daishi,[2] studied with several great Masters in China. When he returned it was his wish that all sects, and the Shintō religion, should be included, for they are all part of the One Universal Being.' He paused for a moment, and then added sincerely: 'I am certain that he would also have included Christianity, Judaism and Islam in his system if he had known of these religions. For him all the great religions were expressions of Dharma Kaya,[3] of the One.'

I was overwhelmed by what he had told me. What supremely transcendent beings these old Chinese Zen Masters and their disciples of the Tang and Sung dynasties must have been. I realised that their attainment of unity with the Absolute (Dharma Kaya) had also given them a universality of spirit, allowing them to eliminate the barriers between different sects.

'Yes,' I replied. 'That is Zen. Apart from the One nothing exists, and everything is united within it.' I paused for a moment; a question had come to my mind.

'But why is it necessary to go into all these other things if everything is contained in Zen?' I asked.

'Ah, but you have 'only' Zen, nothing more,' he replied cryptically, emphasising the word 'only' in a strange way. I was speechless. He placed two brochures on the table.

'They are not very detailed, but they contain some interesting information, especially with regard to our founder,' he said. I thanked him and asked him to write his name in the flyleaves of the brochures, which he was happy to do. I was now determined to find out what he had meant by his strange statement, which had shocked me very deeply, and I asked him to explain it to me.

'You have only Zen, you see,' he replied with an expression of natural good humour, 'but here one can study everything in detail, all the various aspects of the sects I mentioned previously. In addition to this we also have other areas of study, including Zen meditation, the Perfect Doctrine, and the Doctrine of the Commandments.'

'I can imagine,' I replied, 'that it could be extremely interesting for members of the individual sects to be able to study the doctrines of the other sects. But as far as I know the sole objective of all of them, Nembutsu, Yōdo, Rinzai and Sōtō, is the attainment of unity with the One.'

'Yes?' He looked at me intensely, waiting for me to continue.

'Well, from what you say it seems that Tendai is the roof, so to speak, beneath which the various Buddhist systems with their individual paths to salvation meet. But that sounds like what we in the West would refer to as syncretism, and nothing more.'

'We feel that it is more than that,' he replied, his voice serious.

'I would be very happy to learn what this "more" you refer to is. Do you think that that might be possible in the course of my stay here?' He nodded, his face radiant.

Tomorrow, if you wish, you can take part in a *zazen* session in one of the oldest and most famous halls of the Enryaku-ji, the Compon Chudō. Would you like to?'

'Very much,' I replied.

'Good. I shall send my car to pick you up at a quarter past four tomorrow morning.'

The Rōshi was a delightfully warm and refreshingly tolerant man, and I had enjoyed his visit tremendously. Even so, after he had left I sat down on my bed with a bump, feeling miserable. 'Why on earth did you agree to take part in the *zazen* session?' I asked myself. The answer to this question was very simple: when he had made the offer I had assumed that it was going to be an evening *zazen*. I had never ever heard of a Zen temple which held meditation sessions at such an early hour of the morning. The early morning service is usually between four and five, and even during a Great *Zazen* the first 'sitting' doesn't begin before eight, going on until ten thirty. I had come to Mount Hiei to rest and recover my strength, but now it seemed that that was not to be. The fact that the car was going to come to pick me up at quarter past four meant that I would have to get up at a quarter to, at the very latest. My exertions were starting all over again.

I was in despair. My dream of sleeping in had been shattered, and to make matters worse it was even hotter on Mount Hiei than it had been in Shofuku-ji. I could only hope that I had arrived on an exceptional day, and that the temperature would soon drop again. After all, it was unlikely that everyone back in Kobe would have told me to bring warm clothes with me if they hadn't been certain that it really would be cool enough to need them.

The old attendant came and told me that the bath-house was now open for ladies. Since I didn't know where it was I asked her to show me the way, and she guided me along the corridors, which seemed to be endless, through the main hall and into the other wing. There she led me down into the bowels of the building. She pointed at a door, indicating that it was the entrance to the bath-house, and left.

The first room was a kind of large antechamber, which served as a changing room. There were no individual changing cubicles, it was simply a large open room. One left one's kimono there and proceeded directly to the bathroom, which contained a huge pool of steaming hot water, around thirty feet long. The steam was so thick that it was almost impossible to see, and the water was incredibly hot. There were so many naked Japanese women in the pool that there didn't appear to be any more room anywhere. I had seen enough, and I left again without bathing.

'Too full,' I said to the attendant, who was fussing about in my room.

'Later,' she replied. It seemed that there was to be no escape, I was going to have to take a bath in the scalding water if I was not to lose face.

An hour later she appeared at my door again and announced that the bath was now 'empty'. This turned out to be a bit of an exaggeration, for there were still a dozen women frolicking in the water. Even so, there was nothing for it. I had no more excuses, and like it or not I was going to have to go through with it.

The showers where one has to wash oneself off before entering the bath were not so bad; at least it was possible to control the temperature. The water in the pool was another matter, however! I knew that all eyes were upon me, even though the eyelids of the

Japanese women were discreetly lowered, and I daringly dipped one foot into the water. It was out again before I even had time to think about it consciously, as red as a lobster and smarting painfully.

Encouraging cries came from all around me. *'Amari atsui desu!'* ('It's too hot for me'), I shouted in my best Japanese, and fled.

'I don't care if I lose all the face I have for the rest of eternity,' I told myself determinedly, 'I shall never ever enter that room again.'

The unbelievable temperatures which the Japanese are able to bear when they take baths is a subject which I have already discussed in my first book. I have no idea how they manage it; perhaps their skin is different, or perhaps their constitution has become adjusted to the boiling hot water in the course of many generations. Whatever the reason, I had no intention of risking a heart attack or burns – those were souvenirs which I could well do without.

When I returned to my room I found a tray of prettily arranged Japanese dishes on the veranda table. It was my supper. I cautiously tasted a couple of the dishes, and then I put the tray aside and ate a piece of crispbread with cheese.

Completely exhausted from the heat and my strenuous day, I sat down on my bed to rest a little and consider my situation. When I had arrived in the room I had been so tired that I hadn't bothered to look around properly – all I had wanted was to lie down. Now, however, I suddenly realised that there were a couple of things missing, pretty though the little room was. There was no washbasin, and no door.

'No door?' I thought in disbelief as the fact dawned on me, 'that's not possible.' I sprang up from my bed to have a closer look. It *was* possible. The room was in a rather strange position, and to reach it from the corridor one had to walk through a kind of narrow passageway about six paces long, which was open at both ends. Mine was the only room on the corridor with this arrangement. Even if one were to assume that there were no dishonest people in the guest house, which was very crowded, there was still the possibility that someone might mistake the little passageway for the entrance to the toilet, which was next door, and end up in my room instead.

I asked the attendant about it when she came to collect my supper tray. No, she said, it was not possible to close the entrance to my room. There were the usual sliding wooden screens between the room and the veranda (with which I could shut out the wonderful view of the mountains, if I felt like it), but there was no door. It seemed that I was defenceless.

'And where is the washroom?' I asked. She led me down the corridor, in the direction leading away from the main hall this time, to a large room containing a row of seven washbasins. It reminded me of a youth hostel. What kind of place is this, I asked myself in astonishment.

Even so, the knowledge that I was going to have to end my night's rest at half past three the next morning prevented me from wasting any time on being upset about the failure of my planned holiday. Even being unhappy takes a certain amount of energy, and that energy I did not have.

When Rōshi H.'s large limousine pulled up in front of the guest house at exactly quarter past four the next morning I was still drunk with sleep and unsteady on my feet. Luckily, I had brought one of the standard monastery robes with me from Shofuku-ji, and so I was properly and comfortably dressed. The drive along the mountain road to the Compon Chudō took twenty-five minutes. I hadn't had any idea how far away from one another the individual buildings of the temple were. I learned later that the entire Mount Hiei complex is in fact a single Tendai temple city, made up of a total of more than 130 buildings, all of which belong to the main temple, Enryaku-ji.

Two monks were waiting in front of the Compon Chudō when our car pulled up, and their greeting was no less deferential than mine. The car drove away again, and the monks informed me that it was not yet possible for me to enter the meditation hall. I was very happy to hear this, for it meant that I had a few moments to examine my surroundings. What I saw was so breathtakingly beautiful, and so profoundly moving, that my tiredness disappeared in an instant.

I was standing in a perfectly square clearing, high up in the total solitude of the mountains. It was about as large as a small town square, or the square in front of a medieval cathedral, and it was enclosed by thick forests on all sides. The Compon Chudō itself, a meditation hall decorated in red and gold, stood in the trees at one side, its entrance opening onto the clearing. It was originally built in AD 788 by Saichō, the founder of the Tendai sect (Dengyō Daishi was a title which was given to him posthumously), and it was restored to its original state in 1650. It now has the status of a 'national treasure'. It is said that three of the brass lanterns in the hall had provided light for Saichō himself, and that they have never once been extinguished since his time.

The solitude was complete. For twelve hundred years, until around fifty years ago, it must have been a place of total peace and silence, its atmosphere drenched with the pure spirit of seekers after God, the recipients of His grace. In those days the meditation of the monks seeking liberation and unity was never disturbed by any outside influences. All they had to contend with was the inner spiritual struggle. It must have been a wonderful time to be alive. Now the spiritual being which is our earth is withering away, while our technocrats shoot their projectiles into what we used to call the heavens. The old Chinese Zen Masters carried the entire universe in their hearts. They did not need to take so much as a single step to find it; they did not even need to open their eyes.

The monk in front of the hall waved to me. He had opened the heavy doors, and now he showed me inside and led me to the first place in the front row in front of the altar. The hall was about fifty feet long, but very narrow, only wide enough to accommodate a few rows of monks. Nowadays lay students of Zen meditate here more often than monks do. There were thin *zazen* cushions laid out on the floor in the places where the meditators, who had not yet arrived, were going to sit. I asked the monk to give me a second cushion, as we never sat flat on the ground in our temple, and I wasn't used to it. Once I had arranged the cushions to my satisfaction I went outside again. I knew that it would soon be time for the *zazen* session to begin, and I was wondering where the others were. A few moments later I saw a procession of men and women making their way slowly up a forest path towards the Compon Chudō, looking very tired. I looked at my watch. It was five o'clock, and they must have been under way for several hours already.

They looked astonished when they saw me. I hurried back inside and sat down on my cushions. One of the monks led them to their places and showed them how to sit. When everyone was ready the monk who had greeted me upon my arrival walked up to the altar, bowed, and delivered a little talk on 'sitting' properly and on the meaning and purpose of *zazen*. This was followed by silence.

The *zazen* session only lasted for forty minutes, but even this was too long for the majority of the other participants. They fidgeted incessantly on their cushions, and one of the monks walked up and down the aisles for the entire length of the session, helping them to correct their sitting position. Some of them were unable to remain seated for the full forty minutes, and every now and then the monk would quietly usher someone out of the hall. It seemed that I was the only experienced meditator there.

Unfortunately, it was not the kind of *zazen* I had hoped to experience in this noble hall. To put it bluntly, it was a beginners' lesson.

After a little bell had been rung to indicate that the session was over the monk said a few more wise words to the participants, most of whom were surreptitiously rubbing their sore joints. I didn't understand much of what he said, but at one point I heard him mention the name of my temple in Kobe. I assume that he was explaining what this foreigner was doing there in their midst, and telling them which temple I came from. When he had finished speaking the others left the hall and made their way back down the forest path.

I stepped outside. The sun started to rise above the peaks of the mountains. As the first rays struck the roof of the hall the red and gold paintwork started to glow as though it were aflame, and the dark treetops were filled with shimmering showers of light. A few moments later the entire silent square, a place which had been dedicated to the divine for more than a thousand years, was bathed in golden light.

Even the monks had disappeared. I was completely alone. For a few enchanted moments time stopped, and I slipped into a state of unity: I was one with the compon chudō, with the mountain, with the trees, and with the clearing in which I was standing. I knew that this was the way they must have been almost twelve hundred years before, and I knew that nothing had changed. What I experienced was a state of impersonal, cosmic knowing, even though it was restricted to this one place. Was I too the same, unchanged?

I started in surprise as the big limousine suddenly appeared out of the darkness of the trees, but even so I was pleased to see it. The monk at the wheel jumped out and opened the door for me, and I got in. From a moment of eternity I had returned once again into the measurable, human world . . .

The car pulled up in front of the guest house at about seven. Some of the early risers who had come out to enjoy the morning sun looked very surprised at seeing this foreign personage getting out of the private car of the Master of the temple city.

The entire front wall of the main hall of the guest house consisted of a single huge window facing out towards the mountains. There was almost no one about at this early hour, and this gave me a unique opportunity to admire the view without being disturbed. For a change it was unobstructed by the mountain mists. It was a wonderful sight: to the left and right were the huge forested slopes of the mountains, and between them, shining in the morning sun far away below me, was the city of Kyoto.

'It's wonderfully beautiful, isn't it?' said a voice behind me. I turned around, and two Japanese ladies bowed deeply. The older of the two then asked me if it would be all right for her to drop by and see me in my room later in the day.

I realised that the monks at reception had been gossiping about me. It was hardly surprising, really, what with the Rōshi's sensational visit to my room the day before and my arrival in his private limousine early that morning. It was only natural for people to ask who this mysterious European woman was. A little later one of the chambermaids brought me a handful of calling cards, all sent by people wanting to meet me.

Before doing anything else, however, I made myself a good breakfast. The charming old woman hadn't even bothered to bring me a Japanese breakfast – she had realised that Japanese food was not to my liking – she had simply placed the thermos jug full of boiling hot water on the veranda table.

It was wonderfully peaceful. I ate my breakfast happily, enjoying the view, and I was just in the process of deciding that I would go for a walk as soon as I had finished eating, before the heat became too intense, when something happened which almost made me drop my cup of coffee in astonishment: a group of people strolled past in front of my veranda. They did their best to look nonchalant, as if they were going for a morning walk, but their curious glances were very obvious. They were so close that I could have reached out and touched them.

I had already noticed the little path, hardly more than a foot wide, running along in front of the veranda, but I had assumed that it was merely there for safety reasons, because of the steep ravine which dropped down directly behind it, and it hadn't occurred to me to think that it might be open to the public. Now it seemed that I had become an attraction for sightseers, and that there was nothing at all I could do about it. In addition to this, I realised, my room was freely accessible from the veranda as well as from the corridor.

I had come longing for silence, solitude and cool mountain air, and apart from a few magical moments at the Compon Chudō I had found precisely the opposite. I was told that the hot weather was unprecedented, and that no one had experienced anything like it in living memory. For all I know that may be true, but the knowledge that it was unusual didn't help me a bit. The heat was paralysing, cloying and leaden, and the heavy, humid air was trapped between the walls of the mountains. There wasn't so much as the finest breath of wind.

After breakfast I went out for my walk, but by the time I reached the front courtyard of the main temple, Enryaku-ji, I was so exhausted that I decided against joining the crowds of other visitors for a tour of the buildings – I had no desire to collapse in a heap on the ground in the middle of the temple. Then an idea occurred to me: the bus! I decided to take the bus down the hill to the lovely hotel I had seen on the way up, and to relax there for a while.

Seated in a comfortable club chair in the fully air-conditioned reception hall of the hotel I slowly started to come to myself again. 'This is more like it,' I thought, 'if I were to stay here for a while I really would be able to get the rest that I need and recover my energy. Then it would be easier for me to stay the course when I return to Shofuku-ji.' Any worries about the possible expense of such an undertaking were very far from my mind by this point. As it turned out, however, every room in the hotel was booked out until the middle of October, and I was thus protected from my own foolhardiness. My dream burst like a soap-bubble. I hoped that I would at least be able to eat a good solid meal before returning to my guest house, for I knew that my weakness also had a fair amount to do with my crispbread diet. But this too was in vain: European meals were only available for hotel guests, and even they had to order well in advance. I was graciously granted an iced coffee, but that was all.

The next bus from Kyoto to Mount Hiei wasn't due to pass by for another hour. I waited in the delightful coolness of the hotel reception. When I finally got off the oven-like bus at the top of the hill and started to make my slow way back to the guest house I only had one overwhelming desire: to lie down and rest. I had only slept for a total of four hours in the last two days.

I heard the deafening racket as soon as I entered the first corridor leading out of the reception: rock music, played at such a high volume that it seemed that its perpetrators were intent upon entertaining the entire island. The nearer I came to my room the more terrible it was. Now, as I write, I can still feel the shock. It was shattering. Six young students had moved into a large room directly above me. It was unadulterated torment. My earplugs were no match for their music, and when I went to the reception and complained the monks behind the counter simply shrugged their shoulders.

There was a brief break at seven in the evening when the students went to have dinner. After dinner, however, the cacophony started up again, and continued for the rest of the night. The noise was simply incredible, and to judge by the sounds coming from the room above me the students were stamping on the wooden floor in time to the music. In a temple guest house!

At eleven I went and complained to the monks in the reception again. I was worn to a frazzle. I pointed to the clock and demanded that now, at least, something ought to be done about the noise. It was useless, however. They were completely unimpressed by my anger, justified though it was, and they simply shrugged their shoulders again and said something in Japanese. As far as I could make out they were saying that the students were on holiday and that they wanted to enjoy themselves a little. I pointed out that there was nothing wrong with that, but that they didn't have the right to do so at the expense of other paying guests who had come to the guest house to rest. But they simply didn't understand me: the day shift had been relieved, and the night shift monks didn't speak any English at all.

At one in the morning I started to pack my suitcase, getting ready to leave. At five the racket over my head finally stopped, and at nine I called the number of Myokan-ji in Kobe. E. san answered the phone.

'Kaerimasu,' ('I am coming back') I shouted down the line. In the late afternoon of the same day, after being baked in the train for a total of four hours, I was back in my room in Myokan-ji. The temperature in the room was well over a hundred degrees. I lay on my bed, unable to move, one ice pack on my heart and another at the back of my neck.

The young girls were still there. It was the last day of their *zazen* course. When they returned from their 'sitting' in the temple at nine that evening they knocked shyly on my bedroom door and asked if I had any photographs of myself in the temple from my first stay, saying that they would very much like to see them. To their delight I did happen to have a few pictures with me, and it was only with a great deal of effort that I managed to get them back after they had been handed round. Then they asked if I could spare a little of my time for them, as they had many questions which they would like to ask me.

'You can all come and see me tomorrow morning before you leave,' I said. 'At the moment I am still too tired from my journey.'

And I really was feeling very poorly. Quite apart from my exhaustion I had also had another attack of what felt like angina. I tried to reach Dr Imachi (the director of the university clinic) at his private number, but I was informed that he had been called away to Okayama to perform an operation, and that he wouldn't be back until the next day.

Diary, August 28 1967, evening. Oriental Hotel.

I shall explain how I come to be here later. First I want to write an account of my conversation with the Japanese schoolgirls, before I forget any of it.

They came in to see me this morning. There were six of them; the oldest was seventeen and the youngest was fourteen. They sat around me on the mat, and told me how 'terribly happy' they were to be returning home again. I asked them how they were feeling inside, hoping to hear something about the success of the seven-day *zazen* course they had just completed. The answer astonished me:

'We're all exhausted and we're almost dying of hunger. We don't understand anything about Zen at all. That's why we've come to talk to you. We wanted to ask you to explain what the purpose of *zazen* is.'

I had been asked a similar question four years before. A group of high school boys, about the same age as these girls, had been sent to the temple by their parents to spend two weeks of their holidays doing something meaningful.

One of these young lads stopped me on the steps leading up to the temple, with tears in his eyes, and told me that he and his friends were terribly unhappy in the temple. He said that the monks made them work like slaves from morning till night, and that they were not being given any of the spiritual instruction which they had come for. I felt so sorry for him that I could have taken him in my arms, for I understood his sorrow all too well. We had a brief conversation, and I did what I could to try to cheer him up and explain a little about the meaning of Zen. It wasn't much, of course, and by the end of our talk it was very clear that none of these young men was likely to spend their holidays in a Zen temple again if they could possibly avoid it.

It seemed that these intelligent and trusting young schoolgirls, who were all hungry for knowledge and who had been willing to sacrifice part of their holidays for the sake of religious instruction, had been treated in the same way. I felt shocked.

Choosing my words as carefully as I could I started to explain that the spirit of Zen unites all aspects of existence within itself, both spiritual striving and physical action.

'But we've never ever had to work so hard before,' interjected one of the girls, 'and by the time we went to *zazen* in the evenings we were always so tired and stiff that we were hardly able to sit at all.'

I was incensed. The callous way in which the monks had exploited these girls, making them do work which they were to lazy to do themselves, was simply criminal. At the same time I realised that I would have to be careful. It was perfectly all right for me to voice my criticism on my own account, but not in front of these children. In any case, there was no need for me to tell them things which they were intelligent and observant enough to see for themselves. None of them made any bones about the aspects of the course which had displeased them. What they really wanted was a chance to talk, and I had returned from my unfortunate outing just in time to be able to accommodate them.

'Well,' I continued, hoping to be able to change the direction of the conversation a little, 'don't you feel that you have learned something which might be of value to you, in your daily lives?'

'We're really looking forward to being able to eat until we're full and to sleep in in the morning,' replied one of them, and they all giggled. I laughed with them.

'I can understand that. But is that all?'

'Can't you explain what *would* be valuable for us?'

'Yes, I think I can. As I said just now, in Zen one doesn't search for the truth in meditation alone, but also in one's daily life. As I see it, meditation is not the most important thing for you at the moment. What you need now is to find the answer to a question. The question is, "How am I to live my life?" Don't you think so?' They all agreed enthusiastically.

'Let me give you a few simple examples of what I mean,' I continued. 'You're all still at school, aren't you? And you probably have one or two teachers whom you find boring, or whom you don't like for some other reason. And what do you do? You make sure that these teachers know that you don't like them, you are unfriendly to them or you play all sorts of little tricks on them. Am I right?' They all nodded in mischievous delight.

'You see! Now, this is where Buddha's teachings regarding self-discipline and mindfulness come in. Nobody has anything against a little joke, if it is meant well. But enmity which comes from the heart is something else again. The first thing to do is to stop for a moment and examine yourselves and your own motives before you start annoying these teachers. These little moments of awareness will help you to realise that friendliness is better than unfriendliness. Insights like this are very important, and you must listen to them and follow them. If you manage to find the strength to be aware and control yourselves you will profit in two ways: Firstly, it will help your inner spiritual growth, and secondly, you will find that a surprising transformation will take place in the person you had previously tormented. You never know, you may succeed in making a sad and troubled person happy.

'Or take another example: you probably take it for granted that your mothers are the last in the family to go to bed at night and the first to get up early in the morning, to make your breakfast and get everything else which you need ready for you. And I imagine that you are sometimes bad-tempered and moody when you get up in the mornings, and that you sometimes don't answer your mothers when they ask you simple questions, and that you sometimes simply run out of the house without a word of thanks as soon as everything is ready. Hmm?'

They all nodded, looking a little shamefaced.

'Now, if you can manage to teach yourselves to smile at your mothers every morning when you get up – after all, they do love you – and to be patient when they ask you questions and to thank them for making you your breakfast, then you will find that these little things can transform your entire day, and that you start feeling better and happier too.

'But that is only the beginning. Then you could start looking for the countless other little faults that each of us has, and when you find them you could start working on them, slowly, one by one, in order to free yourselves of them. That would be the beginning of a life in Zen. Self-discipline is very important, it is the basis of all true spirituality. Do you understand what I mean, more or less?' They had been listening with rapt attention, and their eyes were glowing.

'It's really quite simple,' said the youngest. I laughed.

'Yes, it is. But remember, one must really *do* it. Now you are all nodding in agreement, and I am sure that for the next few days all of you are going to take great care to keep an eye on yourselves. But I am equally sure that you will soon begin to find it tiresome, and that all your good resolutions will be blown away like feathers in the wind.'

'Oh! Do you have such a poor opinion of us?'

'Not at all. I simply know that it is human to be forgetful. Even Buddha's disciples were forgetful, and he was well aware of it. That is why he told them again and again to be "mindful", that they should practise mindfulness in all their thoughts and actions. Mindfulness, or awareness, is the very basis of spiritual self-discipline, not only in Zen, but in all the religions of the world.'

'Is it wrong to laugh and play and be cheerful?' At this question I laughed so loudly that they all burst out laughing too.

'It would be a sad world if one were not allowed to laugh and play. Of course it's not wrong.'

'What about dancing?'

'Dancing as well. Being mindful doesn't mean that you have to be miserable and serious.'

'Oh, I hope we can manage to remember everything that you have told us, always.'

'I have a suggestion. Why don't you make yourselves a reminder? You could make a little sign to hang in your rooms, with your lovely Japanese calligraphy, and it will always remind you whenever you look at it. Would you like to do that?' They responded with a chorus of yeses. Then there was a brief silence.

'And what should we write on the sign?' They pulled out their notebooks and pens, and six pairs of dark eyes gazed up trustingly into mine. I remained silent for a full minute, and then I said:

'Write this: I want to live in such a way that I can always respect myself.'

They stared at me for a moment, speechless, and then they wrote down what I had said. Suddenly the youngest and liveliest of the six leapt up and flung her arms around my neck, saying, 'Thank you! Thank you! That is so wonderful!' I almost fell off my cushion.

'I think that we were all afraid that you were going to give us some deep spiritual saying or a kōan to solve,' said the oldest. 'This is more difficult, but it is also a thousand times more beautiful. I think it will become the guiding principle of our lives.'

The girls all bowed down to the ground and thanked me.

'Are you hungry?' I asked.
'Oh yes!'
I had bought myself a big fruit loaf full of raisins and nuts at the railway station. I cut it up and spread the slices with plenty of butter. The girls ate like ravenous lions. We all enjoyed ourselves immensely.

Diary, August 28 1967. Oriental Hotel.

I have been here in the Oriental since yesterday afternoon. It is the best hotel in Kobe, and in its own way it is really perfect. When I finally managed to get through to my friend Dr Imachi he came straight out to Myokan-ji to see me himself.

'My God,' he said as he entered my ovenlike room, 'I hadn't imagined that it would be as bad as this. I wouldn't be able to stand it in this furnace for more than ten minutes. You mustn't stay here a moment longer.'

'Would it be possible to arrange for an air-conditioned room in your clinic?' I asked hopefully. He shook his head.

'You know how it is there. Only our offices and the operating theatres have air-conditioning. And in any case, the Japanese food there wouldn't agree with you.' He gave me an injection.

'But I do have another idea,' he continued. 'Why don't you go and stay in the Oriental for a while? It isn't much more expensive than a room in the clinic.' He examined my rash and the bleeding welts, which were the result of my desperate scratching at night. 'The rash is certain to get better as soon as you have been in a cool, air-conditioned room for a while. I know the hotel director, shall I give him a call?'

I had no trouble getting a room, as all the foreigners who did not absolutely have to be in the city on business had fled to cooler parts of the country. Two hours after the professor had left I was lying on a wonderful big bed in a cool and elegantly appointed room.

There is no way of describing just how wonderful it is. I am very glad that I managed to write about my conversation with the schoolgirls last night, because now I am much too tired to do anything. I slept like a log for fourteen hours. I am having my meals brought up to my room. But I can't think clearly, and meditating is out of the question.

Diary, August 30 1967

After eating an excellent breakfast in bed I am now beginning to feel a bit better. The room service waiter who brought me my breakfast also brought me one of the several Japanese newspapers which are published in English, and in it I read that the region around Kobe is still the hottest on the entire planet at the moment, and that there are no signs that the heatwave is likely to die down in the near future.

Reading that gave me pause for thought. Since there is no way I can stay on in this beautiful but extremely expensive hotel until the end of the heatwave which is afflicting all of Japan, I have decided that the only thing I can do is to return to Myokan-ji as soon as possible. The expense is not my only reason for making this decision, however. If it had been I might have thrown caution to the winds for a while longer. My second reason for wanting to go back to my little furnace of a room is that I am completely incapable of meditating here in the hotel. And not only on my first day here: ever since my arrival I seem to have been slipping deeper and deeper into a kind of pleasant, dozy lethargy. I suppose that that is hardly surprising, considering everything I have been through, but I suspect that this condition could last for quite a while, and I simply cannot afford to waste that much time. The task I have set myself is much too important for that.

Diary, September 1 1967. Myokan-ji.

The heat in my room is just as bad as it was before, but nonetheless I was able to sit in *zazen* for two hours this evening, with an ice pack in my lap.

This afternoon I went to see the doctor who treated my rash before I went to Mount Hiei. After three days of peace and quiet in the coolness of the hotel it has now broken out again with a vengeance, much worse than it has been for months. He looked at my arms and shook his head.

'There's nothing more I can do to help you,' he said, 'you must go and see a skin specialist. I will call him and explain the situation. He lives nearby.' Half an hour later I was sitting in the specialist's surgery, where I finally found out what was wrong with me.

'You have the Japanese sun disease,' he said. 'Very many people suffer from this uncomfortable rash with its irritating itching when they are exposed to the Japanese sun. Among the Japanese it is usually only the very small children, whose skin is still very tender, who suffer from this condition. Later on they become immune to it. It is very strange, but only the sun in Japan has this effect. No research has yet been done to find out exactly what the mechanism of the condition is. I am afraid your rash won't get better until the weather gets cooler. All that I can do is to prescribe you some medicine which will alleviate the irritation for a few hours.'

Now that I knew that there was nothing any doctor could do to help me, and that the heat was likely to continue for quite a while longer (the temperature in my room was around 105 today) I was forced to try to think of a way of solving the problem myself. An idea came to me on my way back to Myokan-ji, and as soon as I arrived I tried it out: I filled a bowl with water, added lumps of ice from the refrigerator, and then I soaked some bandages I had brought with me from Germany in the icewater and wrapped them around my arms without wringing them out. I dripped water everywhere, of course, but in this heat it evaporates almost before it hits the ground.

Diary, September 3 1967

The icewater bandages are a complete success, especially at night. Of course, they dry out within about two hours, but then I simply remove them, dip them in the bowl of water which I have standing by my bed and wind them around my arms again. The rash is fading, but as soon as my arms are exposed to the sunlight, even for a moment, it starts blowing up again.

I am terribly grateful for the relief which this gives me at night (the temperature in my room never goes down below a hundred) and in my hours of *zazen* in the early mornings. During the day, however, after about ten in the morning, I sink into a kind of paralysis.

The main temple is almost completely deserted at the moment. Only a couple of monks are still there on guard duty.

Of course, as soon as I returned from Mount Hiei Sakamoto san called me into his office and asked me my reasons for cutting my planned stay so short. I told him the whole story, not making any bones about my outrage at the state of affairs in the temple guest house.

'Japan is no longer Japan,' he said, looking very serious and sad. 'You know what sort of goings-on there are at our universities. The monks up there are simply afraid that the students would smash the place up if they try to prevent them from doing anything.'

He was right. And now I was completely certain that leaving had been the only thing which I could have done. Japan is no longer Japan! This statement is an expression of the inexorable, unstoppable death of the noble heritage of the Japanese past, and of the Japanese religion and tradition, which are now being replaced by something much more coarse and brutal: 'progress', a blind, brute force which strives only for the things of the external world. It is a development which has scarred the country's very best men, the men of Zen. Some of them appear prematurely aged and worn, even though they are still relatively young. Nonetheless, they are still willing to sacrifice their lives (and under the present circumstances this expression is no exaggeration) to save what can be saved, in the spirit of Zen.

No nation on earth has ever respected teachers and Masters so deeply as the Japanese. Now this respect too is dying. Those who have eyes to see watch what is happening in despair, asking themselves where our world is going to now that it has lost its spiritual centre. And the centre has been lost everywhere, not only in Japan. Where is our world going to? It is not a difficult question to answer, for where there is no centre there can be no balance, and he who loses his sense of balance is bound to fall, sooner or later.

There are a few people, here and there, not all of them Masters, who are aware of the fate which is in store for our earth. It is coming closer and closer all the time. They know, but they remain silent. Not because they are afraid of being ridiculed, but because they do not wish to endanger their quiet spiritual work, their attempts to save what can still be saved. But how difficult everything is made for them! And how rare worthy successors have become! There are only a few great Zen Masters still alive, and still fewer who are fortunate enough to find a successor who is really worthy of bearing the venerable title 'Rōshi'. When the others become too old to continue with their work they are forced to take the next best choice, and the process of decay continues.

The spirit of our times is, as we all know, an enemy of the Spirit. Truth can only be sought in silence, but where can one find real silence nowadays? Our planet has been transformed into a monstrous loudspeaker. No shrine, no temple is safe any longer. Even if a Master were to gather his disciples around him in an igloo at the North Pole, I am sure that there would be plenty of people who would make a sport out of pestering them.

The ancient Zen Masters in China, and later in Japan, all adhered strictly to the monastic rule of seclusion and solitude. They and their monks lived in mountain retreats and monasteries, far away from cities and all human settlements. In those days it was still possible for seekers wishing to devote their lives to Zen meditation to find the complete seclusion they needed.

When Saichō (Dengyō Daishi, 762–822) returned to Japan from China and built the first temple on Mount Hiei the location was still completely isolated from the outside world. In that early morning hour which I was fortunate enough to spend at the Compon Chudō I was able to have a brief experience of the magical aura of that wonderful time, which is now gone, and gone forever.

In the years which followed a Tendai temple was even built up on the very highest peak of Mount Hiei. It is still there, and from the guest house where I stayed, which is itself around four thousand feet above sea-level, it was just possible to see it with a telescope or pair of binoculars. But even the solitude of this temple is a thing of the past: a paved road has been built to it, and it is visited daily by busloads of curious tourists.

The Ishiyama Zen Temple, in a breathtakingly beautiful location high above Lake Biva, has also suffered the same sad fate. Far from being secluded, it is now the popular goal of hundreds of day-trippers.

The masses of people and the endless racket of the modern world have completely destroyed the quiet solitude which was necessary for the Masters' work to be really effective. The sad truth of the matter is that today's Masters only have two choices open to them: They can either lower their sights, making concessions to the modern world, or they can choose to adopt an uncompromisingly strict regimen in their temples, something which is extremely unpopular nowadays, even among Zen monks.

Even so, of course, there are still a few seekers who are willing to do everything which their Master asks them to do and to make any sacrifice for the sake of the great goal. If such people are in the majority in a monastic community they can carry their weaker brothers along with them.

The most basic problem in Japan, however, is that the temples receive no financial support of any kind, which means that they must earn the money which they need to survive on their own. How different the situation is in Germany! There every Catholic and every Protestant must pay church tax together with their income tax, and as a result these churches have surpluses of many millions of marks every year.

The beautiful buildings and gardens of those Japanese temples which are no longer in operation have been taken over and restored by the state, which has declared them to be 'national treasures', and their upkeep is financed by the tourist trade. Even though it is unfortunate, it is understandable, under the present circumstances, that many monastic communities have followed the state's example, opening their doors to the public and demanding that visitors pay an entrance fee.

The guest house of the temple complex on Mount Hiei is another example of the methods which some temples have been forced to resort to in order to survive (the temple on Mount Hiei is by no means the only one which operates this type of holiday guest house). Thanks to modern roads even the most out-of-the-way temples are no longer as inaccessible as they used to be, and the tourist trade is often the only alternative to closing down completely.

Compared to the more famous temples our temple in Kobe is small, and its architecture is not interesting enough to attract visitors; nor is it surrounded by the extensive, beautifully-kept gardens which are so popular elsewhere. It is thus not possible for it to support itself by charging admission, something which is both a blessing and a tragedy. The temple does have one very special treasure, however: Rōshi Mumon Yamada, who is acknowledged to be a saint by all living Zen Masters. In order to support his temple and his monks this great man is forced not only to travel all over the country delivering lectures, but also to speak regularly on the radio and on television.

Nowadays both Masters and their disciples must grapple with all the new distractions created by our modern world. They have no other choice, for the environment which is necessary for their inner work has been destroyed, and can no longer be found anywhere. However, no matter how many concessions must be made to the circumstances of our time there is one thing which must be adhered to strictly, at all costs: the monastic code of discipline and morality. For if those desires and passions which are a part of lust have the upper hand, or even if they only appear sporadically, indicating that they have merely been suppressed and not plucked out by the roots, the path to enlightenment is blocked.

Beliefs and opinions are another hindrance to spiritual progress which is often overlooked, particularly by westerners interested in Zen. It doesn't matter whether the beliefs in question are of a religious, philosophical or political nature – political beliefs are particularly popular nowadays – the stubborn insistence that one's own point of view is 'right' is simply another form of desire. In the realm of the Absolute there is neither right nor wrong.

These barriers are all self-made, and it is thus the seeker himself who must tear them down again. Slowly and patiently, step by step, but nonetheless with radical completeness. And this too is only the beginning of the Great Journey.

Even in the past, when the conditions were more or less ideal, travelling this path was a task for spiritual giants. In order to be able to resist the corrupting influences of the world in which we now have to live and suffer, however, the modern seeker must be blessed with inner resources of a truly superhuman order. And these influences are extremely insidious – we breathe them in from the air which surrounds us, so to speak, and it is thus easy to overlook them for a very long time. The only thing which is of any help at all is constant mindfulness.

Life for Zen monks is very difficult nowadays, and they deserve our love and respect even when they occasionally stumble off the path for a while, committing errors which would not have even been possible in earlier times. For if they continue patiently on their way, combating their faults with insight and awareness as they appear, they will one day attain to true realisation. And then all errors, and non-errors, will be completely unimportant.

Before the seeker can receive a kōan from a Master and meditate on it he must first pass through a process of catharsis, in the course of which he must free himself of all the wishes, passions, desires and opinions which are a part of his earthly 'personality'. The famous old dictum, 'Know Thyself', means, in essence, 'Know who you really are, and who you have always been, since time immemorial.' My own painful experiences on the path, the experiences of an entire lifetime, have taught me that this dictum now needs to be amended in order to make it more appropriate for the modern world and modern Man. Nowadays it would perhaps be more fitting to say, 'Above all, know that which *prevents* you from knowing yourself.'

Heaven can only write its message on a *tabula rasa*, an empty page; but once seekers have managed to free themselves of all that holds them back, so that nothing is left, they are free to go where they wish. 'Nothing' cannot be restricted – no boundaries can contain it. And when this almost unimaginable point has been reached kōans are no longer problems; then they are no more than a confirmation of Truth, for they simply dissolve in the emptiness of the seeker.

Of course, young monks who have already subjected themselves to this rigorous self-discipline before entering a Zen monastery are rare indeed. But there is hope even for those who enter as utter novices, for they have a lifetime of meditation before them, and if they manage to stay the course their daily contact with their Master will help them to learn how to free themselves of their faults, one by one.

Westerners should not expect that the occasional visit to East Asia will automatically result in spiritual miracles. Such miracles are always the outcome of one's own efforts. It is one's own Buddha Nature (the 'tiny point' described by Meister Eckhart) which lets one know when the time has come to begin the work of returning to unity, by means of a feeling of constant spiritual restlessness. Whether seekers realise it or not, it is always they themselves who are the source of the call to set out on the journey, to search for answers and to find out what this endless longing is and how others before they have satisfied it.

The call comes from within the seeker. This inner call *is* a miracle; at the same time, however, it is nothing special – after all, everyone has the same potential – and it does not indicate that the seeker who receives it is in any way 'superior' or 'elect'. This is something which it is very important to remember, and which cannot be repeated often enough. The call comes to all of us sooner or later. After one has passed through an endless series of lives, sometimes as a hedonist, sometimes as a sufferer, and always as a learner, one eventually comes to see how empty and shallow a merely material life is, and one begins to wonder about the meaning of one's existence. That is the first step, and for many novice seekers it takes quite a while to go beyond this point, for the new way of thinking which becomes necessary seems wildly 'unrealistic' and 'far-fetched' at first. And then, when they do manage to open their eyes, they have the feeling that they are seeing the world in which they live for the very first time, for everything seems transformed. And here lurks the next danger, for not all of what one sees is pleasant, and the temptation to start criticising the world is very great.

Of course, it is important to be able to see where one is and to understand the nature of the people who populate this planet, and the more complete and deep this understanding the more valuable it is. At the same time seekers should never forget that the world which they see, which they are living in, is a world which they themselves have helped to create, in countless incarnations.

The 'suchness' of the world, in its positive and its negative aspects, is the outcome of all of the past actions of all beings, including the seekers themselves. Knowing this, and understanding their own responsibility for the world as it is, the wise seekers do not allow judgements to enter into their hearts (when I say 'hearts' I mean the 'tiny point' of their Buddha Nature).

It goes without saying that seekers on the path are able to see what is going on around them clearly and objectively, and to discriminate between right and wrong, in human terms at least. For their spiritual progress it is also crucial that they should understand (in their 'hearts') the difference between those who are ahead of them on the path and those who are behind them. The former are their examples, and the latter deserve their pity and love, for they still have many many lives of joy and suffering and learning to live before their eyes will be opened. Fortunately, Existence in its wisdom has made sure that they do not know what lies ahead of them. No seeker ever knows it before the time for their awakening comes.

Since all beings who have ever lived and learned on this planet are responsible for its present state of suchness it behoves every single one of us to accept this responsibility, both for that which has exalted the earth and for that which has dragged it down. Doing so is a deeply shattering inner experience, requiring a high degree of strength and courage, but the rewards in terms of self-knowledge are tremendous. Another effect of the experience is to motivate seekers to do what they can to help heal and liberate the world for which they are responsible.

From the spiritual traditions of the past we have records of many different systems of initiation. All of them guided seekers through numerous difficult trials and tests of their inner strength and courage, all of which brought them, finally, to knowledge of the unity of all Being.

The high priests of ancient Egypt had techniques with which they helped the initiate to leave his physical body for a while in order to experience his own eternity and that of all other beings. From the accounts which have been handed down to us from many great Indian yogis who had similar experiences we know that the so-called astral body, the 'body' which leaves the physical body at such times, is never completely separated from the physical body. They are connected by an ethereal cord which can become endlessly long, depending on how far away the two bodies are from one another. However, it is important that the astral body should return to the physical body in good time, for if it stays away too long this connection can be broken, resulting in the death of the physical body. In practice, though, this is something which almost never happens, as the desire to return is a compulsion which cannot be resisted.

These initiates thus *experienced* their existence – that which we call life – as an unbroken whole, and learned that death in the negative sense of the word does not exist. They came to understand that death is nothing more than a transition from one state to another.

What they did not experience, however, as far as one can tell from these accounts (and this is also something which I have never seen mentioned in any of the writings of the Masters of the East), was the realisation which dawned upon me in my unremitting, endless hours of *zazen* in my ovenlike room in Myokan-ji, my body failing: The knowledge that all of us, as we have been, as we are and as we shall be, are fully responsible for the suchness of our world. The world as it is now is our creation, and we shall continue to form it, for better or worse, until the end of time. Inconceivably wonderful things have been brought into existence, as have inconceivably terrible things, and the latter have almost succeeded in overwhelming the former in their battle for power. Each one of us has contributed his or her part to all of that which is.

In those hours of mindful rapture I experienced the true meaning of the Zen concept of 'being beyond good and evil', both in its absolute sense and in its relevance for us as human beings. Now that I am able to pass this knowledge on to others, I pray that all who receive it may choose the path of love, for each of our lives is a building block in the fabric of the world.

Notes

1. From Chinese *shēn*, 'gods', and *tao*, 'way'.
2. Born AD 767.
3. The 'Body of the Law' or 'Body of Wisdom'.

13

The Great Kōan and its Solution

In the preceding chapters I have only provided a rough outline of the extraordinary spiritual experiences which I had during my first months back in the temple. Although these experiences began more or less directly after my arrival, I nevertheless decided to begin my account by describing the opposition with which I was confronted upon my return, and the unusual course of events associated with that opposition – unusual, at least, in the context of a Zen monastery. My reason for this choice was that it was this uninterrupted and overwhelming sequence of external events, in combination with my spiritual work upon myself, which finally caused me to break asunder.

I should like to draw the reader's attention to the phrase which I have coined here: when I say that I 'broke asunder' I am not talking about breaking *down*, although it is perfectly true that I had many breakdowns in the course of my stay, right up to the very end. But those breakdowns were purely physical phenomena. What I am referring to when I speak of breaking asunder is the attainment of total liberation.

'Why have I returned to the temple?' 'Why have I returned now, at this particular time?' These questions, rising up ceaselessly out of the very depths of my being, turned out to be a kind of great kōan given to me by Heaven itself, a kōan which, together with Jōshū's 'Mu', demanded a solution. These kōans have now been solved – or rather, they have been *dis-solved*. The one in the other, both in me.

Even before beginning to write I know that my account of

how this miracle took place is going to be sketchy and incomplete. The only reason I have decided to make the attempt at all is because I have the help of an invaluable assistant: my diary, in which I recorded the essence of everything which could be expressed in words. There are a few gaps in the diary – on some days I was too exhausted to write in it – but these can be bridged with the help of the telegraphic notes which I wrote in my little pocket calendar.

'You must *become* oneness with "Mu",' the Rōshi had said.

In the course of my meditation my first realisation was that if I was to become one with 'Mu', or 'nothing', then I was going to have to become nothing myself. Understanding that was the first step. The work of inner destruction which I had already performed in Germany prior to my return to Japan in order to prepare myself for the trials which lay ahead now stood me in good stead.

I began as prescribed in the Zen tradition, sending the word 'Mu' downwards into the depths of my being together with my breath. At first I felt completely at a loss, but then, after a few weeks, I set to work to *become* 'nothingness', and I started to feel that I was back on spiritual terra firma again, if I may be allowed the rather strained metaphor.

It is important to point out that this is not something which one can achieve in a few weeks or months, even with an absolutely superhuman effort. In my own case the final experience of realisation was the culmination of an entire lifetime of ceaseless spiritual work. (And who knows how many more lifetimes of spiritual work, and setbacks, preceded this one?) Even though I had many overwhelming experiences on the way, I never allowed myself to be distracted by them. I did not stop to rest after my 'successes', nor did I ever give up, not even when I was in the very direst of straits and everything seemed to be completely stuck. One must simply accept everything choicelessly, the delight and the despair, without ascribing too much importance to anything. In the course of time, in a slow, almost imperceptible process, 'I' became less and less. (I would like to stress that this did not involve any loss of vitality – my vitality and individuality did not disappear, they were simply transformed.) Then, during my first sojourn in the temple, I experienced a series of overwhelming breakthroughs in satori, which left me as empty and fragile as a house of cards. (These experiences are described in detail in my first book.) Now only the slightest tap was needed to transform me into nothing.

What I am trying to make very clear is that this 'Mu', this 'nothing', this wonderful kōan, is not something which can be grasped. Nor is it something which can be experienced, not even with the most refined and highly developed senses. It is something which one must *become*. And when one has become it then one really can pass through the eye of a needle, to express it in Christian terms. Unlike Christianity, however, Zen would never allow a distinction between rich and poor. As far as Zen is concerned a rich man has every right to possess half the world, so long as he administrates his wealth wisely. There is only one very important proviso: he may not cling to anything he possesses, he may not be attached to his wealth, for if he does he cannot be free. And that is no easy task.

The poor, on the other hand, tend to be filled with countless desires born out of the greed to possess more and more and more. This endless pushing and shoving and elbowing, this 'Gimme gimme gimme,' has remained unchanged since the beginning of human history.

Even so, Zen Masters never allow their disciples to make distinctions on the path of liberation. Dualism is not tolerated, and the disciple must eradicate it totally from his being, never stopping until he has attained to realisation within the One. 'The other' has no place in the consciousness of a Zen Master; all that exists is the One, and everything is contained within it.

This knowledge is not an intellectual idea, it is direct, living experience – it has to be – and out of it was born the doctrine of the Void, or undifferentiated Being. What remains when there is no more differentiation? What remains when no meeting between God and man is possible because there is no separation between the two? What remains when nothing distinguishable exists? Nothingness. The Void. The seeker must pass through this nothingness in order to attain to the One, and he himself must break down the barriers which he encounters on his path. Within himself, for they are barriers which only exist within his own being.

During my first long sojourn in the Zen monastery, and after a period of meditative work on myself which demanded the very utmost of me, I was granted a few wonderful seconds in the realm of the Absolute. My first book contains a description of this experience, or rather, an attempted description. It is not really possible to put these things into words; the best one can do is to talk around them.

If that is so, the reader may be asking, if I had already been able to experience the indescribable, then why did I return? Why did I subject myself to this torture all over again? It is a question which many people have asked me. It is also a question which I asked myself. In fact, as I have already indicated, it was this question which turned into my second kōan. The answer to the question came very quickly, much more quickly than I had expected or believed possible.

In my first book I have already done my best to describe the kind of thing which the seeker can experience in the process of becoming one with the two most famous and most difficult kōans of Zen: 'Jōshu's Mu', and 'The Sound of One Hand Clapping'. I say that which one *can* experience because there is no predefined way for 'solving' a kōan, and each individual's reactions and experiences are bound to be different.

What I hadn't suspected during my first stay in the monastery was that the blissful experience of satori was by no means the end of my work with 'Mu'. The next phase of this work, which now began, involved transcending 'nothingness' and moving on to another spiritual plane, a plane where the task of the meditator must be confronted and mastered in utter aloneness.

I had already broken down the barriers of the earthly 'Mu'. Now I had to battle my way through the transcendental 'Mu'. It was an indescribably hard and lonely journey. I had to go on and on until the gates of Heaven finally burst open – until they *had to* burst open – and the nothingness finally disappeared into the One.

This entire process is a mystery. There is no way of explaining it. It is beyond explanation. All I can do is to say that it is a reality, that it really happened, and that it carried me from the depths of despair and suffering into a state of the most perfect bliss. And not only that: in contrast to my earlier experiences, which had been more like sudden flashes of spiritual lightning, what happened now was something much more protracted. It took place over a period of several weeks, repeated again and again almost every day.

For the moment this is all I wish to say on this subject.

In the chapters leading up to this one I have given an account of the outward course of events up until the beginning of September 1967. Having set the stage by describing the situation with which I was confronted and in which I had to live I can now lift the curtain on the inner events which took place at the same time, which I have up until now only hinted at. The following passage from my diary, which was written a mere six weeks after my arrival in the temple, gives an almost frighteningly clear picture of what I am talking about:

Diary, July 3 1967

Everything has changed, nothing is as it was before. I too have changed in the four years I have been away, I have been transformed. Perhaps this is why I have had to travel to the other side of the world: to experience this directly in everything I do, and to learn to see myself clearly.

What has happened to me, in me? Getting to the bottom of this question is of primary importance at the moment, and I meditate upon it ceaselessly. In the course of my meditation, as a precautionary measure, I am making use of 'Mu' as a tool, to destroy all possible resistance hidden within my being: my resistance to everything which has already happened, to everything which is happening at the moment, and to everything which is going to happen during my stay.

It was a good beginning; the energy and severity with which I carried out my programme of meditation and self-discipline made it possible for me to achieve very rapid results. Of course, the attainment of such results within a few short days was only made possible by the lifetime of spiritual work and training which had gone before.

The next words which I wrote in my diary sound very hard, almost brutal:

The naked truth is this: If I chose I could leave the temple and Japan now, today, without shedding a single tear and without looking back. What has happened?

A few days later I came down with a fever, and I was only able to take part in the main *zazen* session of the day in the main temple. Even that was difficult – walking to the temple was a tremendous effort. In my diary I wrote:

I now have time to meditate in peace. Ceaselessly I ask myself the question to which I must find the answer: 'What is it that has driven me to come here?'

After endless hours of tireless self-examination in *zazen*, it suddenly happened: for the space of a moment I felt as though I was being rent asunder, and then I was suddenly catapulted into a state of knowing. I can find no other words to describe it. There was nothing visionary about the experience at all. It was as though I was in a vacuum, in total emptiness. And in that emptiness, that nothingness, knowing came to me. Or was I myself the knowing?

Any attempt to describe an experience like this is doomed to failure. One is simply helpless. The only way one can even come anywhere near conveying something of the exalted nature of such a state of realisation is by using the kind of ecstatic language of praise and adoration to be found in the accounts of our medieval saints and mystics. As in my first account, however, I have decided to say no more than what actually happened. I do not wish to add anything which might be the product of the subjective interpretation of my own mind, after the event.

The illumination which I was granted was this: I realised, or knew – in that moment the process of realisation and the state of knowledge were the same thing – that the only place left to search was within my own being. Here in the proximity of my beloved Master, the great Rōshi, I knew without a shadow of a doubt that either the entire Truth was to be found within me, or it was not to be found anywhere in the universe. Of course, this is something which every Zen Buddhist knows, theoretically. But knowing something theoretically and actually experiencing it are two very different things. One piece of knowledge is the same as any other; the direct experience of the physical reality of that knowledge is a mystical revelation.

Diary, July 7 1967

The true profundity of that which has now happened can only really be comprehended by a Zen Master. In another nocturnal experience of samadhi a new 'knowing' has been chiselled deep into the tissue of my being: I have returned to Japan and to the temple in order to realise that it was not necessary to return . . .

What a paradox! But I understand what it means. It has to do with the dissolution of my inner attachment to the temple. This is something which I was aware of long before I boarded the plane in Berlin, but I resisted accepting it, afraid that it was merely a product of egotism. There was no getting around the fact, even then, but I did not want to admit the truth of it. And in any case I was also plagued by a terrible doubt: how could I be sure that this almost unbelievable detachment from that which I loved above all else was not simply an indication that something was wrong, and that I should return to my Rōshi as soon as possible?

I have returned because of my inborn perfectionism, which is particularly pronounced when it comes to my experiences on the inner path. Even the last tiny shadows of doubt in the most hidden corners of my consciousness must be blotted out.

This desire to eliminate all shadows, this doubt in the truth my own realisation, was to be paid for with a descent into Hell, and with terrible physical suffering. The reader will remember that I felt absolutely nothing as I climbed the steps of the temple upon my return. This fact says everything really, although I did not understand it myself at the time. And I have already described the many trials which followed, one after the other, almost without giving me a chance to pause for breath: the resistance to my presence in the temple, the battles I had to fight in order to obtain a simple little room of my own, the shock of the changes which had taken place in the temple and, after the typhoon, the unprecedented heat and humidity, which lasted for several months.

This morning I read in the newspaper that some workers in Germany were sent home because the temperature in the factory building where they were working had gone up to 100 degrees Fahrenheit. For months on end the temperature in my room in Myokanji never went down below 100, even at night, and during the day it was much higher than that. Unfortunately, hot weather is something which I have never been able to stand well, ever since my childhood.

I remembered Bodhidharma's words: 'The incomparable doctrine of the Buddha can only be understood after a long and hard training, through bearing that which is hardest to bear and through the practice of that which is hardest to practise . . . '

O great Bodhidharma, I thought to myself, it seems that I have reached the point at which I, at least, can bear no more. Perhaps others are stronger than I am, that is not for me to say, but now I only have one wish: I do not want to die here in Japan. And I want to retain enough strength to be able to return home to my own country before it is too late.

Diary, July 7 1967. Later.

Nevertheless, I can accept this 'detour' fully, without any ifs or buts. Once again Existence has demanded the very utmost of me, in order to allow the realisation of my own being to break open within me like an overripe fruit. No sacrifice would have been too great for this. The object of the lesson was to show me that I have to let go of even my very last attachments. No, that is not right. The object of the lesson was to show me that I have *already* let go of even my very last attachments. I had to come back here to see it – for there is nowhere else on this earth where I could possibly have any attachments left. Only here.

Despite my pitiable physical condition I feel calm and serene during the *zazen* sessions in the temple. Nor does the slightest feeling of exhilaration stir within my heart when I go to the Rōshi for *sanzen*. I wonder, does he sense my secret? The Buddha Spirit in him always repeats the same thing, again and again: 'You must become oneness with Non-Being.' He is driving me closer and closer to the point of total dissolution. I must enter ever deeper into the illumination which I have been granted, it must become an absolute reality.

And how am I doing this? By continuing with the process of self-destruction, consciously and willingly. Mu!

The typhoon broke upon us two days after I made the above entry in my diary, leaving a swathe of death and destruction in its wake, and this was soon followed by K. san's tragic suicide. These overwhelming events left me with very little time for myself and my inner work. In the preceding chapters I have already described everything which took place during this time, together with its effects upon me, up until 3 September. Now I shall take up the story again where I left off, beginning with the entry which I made in my diary on 4 September.

Diary, September 4 1967

Is it possible to speak of happiness when one is in such a miserable physical condition as I am now? And yet I am happy. I have managed to find my last remaining spiritual faults, faults which were hidden deep within me and which, it seems, could only be revealed in this extraordinary situation. In ceaseless spiritual work in my *zazen* sessions I ran them all to ground and destroyed them completely. But this description distorts what happened; I didn't find them and then destroy them: To find them was to destroy them, it was one single process.

And then something astounding took place: in the state of samadhi I suddenly received a message from the beyond, giving me permission to return home. It was something which I had neither sought nor invited, and it came in the form of a single sentence, striking down into the wordless silence of my meditation like a bolt of lightning:

'Your task here is now finished!'

I sat there motionlessly in *zazen* for many hours, drunk with happiness. My entire being was happiness and nothing else. Now it is very late, and the ice packs on my knees have become warm. I try to find a few words of my own to say about this overwhelming message, but I must abandon the attempt. There is nothing to be said. 'Your task here is now finished!' This laconic, divine statement does not only refer to my work here in the temple: it includes my entire spiritual search, everything which I have ever done to serve Him and to find Him. I am free. After so many decades of discipline in this life, and who knows how many other lives before this one, He, 'It', has finally released me.

I am too poor in words and too rich in divine joy to be able to say anything more.

Diary, September 12 1967

It is unbelievable. After the terrible heat yesterday, which caused me yet another sleepless night, the temperature has suddenly gone down. Now it is late at night, and in my room it is a mere 68 degrees Fahrenheit. Another typhoon is on the way, 'Typhoon No. 22' they call it. It is heading straight for us, and the cool air is being brought to us by the storm winds which are the heralds of its imminent arrival. All the doors and windows in the house are barricaded, only my window is open halfway. For the moment, at least, I am grateful for the unexpected change in the weather.

Diary, September 13 1967

Today Typhoon No. 22 suddenly changed its course and passed us by, leaving us unscathed.

Diary, September 17 1967

I am in a state of utter happiness and bliss. And yet there is virtually nothing which I can say about my meditation at the moment. It is not really 'my' meditation any more; on the contrary, now it is as though 'It' is meditating. 'It' tells me what I must free myself of, 'It' tells me which forces it wishes to see at work within me.

It is astonishing, but true: no matter how full of troubles and mishaps it is, in my heart every day is now a good day. And not only in my heart. Everything is easy, even when it is difficult. I am filled with radiant cheerfulness and serenity. When I go shopping I walk through the steaming landscape and the cloying heat as though I were floating on air.

It is similar to the way people feel when they are in love. But only similar – there is also a tremendous, and very important difference: when one is awakened one is no longer attached to anything, and one's consciousness is always as clear and unclouded as the purest crystal. One's buoyancy is the result of transcendence, not of anything external. In the words of the Cabbala, 'The lamps have been repositioned.' The light is shining from a different direction, and a new world has become visible.

Diary, September 19 1967

When one's heart has become completely pure, freed of all desires, passions and attachments, when even one's feelings and emotions have ceased to be egocentric, one's heart feels free, light and empty. Only then is transcendence possible, only then is it possible to become united with both the 'One which is without form' and the 'One which is with form'. When this happens the seeker becomes one with the Source, with God; and since God is everything which is, this also means that the seeker has become one with the entire universe and with all beings. One is simply One, within a serene, harmonious totality of love.

And that is the Garden of Eden.

The last sentence of this entry haunts me. Is this state really the Garden of Eden, symbolically at least? Not if one adheres strictly to the story of Adam and Eve in the Old Testament: the paradise which the Old Testament describes and which we all learned about in school was not a real paradise, and it can never be one, for something devilish took place there. If this state is the Garden of Eden, then it can only be a very much 'purified' version of the Biblical Eden. 'Paradise' and 'The Garden of Eden' are terms to which absolute purity are of necessity intrinsic, and falseness cannot exist in purity.

But where did the third person in the drama, the Serpent, come from? In the very moment in which temptation appeared in the form of the Serpent, Paradise ceased to exist. Where temptation is possible there can be no Paradise.

When the attack came Eve was a paradisiacal being, and as such she was in a state of absolute purity. She was innocence incarnate, and she was thus incapable of recognising impurity when she encountered it. Seeing the Serpent, Eve simply assumed that it too came from God. As a pure being living in Paradise she was unable to make any other assumption, for perfect purity is incapable of imagining anything impure. And so she passed the apple and the serpent's words on to her partner.

Adam could have refused the apple. Unfortunately, this idea did not occur to him, and we are all very well aware of the results of Adam's failure. It was definitely Adam who failed, not Eve, for eating the 'apple' required a positive action on Adam's part, not on Eve's, and no matter how sympathetic one is with Adam I do not think that one can possibly say that Eve ate the apple for him.

I know that the entire Biblical story is an allegory; unfortunately, I don't know how this allegory is interpreted by the esoteric Jewish teachings. In practical terms, however, what the esoteric teachings make of the story is not really important. What *is* important is the apparent meaning of the version of the story which has been handed down from generation to generation, and, especially, what trusting children are taught about it in Sunday school, for that is something which can form them for life.

Really it is the author of this allegorical story who destroyed the original meaning of Paradise. When one hears the story the first question one cannot help but ask is, where was God while all this was going on? Didn't he see the evil which was taking place? Or was it his will that this terrible temptation should take place? If it was, then the Garden of Eden was not Paradise, for it is not possible for such things to take place in Paradise.

In addition to this the author of Genesis is also responsible for stigmatising women and the female principle for all time, at least in the Judaeo-Christian religions. The stereotype of women as 'Eve the temptress' still persists today, and there are no signs that this state of affairs is likely to change in the near future.

The picture of men created by the story is a completely different kettle of fish, however. According to the author of Genesis, Adam has been able to pride himself on his innocence. It wasn't his fault, we are told, the 'woman' talked him into it.

The sentence which I wrote in my diary, 'And that is the Garden of Eden', must have welled up from the depths of my childhood memories, for in Zen terms it couldn't be more wrong. In the East, all the way from the Vedas of India to the Zen Buddhism of modern Japan, the only thing which is held to exist at all is the One, both in the form of absolute Non-

Being itself and in the 'ten thousand things' of manifest reality. Everything else is illusion. No differentiations can exist within the One, especially not when they involve value judgements of any sort.

The Westerner might then feel inclined to ask, 'But where does someone who has become free of the shackles of illusion go then, if not to Paradise?' It is an understandable question, in terms of Western logic at least, but I am sure that any monk who had dared to put it to one of the ancient Zen Masters would have received a very gruff brush-off. The answer is that they don't 'go' anywhere. When the seeker becomes free of illusion he simply becomes aware of his own suchness, and he starts to live in that suchness. As I have already pointed out, the process of attaining to freedom is nothing more, or less, than the process of becoming united with the Original Source – with God, if you will – and thus with everything which is.

The reader may feel that this sounds rather austere and unexciting. In reality, however, it is everything, it is absolute abundance. But there is no way of describing this state with the tools of language, which are the tools of differentiation, without distorting it and making it less than it is. Anything which one can say 'about' the absolute Truth cannot help but be light years away from what it really is. The chasm between words and reality is unbridgeable.

I am reminded of a very dear old friend of mine, who is a wonderful, deeply religious woman. When I spoke to her of these things she replied:

'It may very well be so, but I don't want it! I long for Paradise! When I leave my earthly body I want to meet my loved ones again, I want to be able to bow down in adoration before divine beings.'

My response was, why not? What is the problem? There is nothing which does not exist in God's universe. Everything which is 'imaginable' exists, for it is not possible to imagine something which does not exist. And so long as bonds and attachments have not been dissolved they should not be broken suddenly and arbitrarily. That would result in chaos, and would not be in accordance with the nature of life, which develops progressively.

Everything has its own reality. For instance, I know without a shadow of a doubt that my own metaphysical experiences, which I have described in one of the earlier chapters of this book, were also real. At least, they were as 'real' or as 'unreal' as I myself am, for what that is worth. In the terms of Zen, of course, this kind of 'reality' is nothing more than illusion.

In *sanzen* the Rōshi once said to me, 'You are not. I am not. This room in which we are sitting is not. Nothing is. You must *become* that Nothing.'

The seeker who is successful in this process of dissolution, becoming a nothingness within nothingness, comes to realise that the Whole is utterly indivisible.

Of all the great Masters of the past one of those whom I admire and love the most is Plotinus, a man who attained everything which it is possible to attain on the spiritual path, and a Westerner at that. Plotinus travelled through all the levels of spiritual development and bliss, step by step, recording everything which he experienced in glorious, glowing language. Anyone who reads his account of his unique inner journey cannot help but be inspired.

Even when he attained to unity with the *nous* (the One with form, the source of everything which exists), after making his way through the entire gamut of human spiritual experience, Plotinus did not stop. Realising that he and the *nous* were still 'two, not one', he broke through this last barrier too, in order to become united with the endless and absolute abyss, with the One. And just as the One itself is utterly indescribable, as Plotinus himself says, so is the bliss of unity with the One beyond anything which words can even begin to fathom.

In his writings Plotinus, who was regarded as a God by his disciples, addresses himself directly to those seekers who are already travelling towards the One. He is always practical, never theoretical, and his sole objective is to help the elect seeker to reach the Original Source of all Being. No one is better equipped to give such advice than this sublime Master, for he himself had experienced every detail of the spiritual journey from beginning to end. In his own search Plotinus never allowed any experiences on the way to distract him, no matter how wonderful they were; he continued unswervingly until he had reached the final goal of his pilgrimage (which is also the goal of Zen), the state in which observer and observed are one.

The works of this great teacher, philosopher and Master are unique, for he is the only enlightened one in the entire history of religious literature who has written a detailed account of his own spiritual journey, from beginning to end.[1] His writings are a comfort and an inspiration to all seekers who fear that the Void of Zen is too naked, too hard and too absolute.

In absolute terms, of course, Zen does not really reject anything which is in any way a part of Existence. But all the great Masters of the East, including Gautama Buddha himself, have always been very well aware of the dangers involved in lingering too long in pleasurable states of consciousness. For no matter how blissful such intermediate states may be, the disciple must always painfully tear himself away from them again – a process which can take a thousand years, or more, or less – and continue on his way. The Masters saw that this was unnecessary, and they thus chose to teach the way to the One which leads through Nothingness.

Plotinus' path was a different one. He did not travel through Nothingness, he travelled from one state of spiritual glory to another, each more wonderful than the last, until 'he', as an individual, finally disappeared in the blissful abyss of Non-Being. But Plotinus was unique, in many ways. How many of us have his almost superhuman strength? How many of us would be able to resist the temptation of lingering a while in a divine world of sublime joy and ecstasy, instead of continuing on our way? The ancient Masters of India and their successors were well aware of these human weaknesses, and it was for this reason that they chose the way of Nothingness for their disciples.

Plotinus too had a Master. His name was Ammonius Saccas. All that we know about him is that he lived and taught in quiet seclusion somewhere near Alexandria, and that Plotinus was his disciple for eleven years, right up to the time when Ammonius left his earthly body. Nor is it necessary to know anything more; Plotinus is Ammonius' gift and legacy to Humanity, and whenever one thinks of Plotinus one thinks, perhaps without being aware of it, of his great Master, who must have been a truly great servant of the One.

In more recent years the famous Swiss psychologist, the late Carl Gustav Jung, has given us an excellent account of the experience of leaving the physical body and of the intermediate states which one passes through when this happens. This account is to be found in his book of memoirs, *Recollections, Dreams, Reflections*, which I have already mentioned in an earlier chapter. His description of the transcendental experiences which he had during a severe illness is very precise and detailed, and a great comfort to all those who are afraid to trust in the 'reality' of their own experiences because they feel that it is not possible to square them with the findings of science. After all, Jung himself was a very great scientist, and we can be sure that he was well aware of the responsibility which he was taking upon himself by publishing such an account.

The following excerpt is taken from the chapter entitled 'Visions':

> It appeared that I was floating in space, very high up. When I looked down I could see the earth far away below me, a sphere suffused in glorious blue light.
>
> [*We now know that what Jung saw with his inner eye was the same sight which our modern astronauts see when they are orbiting the earth in their spaceships.*]
>
> I later asked an expert in such matters how far out in space one would have to be to be able to see the earth in its entirety like this. His reply: At least 900 miles! The view of the earth from this height was the most wonderful and magical sight which I have ever seen.
>
> After gazing down for a while I turned around [. . .] Something new entered into my field of vision. It wasn't very far away from me, a huge, dark lump of rock, it looked like a meteorite [. . .] This rock was floating in space, just as I was [. . .] There was an entrance in the rock, leading into a small hall or lobby. On the right, sitting on a stone bench in the lotus position, was a black Indian [. . .] It seems that he was waiting for me, in silence [. . .]
>
> As I climbed up the steps in the rock leading up to the entrance I had the strange feeling that I was being stripped of everything connected with the past. All my opinions, all my wishes and thoughts, the entire phantasmagoria of earthly existence, simply fell away from me, or was taken away from me – it was an extremely painful process. But nonetheless, something remained; it was as though everything which had ever happened to me was now here with me [. . .] one could say that I now consisted of these events. I was my own history, and I had the very clear impression that 'I' and it were identical. 'I am this agglomeration of things past and things achieved.' This experience gave me a feeling of extreme poverty, and yet of great satisfaction at the same time [. . .] Everything seemed past, it was simply a *fait accompli*, without any reflexive connection to that which had actually gone before. There was no more feeling of regret that something had fallen away, or been taken away. On the contrary: I had everything which I was, and that was all which I had.
>
> There was something else which preoccupied me, in addition to this: As I had approached the temple I had been absolutely certain that I would come into a brightly illuminated room, where I would

meet all those people to whom I really belong. I would know what had been before I was, why I had come into being, and in what direction my life was going to flow in the future. My life as I had lived it had often seemed like a story to me, a story with no beginning and no end. I felt as though I were a kind of historical pericope, an excerpt from which the preceding and following text passages are missing. It seemed to me as though an invisible pair of scissors had cut my life out of some much longer sequence of events, and as a result I was left many unanswered questions. Why was my life the way it was? Why have I brought these particular abilities with me? What have I made of them? What is the result of what I have done going to be? I was certain that I would receive answers to all these questions as soon as I entered the stone temple. There I would understand why everything had been the way it had been, and not otherwise. I would find the people who know the answers to my questions about that which had gone before and that which was yet to come.

[*What Jung is actually seeking here is confirmation of the Eastern doctrines of karma and reincarnation.*]

I was still thinking about these things when something happened which distracted my attention: A figure rose up from the earth below me, from Europe, coming closer and closer. It was my doctor [. . .] It was like a vision rising up out of the depths below me. He came to a halt directly in front of me, and then he started to communicate with me telepathically. He told me that he had been sent from the earth to bring me a message. Whoever had sent this message objected to the fact that I was in the process of departing. I was not to leave the earth, he said, I had to return. And in that very moment the entire vision disappeared.

I was terribly disappointed; it seemed that everything had been for nothing. I had gone through the painful process of divesting myself of my past in vain, and now I was not to be allowed to enter the temple and meet my people [. . .]

The rhythm of my consciousness during those weeks was very strange. During the day I was usually down and depressed. I felt miserable and weak, hardly daring to move at all, my heart full of grief. My only thought was, 'Now I must return to the greyness of this world.' Towards evening I would go to sleep, sleeping until around midnight. Then I would wake up again, staying awake for around an hour. Now, however, my state of mind was utterly different: ecstatic and blissful. I felt as though I were floating on air, and as though I were completely at home in the womb of the universe – in a gigantic, endless emptiness which was nonetheless filled through and through with a feeling of overwhelming joy.

'This is eternal bliss,' I thought to myself, 'there is no way one can possibly describe it, it is much too wonderful.' [. . .]

The intensity and beauty that I felt during these visions is simply unimaginable. I have never ever experienced anything as vast, before or since. And then the contrast, the daytime which followed! During the day I felt tormented, I was a nervous wreck. Everything irritated me. Everything was too material, too gross and clumsy, too physically and mentally cramped. It seemed that, in order to serve some incomprehensible purpose, the world around me had been artificially restricted to over-narrow boundaries, and even though I had already clearly seen the illusory nature of this world it nonetheless had a kind of hypnotic power, and was able to give me the feeling that it was, despite everything, reality itself.

Ever since then, and despite my revalorised view of reality, I have never really been able to rid myself completely of the impression that 'life' is nothing more than an excerpt from existence, a play performed in a three-dimensional world system created especially for this purpose [. . .]

If I hadn't been through it myself I don't think I would have ever believed that such things were at all possible. Perpetual bliss was not something which squared with the reality I knew. And yet the visions and experiences were absolutely real. There was nothing spurious about them; on the contrary, they had the unmistakable feel of objectivity to them.

One tends to avoid using words like 'eternal', but I can only circumscribe that which I experienced as the bliss of a timeless state of consciousness, a state in which present, past and future have all become one . . . An indescribable whole in which one is inextricably interwoven, and which one can nonetheless observe objectively. (C. G. Jung, *Erinnerungen, Träume, Gedanken* (Memories, Dreams, Reflections) Rascher Verlag, Zurich.)

This is not the sort of thing that people make up, especially not people like Jung. And everyone who has themselves had experiences of this type knows that these 'visions' are more real, and leave a deeper impression on one's consciousness, than anything else with which one is ever confronted in the so-called real world.

In Chapter 4 of this book I described the six visionary dreams which I have been granted in my lifetime. My own experience tallies completely with Jung's description: the overwhelming impression was one of unmistakable, tangible reality. Of course, there are also some important differences between my visions and those of the terminally ill psychologist: in my case each vision gave me a deeper and more intense view and understanding of a phase of spiritual development which lay before me, and thus they had to do with the work which I had yet to carry out in this body. Jung was nearing the end of his life, and his attachment to his body was fading; it is thus appropriate that he was given a vision of that which lay before him after the end of this life: the temple in space, where he would be united with 'his people' in a state of eternal bliss, freed of all earthly restrictions and hindrances. I can imagine that Jung's approach to his impending death was transformed from that moment onwards.

One should not, however, make the mistake of thinking that Jung's vision was universal. After our deaths each of us will experience that which is in accordance with our individual beings and our level of development. To each his own.

As I have already pointed out, Buddhism has never denied the reality of such experiences, in all their endless variations. Gautama Buddha himself was perfectly well aware of all of his own previous incarnations. But because he himself had attained perfect unity with the Original Source of all Being he could see the pitfalls on the way, and he thus taught his disciples to abandon all supports and aids in order that they might reach the ultimate goal of their search more quickly.

Zen, in its glorious totality, does not admit any compromise whatsoever. The dictum of Zen is simply: 'All that is, is nothing.'

I know what Rōshi Mumon's answer would have been if I had ever asked him a question about such visions: 'You yourself are nothing. How can a vision which appears to you be anything other than nothing?' If one remains constantly mindful of one's own Non-Being then, unavoidably, one eventually comes to value non-valuation. The opposite of this statement is equally true.

Any Zen monk who had the temerity to come to his Master with an experience like the one which Jung describes so credibly in his memoirs would be sure to receive a thorough verbal drubbing. 'You will have to wait until the end of the next world cycle to attain to the Truth, or even longer,' the Master would say, 'if you waste so much as a single thought on that kind of rubbish.'

'If you meet Buddha on the way, kill him!' Many people brought up in Christian cultures have a great deal of trouble with this famous Buddhist motto. It is not blasphemy, however, it is simply another example of the total consistency of Buddhism. Any meeting, even with the Cosmic Buddha (or God, in Christian terms), involves duality, and the objective of the spiritual search is to overcome *all* duality. One should also remember that Buddha does not appear to just anyone. It is only the very advanced Zen monk who is blessed with this kind of visitation.

The next question is: how does one 'kill' Buddha when one meets him on the way? The answer is simple. One 'kills' the divine 'other' not by destroying it, but by becoming it, by dissolving the duality and melting into it.

Exalted experiences like this demonstrate, on the one hand, that the untiring efforts of the seeker have been successful; at the same time, however, they also give a clear indication of that which has yet to be overcome.

The path created by Buddha, the father of Zen, leads directly to Buddha himself, without a single detour. And it thereby leads directly to the One, for Buddha and the One are one. Whenever I think about this wonderful gift which he has given us I feel as though my heart were about to burst with joy.

The Zen Master is also one who has become Buddha, and from that moment onwards he is directly aware of the One, both in its absolute sense and in its physical expression, the 'ten thousand things' of manifest reality. He alone is able to show true respect to higher beings, whether they be Buddhas or Bodhisattvas, Masters or saints, for he alone can see them as they really are. In Zen monasteries it is only the Rōshi who is allowed to bow down before the altar bearing the image of Buddha during the early morning service – the monks must sit to one side, reciting sutras with their eyes lowered. Their law is 'Mu'. The Enlightened One, on the other hand, smiles at the universe in perfect peace, seeing it both as it as and as it appears to be in its play of manifestation.

Diary, September 24 1967

Today the great annual ceremony in memory of the dead was held in the temple. It was exactly as I remember it from my first visit. The Rōshi was overwhelming. After the ceremony was over the roughly four hundred participants were given a simple meal.

I saw Sakamoto san this evening, and in the course of our conversation he revealed a surprising piece of news: He began by saying that Dr H., the Rōshi of the Tendai sect (with whom I had a very pleasant conversation while I was staying in the guest house on Mount Hiei), had written a letter to Rōshi Mumon.

'Rōshi H. writes that he would be delighted if you could accompany him and Rōshi Mumon on their international lecture tour in February,' said Sakamoto san cryptically.

'International lecture tour?' I asked in puzzlement.

After making me promise that I wouldn't breathe a word to anyone Sakamoto san told me that these two great Rōshis have decided to go on a lecture tour together with a number of other advanced Zen Masters and their best disciples. The itinerary of the trip (they plan to travel by sea) includes Hong Kong, Bangkok, Formosa, Singapore and India. Rōshi Mumon is to speak on Zen in the mornings, Rōshi H. on *makashikan*, or 'the spirit of Tendai' in the afternoons. Sakamoto san said that Rōshi Mumon had been delighted at the suggestion that I should come along, and that I shouldn't worry about money.

'The Rōshi says that he will pay for your expenses if you cannot afford it yourself,' said Sakamoto san. 'But remember, no one in the monastery must know about the trip before we leave. We do not want any publicity. Only a few very advanced men are to be allowed to participate. You will be the only woman.'

I am completely bewildered. I need time to digest the news before I can decide what I should do.

I don't have the money to pay for the trip myself, of course, but that is not the problem; the Rōshi has offered to pay and I have no objections to accepting his generosity. Everything would be perfectly all right if only the tour were going to take place before the winter begins. But February! If I say yes then I will have to spend the entire winter in the temple, and neither Shofuku-ji nor Myokan-ji are heated. The windows and doors of the meditation hall are always kept open during *zazen* sessions, no matter whether it is freezing or even twenty degrees below freezing, and one must sit there without moving a muscle for hours on end, exposed to the wind and rain and snow. Nor is there any way of warming oneself up afterwards, apart from the little handwarmer full of coals in the First Monk's reception room.

No one seems to have realised that this might actually kill me. This is understandable though: outwardly I always seem very fit and hearty, and I take great care not to allow the suffering which my poor health causes me to show. I don't suppose anybody has any idea just what a terrible state my body has been in for the last few months. Physically, I am just a wreck.

Diary, September 25 1967

I have decided not to think about the lecture tour for the moment. I won't have to make a decision one way or another for a long time yet.

Diary, October 1 1967

The temperature in my room has gone down to 73 degrees Fahrenheit. Strangely enough, I feel chilly, because of the suddenness of the change, I suppose.

Diary, October 2 1967

Again and again the revelation: Union can only be attained in nothingness. It is so blissful.

Diary, October 4 1967

A wonderful ceremony was held in the temple yesterday, to inaugurate the winter semester.

The ceremony began with the sound of the temple drums and gongs, which were shatteringly loud. Then the Zen priests from the temples belonging to Shofuku-ji's 'diocese' entered the *hōndō*, dressed in their wonderful ceremonial robes. Some of them were very old. They were followed by our monks, only fifteen of whom were present. (The others are still away on holiday.) They all took their places on the left of the altar. I stood on the right, all on my own.

Then the rolling and booming of the drums and gongs rose to a wonderful, deafening crescendo and Rōshi Mumon entered the hall, dressed in his flowing red robes. He was a wonderful sight. At the moment when he reached the centre of the *hōndō* the sound of the instruments became even louder still, an ululation of ecstasy rising up to Heaven, and then it ceased abruptly, replaced by total and absolute silence. In that moment we were catapulted from the abundance of manifest reality into total emptiness . . .

The overwhelming ceremony which followed was carried out in silence, a silence so powerful and pregnant that it was almost oppressive. The Rōshi stood there alone in the middle of the *hōndō* in front of the altar, his hands raised in adoration. Then he bowed down and stretched himself out on the ground in front of the altar with the palms of his hands upwards in the gesture of receiving. After a moment's pause he stood up again with amazing speed. This process was repeated three times.

The breathtaking silence in the *hōndō* was the silence of mystic union with the Buddha Spirit, invoked wordlessly by all present.

This is something which one cannot possibly describe, one can only experience it. In this silence the Rōshi then strode to the altar and performed a symbolic ritual of sacrifice. The ritual was divided into several parts, and after completing each part the Rōshi stepped back a few paces and repeated the same series of prostrations he had performed before. When the last prostration was finished he walked to the middle of the room again, and stood there for a moment, absolutely motionless. And then, suddenly, he shattered the now oppressive silence with a lion's roar of an invocation which seemed to shake the *hōndō* to its very foundations:

'May the Buddha Spirit always bless this temple with its presence!'

There was a short silence, and then the monks and priests started to recite a sutra, while the Rōshi performed another series of prostrations in front of the altar, not stopping until the recitation was over. Each time he bowed down he stretched himself out face down on the matting, his forehead resting on the narrow carpet which had been spread out before the altar, his arms spread out in front of him with the palms of his hands facing upwards. After a brief pause he would then leap up again with breathtaking speed and elegance.

I was terribly afraid for him. Even for a young, strong monk in his prime this performance would have been an incredible strain; the Rōshi was neither young nor strong, and I knew all too well how delicate and overworked he was. Nonetheless, to my astonishment his body obeyed the commands of his spirit flawlessly, and without the slightest outward signs of strain.

This breathtaking act of adoration was followed by the ceremonial procession around the *hōndō*, accompanied by the recitation of more sutras. The Rōshi led the way, followed by the venerable priests, in order of their rank, and the monks took up the rear. The route of this procession around the *hōndō* is very complex, involving a large number of different figures which must be executed precisely, and the entire process took a good twenty minutes. When it was over all of the priests and monks were once again standing motionlessly in their original positions, in three rows to the left of the altar. The Rōshi strode up to the altar again and ignited some incense in a large bowl. Then he took a few steps backwards and kneeled down, and one after another the monks came up to the altar and cast a few grains of incense into the bowl, from which fragrant smoke wafted up into the air. I was last of all. That was the end of the ceremony.

Diary, October 5 1967

A great weight has fallen from my heart: The lecture tour has been cancelled. The ship for the trip had been chartered from England, and the closure of the Suez Canal means that it would have to travel all the way around Africa to get here, more than doubling the cost. I have no idea why we didn't charter a ship here in Japan, but whatever the reason, the upshot is that a very difficult decision has been taken out of my hands, and for that I am grateful.

Diary, October 6 1967

It is so wonderful. I cannot find any words to describe this inner joy, this total joy, the joy of union with Eternal Being. It has been there for weeks now, but up until now I haven't dared to admit to myself that it really is that which it obviously and self-evidently is: Absolute Truth. At least, not when I return to the human realm.

Strangely enough it was the Rōshi's wish (passed on to me by his secretary) that I should stay on to participate in the Great *Zazen* in December which finally pricked the bubble of my last doubts, giving me the certainty that that which I have attained is real, beyond any shadow of a doubt.

The December Great *Zazen* is the hardest of the entire year. It is a non-stop period of intense meditation lasting for eight days and eight nights. Sleep is not allowed, and there are only occasional brief breaks to stretch the body and for meals. Four years ago Sakamoto san told me that all the monks who take part in this Great *Zazen* must sign a statement beforehand, saying that neither the Rōshi nor the temple community can be held responsible should they die in the course of the eight days.

The great doors at either end of the *zendō* are opened as soon as the meditation begins, allowing the bitterly cold winter winds to blow through unhindered. The side of the hall which the monks face when they sit is also completely open; there are no walls in our sense of the word, only flimsy paper screens, and these too remain open whenever the monks are sitting in meditation. 'It's not uncommon to see icicles hanging from the noses of the monks,' said Sakamoto san.

The monks must go to the Rōshi four times every day to report on the progress of their meditation. This means that for a period of eight days he must give *sanzen* 120 times a day.

Of course, dozing off or sleeping during *zazen* is strictly forbidden, and this means that the monk overseeing the session must use the Zen stick very frequently to keep the exhausted monks awake.

It says much for the spirit of Zen in this temple that not a single one of the monks ever tries to shirk this Great *Zazen*. Shofuku-ji is one of the last great bastions of Zen. Whatever human, all too human errors the participants may have committed in the course of the rest of the year, during these days and nights of utter renouncement and bitter endurance for the sake of Absolute Truth all their errors and all their delusions simply dissolve into the Void, and their spirits radiate in crystalline clarity.

If I were twenty years younger, or even ten years younger, I know that nothing would be able to prevent me from taking part in this Great *Zazen*. But as it is I don't feel that I have missed anything – back then I was given other tasks and trials, no less difficult and no less exalted. Everything has happened as it should. I have no regrets.

Even so, and even though my reason told me that it would be madness to take part in this marathon session in my present physical condition (I only weigh 120 pounds at the moment, which means that I am a good 27 pounds underweight, and my heart and circulatory system are in a state of near-collapse because of the climate) I sat down to meditate upon the Rōshi's wish that I should participate. I meditated on it for many hours last night, and again, even more intensely, early this morning. The result of this meditation was an inner sensation: I realised that there is no longer any need for me to remain here. I am now one with Eternal Being. There is no more separation between me and It, and wherever I am It, or He, will continue to think, feel and act through me.

I shall write a letter to the Rōshi today, telling him everything.

Here is the letter which I wrote to Rōshi Mumon:

My beloved, most esteemed Rōshi,

I am very sorry to take up your valuable time with this letter, but I feel that it is my duty to inform you of several things.

In every *sanzen* session which you in your compassion were good enough to grant me you have driven me deeper and deeper into the nothingness of the Void. 'Be oneness with the "Mu"!' you have told me again and again.

In order to attain to this oneness I began, once again, with self-purification. I destroyed myself and everything which arose within my being, using the 'Mu' which you had given me as a tool. I drove myself very hard, to the brink of total exhaustion and beyond.

And then, one day, during a meditation session, everything was suddenly transformed. I had nothing to do with this transformation, 'It' acted. It became utterly impossible for me to become the 'Mu' – the One displaced it, and then, later, 'Mu' and the One dissolved into one another and became one. The One was the nothingness and the nothingness was the One.

I continued to 'sit', day after day. And then it happened. Suddenly, with a feeling of overwhelming shock and and indescribable bliss, I *knew*: I am one with the One and – I am free.

For several weeks I tested myself and my realisation very severely, in order to be sure that I was not suffering from a delusion. But the blissful knowledge of my liberation remained, and became deeper and deeper every day. Not only during my meditation, all the time. This freedom is total, absolute and perfect.

My beloved Rōshi, I am certain that you will understand what I mean when I say this, for it is Truth: I am even free from our temple, and free from you, my most deeply respected and beloved Master.

When I left you and returned to Germany four years ago my attachment to you was very deep. For all this time my only thought and my only wish was to return to you, and to be in your presence again. I gave up concerts, theatres and the cinema. I saved every penny I had, and as soon as I received the money for my book I scraped everything together and booked my flight to Japan, back to you.

Now I am free. One with the Non-Being Being. All bonds, all attachments have dissolved. Now I *know*: No matter where I am, no matter where I go, I am one with the One.

My Rōshi, this happiness is your doing, and yours alone. My heart is overflowing with gratitude and holy love for you. My heart knows that we shall never ever be parted again. We are one, for the rest of Eternity. That is all.

Your blissfully happy,
devoted and grateful
sister and disciple,

Gerta

Diary, October 7 1967

The letter! I had to write it. I brought it to the Rōshi's attendant monk, Nan san, early this morning. My heart beats wildly whenever I stop to wonder how the Rōshi will react to it.

Diary, October 9 1967

Sakamoto san just left. He brought me a basket of fruit, a present from the Rōshi.

'Has the Rōshi read my letter?' I asked him in trepidation.

'Yes,' he replied. 'I was present when he read it. He said, "Ital san is neither my guest nor my disciple. She is my sister in Buddha. Thus, whatever I own is also hers, and whatever she owns is also mine. Tell her, if she needs money she can have anything she wishes. It belongs to her, no less than to me." '

It would not be fitting to make any comment on this statement. All one can do is bow down in respect.

Diary, October 10 1967

Unity can only be attained within the Void.

Diary, October 11 1967

Everything is one: my own suffering, the animosity towards me, the misunderstandings, the divine liberation which I have been granted, and the understanding of the connections between all of these things. It is all one. Even our enemies are contained within this unity. Especially our enemies, for they are our best teachers.

Later:

There is one Zen story which I have always found very strange and confusing, but now I understand it. The story is about a monk who attains to satori, and his first response to the experience is to say that his Master's enlightenment isn't worth much. This sounds very cold and ungrateful to Western ears, and even D. T. Suzuki refrains from making any comment on the story in the book in which he cites it.

From my own experience I can now confirm that the monk's statement was neither cold nor ungrateful, no matter how strange it may sound to us, and that he was not in any way denigrating his Master. On the contrary, his response demonstrates that he had realised a very profound truth: He (the Master) has 'It', I have 'It', and there is no living being which cannot have 'It'. It is simply the way things are. So what is all the fuss about?

The same thing applies to the famous story about the Zen monk who – in the moment of enlightenment – suddenly hit back when his Master slapped him. This monk didn't strike his Master because he was angry or insulted, far from it. He simply felt so blissful in the experience of the Ultimate that there was nothing else he could do, and I am certain that his Master was able to see the joy in his being. The monk's blow also expressed something else: the barrier between the two of them had been dissolved, and now there was no difference between Master and disciple.

When I had to leave the temple to return to Germany four years ago I left in sadness and regret, and the pain of parting was immense. This time I shall leave with joy in my heart.

Diary, October 12 1967

The famous Japanese October weather has begun. It is beautifully sunny and mild during the day and cold at night. We still have a few days of holiday left, and I suppose that I could make another trip to Nara or Kyoto or to the seaside if I wanted. But such things now seem completely unimportant and unsubstantial. 'The lamps have been repositioned.'

Diary, October 14 1967

The silent ceremony marking the resumption of *zazen* and the beginning of the work of the winter semester took place in the *hōndō* this evening. It started at six. The outward form of the ceremony was the same as it was four years ago, but nonetheless it was different. Last time the only light in the *hōndō* was a single lantern, standing in the corner directly in front of the kneeling Rōshi and casting flickering shadows on the white walls. Today all the lights in the *hōndō* were on, and the atmosphere was not nearly so mysterious and magical. Last time the ceremony moved me very deeply; today I felt cool and detached.

Why was everything so different this time? The answer to this question is simple: The new First Monk who conducted the ceremony doesn't have any feeling for such things. Four years ago Gan san was First Monk. He is a noble and profound soul, and it is him I have to thank for the overwhelming experience which I had then. He is in Myōshin-ji in Kyoto at the moment, where he has a responsible position. (Rōshi Mumon is also the Master of the monks in Myōshin-ji.)

Tomorrow is Sunday. The ceremony inaugurating the Rōshi's next series of lectures is to take place at ten in the morning. The first session of the next Great *Zazen* begins in the afternoon at five, and is to last until ten p.m.

Something terrible has happened: since this morning I have had excruciating pains in my left ankle, radiating all the way up to the knee. And the Great *Zazen* is due to start tomorrow! It seems that sitting in *zazen* for months on end has caused the joint to become inflamed. I always sit in the lotus position, with my left foot resting high up on my right thigh, and this means that the ankle is twisted sideways for several hours every day.

Diary, October 15 1967

It was a terrible, exhausting day. The pain in my ankle was unbelievable, and I have no idea how I managed to hold out without either giving up or collapsing completely. Even the little breaks during the five-hour *zazen* session were torture. We have to walk around the *zendō* during the breaks, and with my bad foot I was only able to hobble painfully. I shan't go to the early morning service at four tomorrow – if I do I won't have a chance of being able to make it through the day. Tomorrow there are three sessions, one from 8.00 to 10.30, one from 1.00 to 3.30 and one from 5.00 to 9.30.

Diary, October 16th 1967

I bandaged my foot tightly this morning and took some very strong painkillers before each *zazen* session, but it is still torture. Between the second session and the third I hobbled down to Sakamoto san's office and asked him to ask the Rōshi if it would be all right for me to use my own sandals in the *zendō*. My foot is so swollen that it's simply impossible to get it into any of the temple sandals. He nodded understandingly and went to see the Rōshi. A little later he came back and told me that the Rōshi had assented.

'Please tell the First Monk,' I said, knowing that there would be trouble if he didn't. Sakamoto san laughed.

'It has already been done,' he replied. 'He knows that it is all right.'

Relieved, I wore my own sandals to the evening *zazen* session. The floor of the *zendō* is made of stone, and, as I have already mentioned, one is not allowed to touch it with one's bare feet. As I was arranging my cushion on the bench some of the monks pointed at my sandals, assuming that I had forgotten to change them, but when I pointed to my bandaged foot and explained that the Rōshi had given me his permission to use my own sandals they laughed and nodded, as if to say, 'That's all right then.'

After an hour and a quarter the Rōshi's little bell rang, indicating that it was time to go in for *sanzen*. All the monks leapt up and rushed out through the door of the *zendō* and into the open as though they were being chased by the Devil himself. I hobbled after them as quickly as I could, following them along the long stone path to the narrow wooden gallery outside the *sanzen* room, where we all sat down and waited until it was our turn to go in.

The entire length of the stone path leading to the terrace was dotted with straw sandals which the monks had lost in their race to get to the front of the line. The rest of the sandals lay at the foot of the steps, for just as it was not permitted to touch the stone floor of the *zendō* with one's bare feet it was also not permitted to touch the wooden floor with one's sandals. I was the last in line, of course, and I had to wait for about forty minutes before I could go in to the Rōshi for *sanzen*.

When I knelt down before him the Rōshi asked me to describe my

Buddha Nature. My answer was similar to the letter which I had written him. He breathed deeply.

'Yes,' he replied with a loving smile, and rang his bell.

This *sanzen* was a momentous, profound inner experience. Everything was filled with an aura of the divine. It radiated from the Rōshi, it was in me and the room in which we sat. This *sanzen* marked the final end of 'Mu'.

I was also the last to return to the *zendō*, of course, since I had been the last in the *sanzen* room. All the other monks were already sitting in their places. This was perfectly normal, as it is the rule that one has to return to the *zendō* and sit down as soon as one's *sanzen* with the Rōshi is finished. The moment I stepped across the threshold, however, I was stopped in my tracks by a terrible, blood-curdling cry. It came from the Jikihitsu's place. ('Jikihitsu' means 'Sun in the Hall', and is the title of the monk who oversees the meditation sessions.) One would never think it possible that a Japanese is capable of roaring like a giant, but this Jikihitsu is big and fat, and in addition to this he has always been one of the bitterest opponents of my presence here in the temple, and that gave him plenty of energy. The shock of that moment couldn't have been greater if a bolt of lightning had struck me. Almost fainting with fright I looked up to see what was the matter. He pointed at my sandals, still shouting like a madman. I took a step backwards, assuming that he wasn't going to let me enter the *zendō*.

'Return to your place!' he shouted, in a tone of absolute command. I hobbled to my place at the back of the hall, running the gauntlet between the two rows of monks.

After the *zazen* session was over I went to see the First Monk of the winter semester. This semester the post has been given to a monk who is an old aquaintance of mine. (He hadn't been present during the scene with the Jikihitsu, of course. The First Monk of the semester never takes part in *zazen*, as he is required to devote himself exclusively to the duties of his office.) I was still trembling from the shock. In my halting Japanese I explained what had happened.

'Don't worry,' he said, laughing. 'You go on wearing your sandals. I will go to the Jikihitsu again and tell him that it is allowed.'

Now it is long past midnight and I suddenly feel very tired. Even so, I want to write a little more before I go to bed.

Once again, it seems, one of the monks is simply ignoring the Rōshi's wishes. I wonder what is going to happen tomorrow?

Before I sat down to write in my diary I bathed my poor foot in hot water to help relieve the pain and swelling after the day's exertions. As I sat there with my foot in the bowl of water I started thinking back over what had happened. I suddenly burst out into peals of merry laughter: even though the shock which the 'Sun in the Hall' gave me really was shattering, he also unwittingly gave me a profound experience of true Zen.

After my exalted, deeply moving experience with the Rōshi I had come out of the *sanzen* room in a very elevated state of consciousness. I should perhaps mention that all the monks who come out of the *sanzen* room always walk back to the *zendō* very slowly, with their eyes lowered and their hands folded in front of them. Even if nothing of note happens, *sanzen* with an enlightened Zen Master is always an overwhelming experience.

From my state of blissful absorption in the Beyond the Jikihitsu's shrieks of rage then catapulted me back to reality with a speed and suddenness which took my breath away. Even now, my body starts to tremble as soon as I think of that moment of shock. But in that moment I was granted a thrilling, direct vision of the way in which the pure Spirit and that which we call 'reality' are eternally interwoven within one another. I am sure that that was not his intention, but that is what happened, and it was the suddenness and intensity of his outburst which made it possible.

Diary, October 17 1967

The pain during *zazen* was no better today, but nonetheless I managed to make it through all three sessions without collapsing. When I hobbled out of the Rōshi's room after evening *sanzen* – I was last, as usual – I found that my sandals had disappeared from the stone steps where I had left them. I looked for them everywhere, feeling more and more desperate all the time, but it was no good. They were nowhere to be found. It wasn't difficult to guess who was responsible for their disappearance.

I couldn't walk back to the *zendō* barefoot, and so I went to see the First Monk in his office, which is next door to the *hōndō*. He was unwilling to believe me at first, and he came to the steps outside the *sanzen* room with me to look for himself. I showed him where I had left the sandals, and he looked for them everywhere, just as I had, but he couldn't find them either.

'I am sorry to trouble you,' I said, 'but since I am unable to walk on the stones without any shoes I am afraid I must ask you to bring me my street shoes and my torch. They are under the bench outside the *zendō*. Otherwise I shan't be able to return home tonight.' He agreed immediately, and when he had brought me my shoes I went to see the Rōshi's secretary.

I was furiously angry, and I didn't try to hide the fact. First the scene in the meditation hall yesterday, then this infamous trick today. I had had more than enough. Sakamoto san was very upset.

'There are only one or two monks, at the very most, who still insist on maintaining the strictly orthodox point of view,' he said. 'They are simply not willing to accept that a woman can be a full member of the temple community and their equal, even if she is a guest of the Rōshi's. But all of the others like you and respect you. You know that.'

'I know,' I replied, 'but this is not only malicious and spiteful, it is also stupid and childish, and it has nothing whatsoever to do with the spirit of Zen.'

'Please be patient. The First Monk will deal with the matter.'

'I have had to be patient ever since I arrived here. My dear Sakamoto san,' I said, taking a deep breath, 'please understand me. This is really the last straw. I shall now start making my preparations for my return to Germany.'

Diary, October 18 1967

My sandals have turned up again. One of the monks brought them back early this morning. Someone had thrown them into the garden where it was impossible to see them at night. Even so, I didn't go to the first *zazen* session today. First I wanted to make sure that I would be able to sit in the *zendō* without being troubled.

I saw Sakamoto san later, and he told me that there had been a terrible row. He said that the Rōshi had called the Jikihitsu to his room, and that it had turned out that he hadn't known that I had been given permission to wear my own sandals. It seems that the First Monk had simply forgotten to tell him about it.

Sakamoto san also told me that the Rōshi had said that my practice of *zazen* is 'strict and exemplary', and that it was his personal wish that I should not be disturbed or molested in any way. He also ordered that I should not be struck with the Zen stick any more. Now I can meditate in the *zendō* without feeling afraid.

The next *zazen* session was wonderful. I was unable to walk around the *zendō* during the break; I had to sit on the narrow bench outside, with my left leg stretched out beside me, and quite a few of the monks came and showed me their sympathy in sign language. (No speaking is permitted during *zazen*, of course.) Katsu san was particularly loving. It made me very happy.

The Rōshi only gave one *sanzen* session today, at four in the morning, as he had to leave for Kyoto directly afterwards.

Diary, October 20 1967

I haven't been able to use my icewater bandages since the beginning of the new semester – I can hardly carry a bowl of icewater into the *zendō* with me – and as a result of this my heat rash has got much worse again. It's driving me mad. And as if that wasn't bad enough the pain in my ankle and leg is getting worse and worse all the time. I shall have to go and see the doctor when the Great *Zazen* is over. Perhaps he can at least give me something for the pain, which is making sitting in *zazen* terribly difficult.

Diary, October 21 1967

The Rōshi gave *sanzen* again yesterday.

With my bad foot the opening ritual was rather difficult for me, and it took a long time before I was finished. When I finally kneeled down before him there was a long silence. I always feel that this moment of silence at the beginning of *sanzen* is very special: it is a silence pregnant with meditative ecstasy.

Finally the Rōshi breathed the Great Breath, voicing it with a sound that penetrated his entire being. Then there was silence again.

Then, suddenly and without any warning, his question crashed out at me like a bolt of lightning:

'How do you live your Buddha Nature?'

As usual I was speechless for several seconds, as if I had been given an electric shock. But then my answer came of its own accord, unaccompanied by the slightest thought on my part, and with such vehemence that I myself was startled.

'I do that which needs to be done!'

The Rōshi smiled, breathed deeply, and rang his little bell.

I wasn't particularly worried about what he might ask me when I went in for *sanzen* today. I knew what I can expect from now on: test questions, probing the depth and breadth of my satori. And I was right. After the period of silence and the Rōshi's Great Breath he looked me straight in the eyes, with an enigmatic and yet mischievous smile on his face, and asked:

'What needs to be done?'

I almost broke out laughing at my own cheeky answer:

'At the moment, *sanzen*!'

After a split second of astonishment the Rōshi burst out into peals of laughter. 'Yes,' he said, and rang his bell.

To receive a 'yes' from one's Rōshi in *sanzen* is a rare occurrence, a small sensation for both Master and disciple. Such confirmation of the success of one's spiritual efforts is always a source of great joy.

That the Rōshi should laugh, however, is rarer still. The last time I experienced his laughter during *sanzen* was four years ago, when the kōan of 'The Sound of One Hand Clapping' finally exploded into a Great Satori, after months of gruelling meditation.

Today too I was overflowing with bliss and joy when I returned to the *zendō*. It had been the last *sanzen* of the seven days of the Great *Zazen*, crowning it with glory, so to speak. After the end of the last 'sitting' at ten p.m. two monks rushed into the *zendō* and distributed bowls of tea and little cakes. We drank the tea and ate the cakes quickly and then we filed out of the *zendō* with our cushions under our arms, completely exhausted.

Tomorrow is Sunday, but sleeping in is out of the question, as the Rōshi's lecture begins at seven a.m. In addition to the monks the Rōshi's lay disciples and a number of other visitors are going to be present, and I am expected to attend, even though I shan't be able to understand a single word of what he says.

Diary, October 22 1967

It is still warm during the daytime, but it is icy cold at night and in the evenings and early mornings. On the radio they said that the weather is unprecedented for this time of year, and that the temperature doesn't usually go down this far until December.

I shivered with cold during the Rōshi's lecture in the *hōndō* this morning. The monks are now wearing their winter robes. They are exactly the same as the summer robes, except that they are made of much thicker cloth.

Afterwards I visited the Rōshi in his private quarters, as I wanted to thank him personally for all the loving messages he had sent me. Nan san went in and announced my arrival, and I was admitted immediately. Not into the Rōshi's delightful little study, as I had expected, but into the large reception room next door. (This is the room which I lived in for several months last time I was here. It was a great honour to be able to live so close to him for so long.)

I wasn't the only visitor, of course. Three of the Rōshi's most devoted lay disciples were also there, sitting at a respectful distance from their Master's seat. They are men who have never hesitated to offer the Rōshi their help whenever he has needed it, even though they are not at all wealthy.

The Rōshi was sitting on his heels in *suwari*, with a brush in his hand. In front of him was a white rectangle of artist's pasteboard, which he was decorating with complicated Chinese characters. Other pieces of pasteboard, some white and some golden, were spread out in rows on the floor to dry. His calligraphy was exquisite.

I bowed down to the ground, and after greeting me warmly in return the Rōshi had his attendant bring me tea and cakes. Then he returned to his work, saying that he had more than 1,500 orders from temples and lay disciples all over Japan.

'I saw Professor Imachi recently,' I said. 'He said that he too would dearly love to have one of these pictures, a large one if possible, for his private office in the hospital, and he asked me to convey his wish to you.' (Professor Imachi is the director of the university hospital.)

'He will have to wait for at least nine months,' replied the Rōshi.

'I shall tell him. He also asked me if it would be all right for him to remind you of it again in a few months' time.' The Rōshi nodded in assent, smiling.

It was the first time I have ever actually seen him at work on these famous calligraphic pictures of his. It was fascinating. The four of us sat there in total silence, not moving a muscle; I in the lotus position, of course, and the others in *suwari*. The Rōshi never hurried and never paused, producing one perfect picture after another and laying it aside to dry. It was unbelievable. I have never seen anything like it, before or since.

The brush which the Rōshi held in his hand was a good inch and a half broad. The material for preparing the drawing ink lay to one side. He would begin by gazing at the white or gold pasteboard before him in silence for a few moments. Then, in a single flowing movement, he would dip the brush in the ink and produce the finished character, beginning with the full width of the brush and reducing the pressure progressively as he came to the more complex details. The result was always perfect, always 'just so'.

He would then draw the fine characters on the left hand side of the picture, using the same broad brush. These characters usually comprise the Rōshi's explanation of the meaning of the main character, or a question designed to stimulate meditation on the character. Finally, he would apply the red stamps, in the bottom left and top right corners.

He produced a total of five of these pictures while I was there, each of them perfect, each of them a matchless totality in itself. Some of them were characters which I recognised, for he has already given me several of these pictures as presents. The unerring certainty with which his brush moved across the surface of the pasteboard was magical. I wouldn't have believed it if I hadn't seen it with my own eyes. I have seen the calligraphic work of many of the famous Masters of the past, but none of it matches the power and delicacy of Rōshi Mumon's characters. And I do not say that simply because I love the Rōshi, it is really so.

While he was taking a short break to prepare fresh ink I took the liberty of pointing to a character which I found particularly startling and unusual, and asked him what its meaning was. He laughed.

'Mu!' he said, handing me the rectangle of pasteboard. I was flabbergasted.

I was already well aware of the fact that the various Masters all draw the characters differently, in accordance with the nature of their individual beings. 'Mu', in particular, has been rendered in a very wide variety of different ways. (I already have one particularly beautiful example, given to me by Master Osaka in Tokyo.) But the 'Mu' which I now held in my hands, and which the Rōshi gave me to keep, is truly unprecedented; I have never seen anything like it. It is a broad, hard line of annihilation, cutting through everything. The Rōshi dipped the brush in the fresh ink, and glanced at me briefly. Then he turned his gaze to the empty rectangle before him and breathed deeply for a few moments before beginning to draw. I and the lay disciples all leaned forwards as he did so, as if pulled by an invisible, magnetic force. I found it difficult to contain my excitement at what I saw.

In a single magnificent swoop, moving as though it had a life of its own, the brush described a perfect circle on the piece of pasteboard. It was a good inch and a half broad and filled the rectangle almost completely.

The Rōshi regarded his work in silence for a moment, then he drew a few small characters on the left hand side of the pasteboard, applied the red stamps and held it up so that I could see it.

'What is that?' he asked.

I answered without the slightest hesitation, my heart overflowing with joy.

'Yes,' he said, satisfied. Then he picked up the brush again and wrote a couple of words along the lower edge of the picture.

'That is yours,' he said softly, handing me the masterpiece. His words were simple, but his true message lay in the tone of his voice, his movements, and the gentle expression in his eyes. I gazed at the picture, my heart full of joy.

'And I believe you know that it is yours,' he said as I looked up into his eyes again.

The Rōshi then stood up, took his leave of us, and walked into his private room next door.

The three lay disciples, who had stood up at the same time as I had to bow to the Rōshi as he left, were all awestruck. One of them examined the words which the Rōshi had written along the bottom of the picture and translated them for the others.

'Do you know what this means?' he asked me. They hadn't understood our conversation, as both the Rōshi and I had spoken in English. I hid my treasure in my kimono.

'Excuse me please,' I replied softly, 'but I don't want to say anything just now.'

The words which Rōshi Mumon had written beneath the eternal circle were as follows:

To Miss Ital, from Mumon

In reality only the Rōshi and I know the true meaning of what transpired between us. The two characters he drew for me are the symbolic expression of a lifetime of spiritual struggle and searching, devoted to the attainment of the Ultimate: First he gave me 'Mu' ('nothing'), then he drew the character for the One, the Original Source, his infallible heart guiding his hand.

To know that these two are really eternally one is the greatest experience of all, an experience which is only granted to those who have themselves become nothingness, and who have awakened to their own Truth.

Diary, October 23 1967

There is no *zazen* today or tomorrow. I went to Osaka this afternoon, where I arranged the details of my flight back to Germany with the manager of the Lufthansa office there. All I had to do was confirm the route I want to take, as I bought the ticket and paid for it before I left Berlin.

I am going to fly back via America, as I had originally planned. Before I left for Japan some dear friends of mine in Honolulu invited me to come and visit them for a while on my way home, and I had put off my final decision about the route until I heard from them, as I wasn't sure whether the invitation still stood. A few days ago, however, I received a letter from them in response to my query, saying that they would be delighted to have me. They also wrote that they are going to be away in Australia for several weeks starting in mid-December, and that they are expecting me in the second half of November. That put a pleasant end to all my indecision about the date of my departure.

So, Honolulu it is! My next stop after Honolulu is San Francisco, where Lufthansa is going to reserve a hotel room for me, and after three days in San Francisco I am going to fly on to Mexico City, where I plan to visit the remains of the famous Aztec buildings which have been dug up in Teotihuacan, and the Olmec and Toltec sites as well, if I have time. I shall have a total of ten days in Mexico City, after which I shall fly south to Merida, the capital of Yucatan, for it is there that the most magnificent Maya sites are to be found, in Chichen-Itza and Uxmal.

I knew that this itinerary was going to be extremely strenuous when I planned it in Berlin; that is why I took care to leave my ticket open. I wanted to be absolutely sure that I would be able to stop in Honolulu and rest before confirming the other bookings, as I knew that I wouldn't have the strength to go through with it otherwise.

All afternoon in Osaka I kept a careful eye on my inner world, watching to see if there would be any reactions to these preparations, and on my way back to Kobe in the express train I once again subjected my consciousness to a thorough examination. Nothing had changed: I could not find any sadness, or any feeling of pain at my impending departure from the temple and from Japan. When I compare the way I feel now with the almost desperate state I was in when I was getting ready to leave four years ago, I can hardly believe that such a transformation is really possible. This outward test of my attainment has proved it once again, beyond any shadow of a doubt: I am really, truly free, both inwardly and outwardly.

'Your task here is now finished!' These divine words are being confirmed again and again, in the simplest, most everyday things.

Diary, October 24 1967

This morning I was called in to see the First Monk. A senior Buddhist abbot from China had come to visit our temple. The monks had told him about me, of course, and he had expressed the wish to meet me. He was a tall, strongly-built man, radiant with good health and warm-heartedness. His own monastery was in Hong Kong, and his visiting card revealed that he held a great many very senior titles.

The abbot invited me to accompany him on a visit to a Chinese temple in a part of the city I had never been in before. It was breathtakingly beautiful, and my feeling of wonder at the sights I saw there was mixed with astonishment at the fact that I haven't heard so much as a single mention of the temple's existence in all the time I have spent here in Kobe.

On either side of the gateway to the temple complex stood the traditional Chinese guardian figures. The buildings themselves were decorated with wonderfully colourful enamel work. The predominant colours were green, yellow and red. It is a great pity that the abbot only spoke very broken English, even though he lives in Hong Kong (his Japanese was no better), as it made it impossible for him to explain the meaning of all the wonderful works of art to me. Even so, my intimate aquaintance with Erwin Rousselle's wonderful book on Chinese art[2] stood me in good stead.

The difference between this temple and Japanese Buddhist temples (and Japanese Zen Buddhist temples in particular) is very striking. The visitor here is presented first with a cornucopia of exquisitely beautiful colours, works of art and symbols, designed to express the endless, divine variety of manifest existence. When one enters inside and walks towards the middle of the building one passes by the countless images of all the Buddhas and Bodhisattvas of the past. Then, at the very centre of the temple, one comes to the Holy of Holies: a completely empty room. According to the Buddhists, this design symbolises millions of years of being. I almost wrote 'millions of years of development' – but then, what do we know about development? The few thousand years which make up our written history are, in reality, a pitifully small span of time, and they cannot tell us anything about the many high civilisations which have gone before and which have now disappeared without a trace, covered by the sands of time. In our ludicrous arrogance we assume that no culture has ever been so advanced as ours, but perhaps, some day, a great earthquake or some other natural disaster will reveal things which will force us to change our minds.

In the course of our visit I was also introduced to the abbot of the temple. He invited us in to his private study, where he played us some wonderful gramophone recordings of old Chinese Buddhist texts, recited by monks in a kind of chanting sing song. Even though I have never heard anything like them before, I couldn't get rid of the feeling that they were somehow familiar.

I still can't get over the fact that I have never heard of this temple before, even though the abbot of the temple and Rōshi Mumon apparently know one another quite well. It's not mentioned in any of the tourist guides.

The abbot from Hong Kong was terribly kind, and he gave me several presents: a delightful little bronze Buddha, a yellow monk's robe and a small badge. He asked me to wear the badge on my lapel, as a sign of membership in his order. This is a very great honour, of course, but unfortunately the symbol on the badge is a swastika, so I can't possibly wear it at home in Germany! (The swastika is actually a very ancient and very sacred eastern symbol, and I am sure that the good abbot has no idea of the connotations which it now has in the West.)

My friend Miss O. then arrived, as expected. This was a great relief, as it meant that she could talk to one of the two Chinese abbots; dealing with both of them at once had been getting to be a bit much for me.

We drove to a very exclusive Chinese club for lunch. A private room had been reserved for us in advance. The food was magnificent, infinitely better than anything I have ever eaten in Chinese restaurants in Europe, or in Japan for that matter. The Chinese really know how to live. But then, their culture is very much older than ours, and in any case it is not often that one is the private guest of two very senior Chinese Buddhist dignitaries. The meal lasted for several hours, and even though I ate a great deal I had no feeling of satiety. It must have cost a fortune.

To my great surprise the abbot of the Chinese temple knew that this was my second stay in the Zen monastery here in Kobe, and he even knew that I had practised *zazen* under the tutelage of a Master in Tokyo last time I was in Japan. I didn't manage to find out who had told him all these things – the Chinese always seem to know everything.

After we had finally finished eating, the two abbots then brought me back to the monastery. It was a wonderful, deeply fulfilling day, our second 'day off'. I have been writing for several hours now – I wanted to put it all down on paper before I forget anything.

Diary, October 27 1967

Another typhoon!

I attended the Rōshi's lecture at seven this morning. It was bitterly cold. At midday I went to the hospital to have my foot examined, as the pain is getting to be really unbearable. It is hardly surprising really, considering all the strain I am putting on it. The doctor who examined me said that I should rest the foot completely for a few weeks, moving it as little as possible. That was all: I could have told him that myself. The doctor also said that it would be madness to go on putting such a strain on my foot and leg. I continued with my 'madness' this afternoon, going to five o'clock *zazen* in the *zendō*. By then the typhoon was raging with full force, hurricane-like winds combining with an endless deluge of water falling from the sky. It got worse and worse. The doors of the *zendō* were open as usual, allowing the icy cold wind to howl through the hall unhindered. It wasn't easy, but I managed to stick it out, despite the cold and the pain. I thought of Bodhidharma, who had meditated sitting in the snow. Later on it occurred to me to wonder whether he had been able to produce his own warmth, simply by concentrating, like the Tibetans described by the late Alexandra David Neel in her fascinating travelogue. She says that they could sit naked in the snow and ice, without feeling the cold or suffering any adverse effects.

Zazen in the *zendō* started again yesterday. *Sanzen* with the Rōshi today was a joy. Every day now he presents me with a fresh problem, which has to be solved immediately while I am still in *sanzen*. All the questions he puts now have to do with the effects of my work with 'Mu'.

Diary, October 28 1967

The manager of the Lufthansa office in Osaka called me on the phone today. He is a charming man. He told me that he had received a telex from Lufthansa in Mexico City confirming that a good and inexpensive private room had been reserved for me there. It is a great relief to hear that, and I am very grateful for all the wonderful help of the Lufthansa staff. The omens are good – it looks as though I have chosen the right time for my trip.

Zazen without *sanzen* today. Storms and rain. I was wet through when I arrived at the *zendō*.

Diary, November 1 1967

On the days when we only have one *zazen* session (in the evening) I often drop by on Sakamoto san in his office beforehand. Today he told me that he has succeeded in organising an audience for me with the Rōshi of the Nansen-ji temple in Kyoto on the fourth of November, the day before the next *sesshin* (Great *Zazen*) is due to begin in all Japanese Zen temples. Sakamoto san grew up in the Nansen-ji temple – his father has a position there, and his mother conducts the tea ceremonies – and so arranging the audience was easy for him. When Sakamoto san was a child thc Rōshi was a simple monk, and for him his secretary is still the little 'son of the temple' who can always come and see him whenever he wishes.

To my great surprise Sakamoto san then pulled out a large parcel and handed it to me. (He knows all about my impending departure, of course.) It contained a large, round cake box finished in black lacquer. The lid is decorated with beautiful flowers, made up of myriads of tiny, brightly-coloured stones. His calling card lay on top of the box, and on the back of the card he had written the following words:

To G. Ital Lady Rōshi
This is the memorial
'Japan' of our friendliness.

I. Sakamoto

Now my heart really does feel touched . . . I shall have to pull myself together.

Diary, November 4 1967. Late.

My visit to the Rōshi of Nansen-ji temple was deeply moving. It was a wonderful, warm autumn day. The world was bathed in soft golden sunlight, and looked as clear and transparent and luminous as the experience which I was to have in the temple.

The journey from Kobe to Kyoto on the express train took an hour. In Kyoto I boarded a tram, showing the conductress the slip of paper on which Sakamoto san had written the name of the stop I had to get off at in Japanese. The tram drove through the hustle and bustle of the Kyoto suburbs, and several times I leapt up as the walls of one walled temple park after another hove into view, thinking that I had arrived, but the conductress waved me back, indicating that we still had a long way to go. Many stops later she finally pointed to the door of the tram, indicating that I had arrived at my destination.

Sakamoto san had also drawn me a little map, showing me where to go when I got off the tram. Even so, I had to ask directions several times, the last time in a garden restaurant which turned out to be almost directly opposite the temple. It is typical of modern Japan that the waiters didn't know that one of the most famous temples in the country was just a few yards away from their place of work.

Rōshi Shibayama's beautiful little house, surrounded by a garden full of flowers, was located a little distance away from the temple grounds, not within them. I rang the bell, and the Rōshi's attendant monk opened the door and ushered me inside. He had been expecting me, and he asked me to wait while he went to get Miss K., the Rōshi's secretary.

Miss K., a very pretty young lady, is both the Rōshi's disciple and his interpreter. He only speaks Japanese, and she accompanies him everywhere, even on his journeys abroad. She was very friendly, but she said that it was a little early yet, and asked me if I had visited the temple. When I replied that I hadn't she asked me to do so, and to come back in three-quarters of an hour.

The entrance to the temple grounds was only about a hundred paces away from the Rōshi's residence. I bought a ticket at the gate and walked inside, into an endless expanse of gorgeous parks which served as a setting for temple buildings of breathtaking beauty. Needless to say, the grounds were full of visitors and tourists. On the nearby terraces sat several groups of schoolchildren engaged in drawing and painting, their transistor radios blaring.

The first building on this site was the palace of Emperor Kamayama, which he built in 1264. The emperor later became a student of Zen, and he gave the palace to his Master, Kokushi, to use as a Zen temple. This temple was destroyed by fire three times, and rebuilt again each time as a perfect copy of the original. The main building on the temple grounds now has the status of a national monument. It was built when Kyoto was still the capital of Japan, and it became a part of Nansen-ji in 1611.

The main temple is now open to visitors, although one must follow a prescribed route through the building, of course. The rooms of the temple are all utterly empty of any objects or furniture, the sliding screens in front of the doors and windows decorated with the priceless work of great master painters of the past. The Buddha on the altar of the main hall of the temple is Kwannon (known as Kuan Yin in China), Buddha's female aspect.

I found Kano Tanyu's famous painting, *Tiger Drinking Water*, on one of these sliding screens in a building behind the main hall. The attendant in this building told me that the grounds contained a total of twelve more temples. This gives one some idea of just how large the grounds are, for none of the other temples is visible from the main building, and one really has to walk a long way to find them at all.

The monastery buildings in which the Zen monks live are located quite a way away from the main temple complex, and they are not open to visitors. I didn't see a single monk anywhere the whole time I was there; it seems that they live in total seclusion, not coming into contact with the outside world at all. (Nansen-ji was only opened to visitors after the Second World War, and then too under duress.)

The entire temple complex radiates an atmosphere of grandeur and splendid magnificence. Nonetheless, even after seeing Nansen-ji I still feel that the beauty of Kinkaku-ji (the Golden Temple) is unrivalled anywhere. The latter is not grandiose – its magic lies in its simplicity. No sensitive visitor can help being struck dumb, ecstatically so, by the sight of the divine harmony of Kinkaku-ji and its reflection in the still waters of the perfectly dimensioned artificial lake in front of it.

Like Shofuku-ji in Kobe Nansen-ji belongs to the famous and very strict Rinzai sect. It is the chief temple of the Rinzai sect in Japan, and its abbot is always that Rinzai Zen Master who is recognised by all others to be the most advanced and perfect among them. All other Rinzai temples are thus, in a certain sense, subject to his authority, although one should not make the mistake of thinking that this authority has anything to do with 'power' in the temporal sense. The abbot and Master of Nansen-ji is *primus inter pares*, but *primus*, nonetheless.

Sakamoto san informed me that the next most 'senior' temple in the hierarchy of the Rinzai sect is Shofuku-ji in Kobe, our own temple. This didn't surprise me in the least, considering the great esteem in which it is held everywhere.

I mention this in order to make it clear what a singular and rare honour it was to be granted an audience with Rōshi Shibayama, the abbot and Master of Nansen-ji. Sakamoto san had told me that the Rōshi had agreed to see me for thirty minutes, but as it turned out I stayed for more than two hours.

I arrived punctually at the appointed time, and the attendant monk now ushered me directly into the antechamber, where I removed my shoes. Then Miss K. came in and showed me to the visitors' room. It was completely empty, of course, apart from a long table in the middle of the room and four chairs. The entire house was decorated in the Japanese style. It was beautifully appointed and cared-for, and it radiated an atmosphere of silence and refined elegance.

A few moments later the Rōshi entered the room. I sprang up from my seat and made the ritual prostrations due to his station, which he received with an astonished exclamation. I then thanked him for being kind enough to grant me an audience. Meanwhile, the attendant monk served tea and cakes.

Rōshi Shibayama is a slim man, with an ageless face. He looks very fit. He was an attentive listener, and Miss K. was a superb and very experienced interpreter.

At the beginning of our talk the Rōshi mentioned that he had resigned his position as abbot of the temple a little while before, and that his successor had now 'taken over'. Miss K. then explained that the Rōshi's successor is still relatively young – he is in his early forties – but that he is very capable and a superb teacher for the monks in his care. Nonetheless, Rōshi Shibayama still keeps an eye on him and his work, and their Master-disciple relationship continues uninterrupted. The Rōshi, who recently celebrated his 70th birthday, is now able to devote his time to other important tasks.

'Training a worthy successor is the greatest problem faced by Zen abbots nowadays,' sighed Miss K. with feeling. 'For some it has become almost insoluble.'

'As you probably know,' I replied, 'this is also a particularly serious problem in my own Rōshi's case. Under the present unfortunate circumstances it looks as though it is not likely to be solved at all, not in the near future, at any rate.'

It turned out that Rōshi Shibayama was very well informed about the new laxity of discipline in Shofuku-ji – lax, that is, in the unbelievably strict terms of a traditional Zen monastery. I mentioned the American I had met in the café after the typhoon, explaining that it had been he who had talked the experienced monk X. san into running away to America, and who had poisoned the mind of Rōshi Mumon's most gifted monk, K. san, who had later taken his own life. Then I asked him if seekers from the West were ever admitted to Nansen-ji. His reply was emphatic:

'That is out of the question! We make no exceptions here. The discipline in Nansen-ji is the strictest in all Japan. The spiritual and physical training of our monks begins at four in the morning and ends late at night. They must be completely alert and mindful all the time. In any case, there is no room here in the monastery. It is true that monks do sometimes leave – but there are many others waiting for admission in Zen monasteries all over Japan. Dealing with these applications alone will take many years, many decades.'

I thought of a very gifted pupil of mine back in Germany, a true disciple of Zen.

'But suppose the aspirant were very sincere and devoted; would it not be possible for him to live outside the monastery and to take part in *zazen*, if he were to prove his worthiness?' The Rōshi's answer to this question was even more severe:

'It is not possible to take part in *zazen* here without being a full member of the monastic community. All of the monks' work, from dawn to dusk, is a part of their training, both their physical work and their spiritual work. In addition to this only Japanese is spoken in Nansen-ji. We demand from our monks the same total and absolute commitment which used to be a matter of course in all of the Zen monasteries of the past. Believe me, it is not only Westerners for whom our discipline is too hard; it is also too much for many Japanese monks. Many have to leave.'

I bowed down in respect and admiration.

'I am afraid that I cannot say that the monks in Shofuku-ji have this commitment,' I said, expressing the sorrow which I have been carrying in my heart for months now, 'and this is something which I find inexplicable, all the more so since Rōshi Mumon is a very great enlightened Master.' In his reply to this comment of mine Rōshi Shibayama repeated something which I had already heard from Dr H., the Rōshi of the Tendai sect on Mount Hiei:

'Rōshi Mumon is above all a teacher,' he said.

It is certainly true that he is a good teacher – in his position as President of the Zen University in Kyoto he has become very famous and widely respected. Perhaps, I thought to myself, being a teacher really is more in accordance with his gentle nature than being in charge of a monastery. The Master of a Zen monastery must be very strict and hard. I thought about this for a moment. Considering everything which I had seen in his temple during my two long visits it seemed very likely that this was the case. I decided to go into the subject of discipline at Shofuku-ji in more detail.

'Please forgive me if you feel that I am trying to be more Catholic than the Pope, as we say where I come from,' I began, 'but there are some things in our temple which do not seem right to me. Even four years ago there were some goings-on which I found very upsetting, and now it has become much worse.'

Without mentioning any details I expressed my astonishment and incomprehension at the way in which all the breaches of discipline in the monastery are kept secret from Rōshi Mumon. 'We are well aware of everything which has been going on in Shofuku-ji,' said Miss K., translating Rōshi Shibayama's answer. 'Perhaps things would be different if your Rōshi were not weighed down by the duties of so many different offices. It is unfortunate that he must be away from the temple so often; too often in our opinion. Even so, we receive complaints of this kind from almost all Zen monasteries, even those whose abbots are always in residence, and the situation is likely to deteriorate still further in the future.

'Here in Nansen-ji we are absolutely uncompromising. But if all monasteries were as strict as we are then they would probably be empty. This rebellion, the reasons for which are unclear, is spreading like an epidemic.'

'I have another question I should like to ask,' I said, 'if it is permitted.' Rōshi Shibayama nodded. 'A while ago Rōshi Mumon built a small temple in the memory of Mrs M., in order to provide a place to stay for the Zen nuns who sometimes pass through or take part in meditations in the temple. I have been living there myself since my return from Germany. The nun E. san has been appointed to be the housekeeper of this temple, and since then she has been able to do as she pleases. She lives her own private life, and does not appear to be subject to anyone's authority.'

Both Miss K. and Rōshi Shibayama smiled ironically at the mention of E. san's name. Sakamoto san had already told me that the Rōshi of Nansen-ji was well aware of E. san's activities.

'One day some workers came and installed an antenna on the roof of the temple, and then a huge television set was delivered and placed in E. san's room, which opens onto the garden. Ever since then E. san and her sister and everyone else who comes to stay in Myokan-ji have been spending their evenings in front of this machine. Their laughter echoes through the entire temple. I can even hear them in my secluded little room upstairs. I started to wonder whether I was really living in a Zen temple, and I asked Rōshi Mumon's secretary if such things were allowed, and, if so, since when they had been allowed. He told me that he hadn't known anything about it. It seems that no one had known anything about it. E. san herself simply said that the television set had been a present. Even so, nothing was done about it. The television set is still there, and it is still on every night. I feel very shocked at this, but perhaps I am being too strict?'

'No,' replied Rōshi Shibayama, 'you are not too strict. Not at all. You are right to miss the discipline which used to be the rule in Zen monasteries, before the Second World War. In Nansen-ji we still insist on that same strict standard of discipline, and as I have already said, those who find it too hard must leave our temple. The time may come when Zen Masters will be forced to become even stricter in their selection of their disciples. That is one possible solution to this problem: for the Masters to work only with a very small group of totally committed monks, monks who are not willing to allow anything to distract them from their goal.

'As things are now the Masters in charge of monastic communities must be men of iron, with great energy. They must be men whose word is respected and feared. Rōshi Mumon is not such a man. He is too loving. His heart is too soft. Nowadays, unfortunately, anyone with a loving heart is bound to be exploited ruthlessly.'

Rōshi Shibayama then went on to tell me an anecdote about his own training in Nansen-ji, under the tutelage of his Master, Bukai. It took my breath away.

As I got up to leave he handed me a present: two little books of his on Zen, which had been printed privately. He wrote his name and a dedication in the flyleaf of each book before giving it to me. I found it difficult to tear myself away from this great man. He is one of the last great pillars of Zen.

Miss K. then ushered me out, showing me the monastery vegetable garden on the way. The monks were all hard at work in the burning sun. She pointed to one of the monks.

'That is the new abbot,' she said, 'as you see, there are no exceptions.' I stared at him in amazement. He was working just as hard as all the others, and outwardly he seemed no different from them.

The anecdote which Rōshi Shibayama told me is a perfect example of the degree of commitment to the One which is demanded of the true disciple of Zen. It is a commitment which must be lived totally, every moment of the disciple's life, without stopping. I shall try to write the story down exactly as he told it:

'Rōshi Bukai owned a private house near to the temple. He had rented it out for a while in order to obtain money which the temple needed. The house was in the temple grounds, of course, and it looked like a miniature temple itself. When the house became empty again my Master, Rōshi Bukai, told me to go and clean it from top to bottom.

'The sight which met my eyes when I entered the house was a great shock. The people who had been living there had left it in a terrible state. Somehow, I managed to tidy up and get everything clean. But then I came to the toilet. It was awful, unbelievable.'

(I should mention that Japanese toilets are usually no more than a kind of hole in the floor, and that flushing systems have only been introduced very recently.)

'There was not a single square inch of the room which was not filthy, and to make matters worse it was a blisteringly hot August day. The smell would have been bad enough even in winter, but in that heat it was overpowering. I started back in horror. My movement, and the expression on my face must have betrayed my unwillingness to have anything to do with something which I found so disgusting.

'I hadn't noticed that Bukai Rōshi, my Master, had quietly walked up behind me. Without saying a single word he pushed me aside, lifted up his robes, snatched the wet cloth from my hand, walked into the room, barefoot, and set about cleaning the toilet.

'For a few moments I stood rooted to the spot, unable to say or do anything. But then I jumped forward and took the cloth out of his hands and started scrubbing. A moment later I lost my self-awareness.

'My Rōshi watched me for a while, without saying anything. Then, in a quiet voice, he said, "So. The contrast between dirt and cleanliness is too much for you. With this wet cloth in your hand you are incapable of remaining *one*. Are you not ashamed? Has all your practice been for nothing?" '

'I shall never forget how deeply these words of my teacher and Master wounded me.'

The disciple must overcome all inhibitions, no matter what they are, he must be able to remain One in each and every situation. He must be happiness, and nothing else, in happiness; sadness, and nothing else, in sadness; meditation, and nothing else, in meditation. That is the true discipline: to be one with the moment, no matter where one is, no matter what one is doing. It is not an easy task. But it is the duty of all disciples of Zen, it is our vow and our faith, and it must be practised ceaselessly, day and night.

Diary, November 6 1967

It is icy cold in the *zendō* at the moment. I have started wearing several layers of woollen clothes under my robes, but with both the doors of the meditation hall open and the open window behind my back it doesn't help much. It is only a problem at the beginning of the *zazen* sessions though; as soon as I enter into a state of meditation all physical feelings of cold disappear completely.

There was no *sanzen* yesterday or today, unfortunately. The Rōshi is away, and he is not due to come back until late this evening. He is going to deliver a lecture tomorrow morning.

Yesterday and today I spent many hours in desperate meditation in my freezing room in Myokan-ji. Without allowing any opinion of my own to seep in I examined all the pros and cons of my departure once again. Why? After all, Heaven itself has already given me its answer. It is because of Rōshi Mumon. It wounds me to leave him now, he has had to suffer so much this year, and has had so many painful disappointments and losses.

It is very important to transcend the confines of one's ego when one performs this kind of meditation, at least if one wishes to receive a pure answer. One must become a zero, a nothing, and allow one's questions to sink deep into the depths of this nothing, waiting patiently for Existence to answer. And when the answer comes one must be prepared to accept it, totally, no matter what it is.

And so I sent the question which had been tormenting my human heart on its way, without thinking 'about' it, of course, and waited for the answer to come, in a state of total silence and inner emptiness. (When I was finished today I looked at the clock and realised that I had been in this state for at least two hours.)

All bodily sensations disappeared. How can I describe it? It is difficult. Since the intellect also disappears when one is in this state it must be something else which is aware of what is taking place. It is consciousness, free of all disturbances, consciousness aware of its own existence.

The disappearance of the feelings of solidity and weight associated with one's awareness of one's physical body is in itself a source of great bliss. However, if one's consciousness is able to avoid paying attention to this bliss – that is, if one can resist the temptation to 'enjoy' the feeling – the bliss is then followed by a state of profound silence. It is indescribable really. The closest I can come to describing it is to say that the silence becomes larger, that it becomes hyper-silence. But that too is only a poor label for something for which there are no words.

Then, in this state of silence (my silence), within the greater hyper-silence, something happened which I can only describe as an explosion, in which all boundaries disappeared: I was suddenly in my original state, in the Whole, in Unity. Now words really do fail me. There is nothing at all I can say about this state.

When I returned to normal consciousness streams of tears were pouring from my eyes. All my clothes were soaked through, it was as though my entire body was crying, crying with bliss.

Diary, November 7 1967

The bliss is still there. It is incomparably more intense than anything which I have ever experienced before, more intense even than my satori four years ago. The reason is that now I have been liberated from myself, completely. And that means that I have been liberated from everything.

I am struggling to find the right words to express it, to make it comprehensible. Now that I have returned to 'real life' the person I was before yesterday's event has disappeared completely. I am no longer the same.

In all of the Zen literature which I have read I have not been able to find a single word explaining what it is that one experiences when this happens. There are two reasons for this: Firstly, one *should* not speak about it, and secondly, one *cannot* speak about it, even if one wants to. This greatest of all experiences cannot be contained within the puny confines of words. And the harder one tries the clearer it becomes that everything which can be said is far, far away from the actuality of the Truth.

Nor is it possible to answer questions about it. Any answer one gives is bound to be unsatisfactory, and the questioner will remain unsatisfied until he himself has experienced. And then he too will become silent.

This much I can say, although it is not much: I have become lighter. That is to say, I no longer have a past. What used to be my past is now weightless and insignificant, it is like a film which has nothing at all to do with me.

Now I know what liberation is: it is being free of one's past. Even if one has never wasted a single thought on one's past life one still carries it in one's being. It is only when one attains to the Great Liberation that one realises just what a burden it has always been.

That is why I say that I have become lighter.

Notes

1. Plotinus, *Life of Plotinus* (Loeb Classical Library, 1966).
2. E. Rousselle, *Vom Sinn der Buddhistischen Bildwerke in China* (The Buddhist Visual Arts in China: Their Meaning and Significance), Genter Verlag, Darmstadt. According to the British Museum Catalogue of Books there is no English translation of this work.

14

Farewell to the Rōshi and Japan

Diary, November 22 1967. Honolulu.

I am sitting on the terrace of my friends' house, high up on the slope of the mountain, with a breathtaking view of the city of Honolulu, the Pacific Ocean, and the Diamond Head Crater, the island's most famous landmark, which is set into the landscape as though it had been carefully placed by a master artist. Being here is a wonderful, divine gift. I can hardly believe that it is really true – it still feels as though it were a dream. The beautifully temperate climate of Hawaii is like balm for my poor battered body after the terrible cold in Japan, and I am enjoying every moment with a heart full of gratitude. Ilse and Werner's hospitality is so warm and natural, I feel really at home here.

After the extreme physical and mental strain of the months which had gone before, a regimen which would have reduced even a strong man to a wreck, I was much less than a mere shadow of myself – I was a shadow of my shadow.

This holiday in the warm climate and the relaxed atmosphere of Ilse and Werner's home perched up on the slopes of the mountain in Honolulu was exactly what I needed to recover my strength. I went swimming in the sea and I bathed in the wonderful natural beauty of the surroundings; I felt as though I had been given a hundred injections of vitamins all at once. My health returned, and I began to exist once again as a physical being. Without this glorious, gentle rest and Ilse and Werner's help I would never have been able to go through with my tour of Mexico, at least, not without eliminating a great deal from my itinerary.

This holiday was one of those wonderful healing interludes which are needed in everyone's life: looked at objectively they may seem small and insignificant, but we cannot survive without them. They serve to preserve and restore our inner balance, giving us the strength we need to go on. Other people, people who are there in the right place at the right time, always play a role in making these interludes possible, guided by the hand of fate.

Of course, one has to be 'poor' oneself in order to be able to appreciate the riches of this world and the blessing of being alive in such a world, even when it is darkened by confusion.

Diary, November 1967. Honolulu.

I didn't manage to write much during my last two weeks in Japan – I was much too busy making parcels (I sent a large number of things home by post) and packing the suitcases which I was going to take with me on my journey. Now I can write an account of the most important events which took place during that time.

After the experience which I was granted between 6 and 7 November (I wrote a precise description of this directly after it happened) I passed through everything which took place up until my departure with a feeling of lightness and weightlessness.

On the 7th I went to see Rōshi Mumon in his private study. I told him everything which had happened and asked him to give me his permission to return home. Once again, there was no *sanzen* during *zazen* that evening. It seems that the Rōshi was too exhausted to be able to go through with it: The next few evenings, after he had rung his bell to signal the beginning of *sanzen* and we had all gathered in the freezing cold on the open terrace outside the *sanzen* room, only the first five monks were admitted. The rest of us were sent back to the *zendō*. Every time it happened I felt a cold shock of fear run through me, for I felt certain that the Rōshi must be ill. I knew him ell enough to be sure, beyond any shadow of a doubt, that only absolute, total exhaustion could possibly keep him from fulfilling the duties of his office – the office of a living Buddha.

During my last days in the temple I always left the *zendō* before the last hour of *zazen* began. The Jikihitsu who had screamed at me because I had worn my own sandals was responsible for wielding the Zen stick during this hour, and although I was taboo for him the ceaseless brutality with which he struck the other monks was simply too much for me to bear. He managed to demolish six of the long sticks, which are extremely sturdy, on the backs of the poor monks in the course of ten days. I was told that this was something which had never happened before in the entire history of the temple, and he was removed from his post soon afterwards. I suppose he may have thought that it was necessary to hit harder now that the monks were wearing their thick winter clothes, but whatever his reason I preferred to return to my room in Myokan-ji and continue with my meditation there.

I went to see Sakamoto san and told him how worried I was about the Rōshi's health. He informed me that the Rōshi had decided to resign from all his posts in Kyoto, starting next semester, and to devote all his time to the training of his monks in Shofuku-ji.

'That will be the beginning of a much harder life for the monks here,' said Sakamoto san, 'but it will also be much more fulfilling. I can imagine that some of them will leave the monastery, but those who stay will experience wonderful things. And the Rōshi has also made another decision, an even more important one: In future no outsiders will be permitted to set foot in the temple.'

'Has the Rōshi already handed in his resignation?' I asked. I wasn't quite ready to believe it.

'That's the problem. The students at the university are terribly upset. Ever since the news has got out they have been pestering him, day and night, begging him to stay.'

I can only hope and pray that the Rōshi doesn't allow his kind heart to get the better of him and prevent him from making the right decision. It is absolutely essential that a worthy successor should be trained before it is too late.

Again and again I wonder at the strange combination of qualities which go to make up Rōshi Mumon: on the one hand the spellbinding and yet implacable power of the great Zen Master, his enlightened and thus infallible Buddha-wisdom, and on the other his human qualities, qualities which make him 'too good' and 'too soft' in Rōshi Shibayama's eyes. How can one reconcile the two? One would not think that such a paradox is possible in an enlightened Zen Master, but Rōshi Mumon is the living proof of it.

Unfortunately, I was never able to accompany the Rōshi when he visited prisons, but Sakamoto san was always with him. He told me that the Rōshi would often stop in the middle of a sentence when he was speaking with the prisoners, rendered speechless by the sheer force of his overwhelming compassion. Sakamoto san's own voice trembled with emotion as he told me about it.

Every two years, Sakamoto san told me, he visits the little island off the coast where the lepers live, the hold of his boat filled with crates of books and other presents. The lepers' colony is completely cut off from the rest of the world, and he is their only comfort. Hundreds of them gather to wait on the quay hours before his boat is due to arrive, and when he steps down the gangplank they stretch out their deformed hands to him and he takes their hands tenderly in his own and gazes into their eyes. Those who have no hands to hold lean their heads on his shoulder and he takes them in his arms. The most wretched among them, said Sakamoto san, can always be sure of a particularly warm and tender greeting. It seems that Rōshi Mumon is not in the least bit afraid of becoming infected himself, nor is he shocked by ugliness. For a man who lives in the eternal Buddha Spirit there is neither ugliness nor beauty, there is only the One.

His visits to the lepers' island always last for several days. He lives with them in their houses, delivers two lectures every day, and receives everyone who wished to speak with him. He shares their suffering, and showers them with his love. Who knows – perhaps some of his best disciples are to be found among those poor souls on the lepers' island. Whether this is true or not, however, I am certain that while he is there that island of unimaginable suffering is transformed into a place of love. Not 'charity', but love, in its purest sense. The luminous, unconditional love of a true saint, flowing everywhere and transforming everything, and, in response, the love and gratitude of the ill-fated residents of the island, their hearts opened for the universal love of the Eternal by the being of light in their midst.

Rōshi Mumon is a saint. And how can a saint suspect malice, cunningness and hypocrisy in the robes of holiness? They are simply too far removed from the world in which he lives for him to be able to imagine them. The nature of his being is purity, and nothing else, and in those moments where he is confronted with iniquity it wounds him so deeply that he must turn his face aside.

I know that this will seem incredible to some readers, but it is truly so. I know Rōshi Mumon very well, probably better than most of his own monks do. He himself has said that I am his sister in Buddha, and that means that we are one in spirit.

A completely enlightened being is one with all which is. That is the essence of Zen. Rōshi Mumon is so perfectly enlightened that he is one with everything with which he comes into contact, no matter whether it is positive or negative. If he comes into contact with wrongs, then there are no barriers between him and the perpetrator, or between him and the wrong itself, and he feels the burden of guilt just as much as the perpetrator, perhaps more. Not out of sympathy or pity, but simply because that is the way it is. That is the suchness of his nature.

It is not possible to be one with Universal Love without, at the same time, being one with its opposite. To paraphrase the old saying: When you laugh, the entire universe laughs with you, and when you cry you do not cry alone, for you are the universe and the universe cries with you too, just as it laughs.

This is not something which can be understood with the rational mind. It goes beyond the mind; it is meta-physics. The first and last truth of the Zen experience is this: There are no opposites within the One. Dissolving into this 'One' is the most ardent longing of all disciples of Zen, and it is the goal towards which their Masters tirelessly drive them.

But then, one may ask, what about an enlightened Master like Rōshi Mumon who feels the guilt of the guilty? Is that not a paradox? How is that possible if his home is the One, where there are no opposites? The answer is that he also lives in the world of differentiation.

One continues to walk on the earth after enlightenment, one doesn't dissolve in a puff of smoke, but as of that moment one walks in the unity of Buddha Being. One's spirit is enlightened but one's feet remain on the ground. A blow, no matter whether it is physical or spiritual, is just as real as a revelation. The enlightened being feels the blow, but he also accepts it. That is the mystery and the wonder of living within the One while one is still on this earth.

I suffer, but without suffering. I am happy, but without being happy. I am wounded, and yet I am unscathed.

I know that the above is confused and unclear, but it is the best I can do. My wish was to explain, from my own experience, the nature of the great Rōshi who is described as being 'too good'.

I went to see the Rōshi two days before my departure. He gave me two of his wonderful calligraphic pictures, which he had prepared especially for me. One was the character for 'happiness'. The Chinese characters which he had written down the left hand side of this picture meant, 'As deep and as wide as the endless ocean.' The other picture was the character for 'long life'. The comment he had written here was, 'Like the Himalayas.' These two characters can be interpreted both in the context of this world and of the beyond.

After expressing my thanks I produced the short staff made of red-lacquered wood which I had been given a few days before, without any ceremony or comment, and held it up before him. These staffs are the symbol of a Rōshi's office, and no-one else is allowed to hold or use them.

'May I really keep this staff? Does it belong to me?' I asked. The Rōshi responded with peals of laughter. I had not heard such merry laughter from him for a very, very long time.

'Of course it belongs to you,' he replied at last, as his laughter died down. Then he invited me to come to his room for supper later that evening.

Supper consisted of the only alternative to rice on the monastic menu: Japanese macaroni. After I had expressed my thanks for everything he had done for me there wasn't much more to say. One is not interested in mere words when the beating of the inner heart is filling the room like the pealing of a thousand divine bells.

The Rōshi gave me a photograph of himself and a few other small presents. I have them with me now. Even though I did not know whether we would ever meet again, on this earth at least, my feeling of lightness and weightlessness continued unabated. I can find no other way of expressing it, for it is the simple truth. I love and respect Rōshi Mumon more than any other being on this earth, and yet, in the hour of our parting, I felt only calm equanimity. This was the living proof of the transformation which had taken place within me. I was really free. No pain, not a single tear. But a profound understanding of the nature of non-pain.

I sat in the super express from Kobe to Tokyo and watched the Japanese landscape rush past the window. When I had left the Rōshi and the temple four years before the pain of parting had almost broken me. This time I had not even looked back. I was in the present, here, and now.

In Tokyo the winter had already set in in earnest. I had written a letter to Master Osaka, who had been my first Master in Japan, telling him that I would arrange my stopover in Tokyo so that I could come and see him, and he had sent me a telegram telling me when he would be free. At the appointed time I took a taxi to his home, which is in an outlying suburb of the city.

It was wonderful to see him. I told him everything which had happened to me since we had last seen one another. He nodded, his eyes radiant.

'I saw it at once. I share your happiness.'

After we had taken tea together I asked him if he would be good enough to show me his *dōjō* once again. He was delighted, and he got up at once and led the way. Even though the *dōjō* was empty I made the prescribed prostrations, as though *zazen* were about to begin. I felt the need to express my gratitude here as well.

When we reached the altar Master Osaka pointed to the place in the corner. 'That is where you used to sit,' he said quietly. We kneeled down in silence before the altar.

Epilogue

I have already said everything that there is to be said really. Even so, I should nonetheless like to add a few words on the subject of Zen in general. I should hasten to add that I have no intention of writing a 'history' of Zen, however brief: D. T. Suzuki and a number of very learned Jesuits have written excellent works on this subject, and I can highly recommend their books to anyone who is interested in finding out more.

Suzuki was a true Japanese Zen Master and scholar, and as such he was not willing to provide the kind of analytical, 'exhaustive' interpretation of the more profound secrets of Zen which the intellectual western mind demands. For a Master like him, of course, it would not have been difficult to distill such an interpretation from the recorded actions, responses and replies of the great Zen Masters of the past, but Suzuki declined to do so. I had the honour of making his aquaintance on several occasions, and in the light of my own experiences I can now understand the reasons for this endlessly kind and unassuming man's reticence. In fact, it wasn't really reticence at all: as an enlightened man he understood that explanations, however detailed and accurate they are, do not help people who do not themselves 'know'.

Now, when I reread the works of Suzuki and other living Zen Masters I often have the experience that the meaning of statements which had seemed totally obscure to me before suddenly becomes crystal clear; it is as though scales have fallen from my eyes. This demonstrates the truth of the old Zen adage, in which it is said that the disciple who solves one great kōan has solved them all. Master Osaka in Tokyo had also given me 'Jōshū's Mu' as my kōan, and when it finally dissolved in a shattering experience of satori his comment was: 'Now everything is settled. The main work has been done.'

One should not misunderstand this statement, however. Everything was only 'settled' so long as I continued to delve ever deeper into the Truth. Both from his own experience and from a tradition which was many centuries old Suzuki was very well aware of the fact that it is not possible to serve anyone the truth on a platter, and that it would in any case be wrong to try to do so. The most that anyone can do is to point the way.

Goethe expresses this truth in another way: 'God provides the nuts, but he doesn't crack 'em.' However, once one has, after many attempts, managed to crack the main nut, then the rest are no longer difficult, for one has acquired the knack of finding the solution. Suddenly the seeker who has struggled so long and hard to discover the great secret is able to find all the remaining solutions with almost no effort and then – then, to his surprise, they no longer interest him. This is something which I can confirm from my own experience. Now I understand the stories about disciples of great Masters who, after attaining enlightenment, reacted in ways which I used to think were churlish and ungrateful, for my own inner reaction was no different: 'What on earth is all the fuss about?' I thought. 'There is nothing to be said about it and nothing special about it.' And this has been the reaction of everyone who has ever been granted this experience, all down the centuries.

Of course, one should also remember that the kind of exchanges described in the Zen stories referred to above are only possible between a Master and his disciple, or between two people who have both had the same experience of enlightenment: all of the absurd and paradoxical statements to be found in Zen should be seen within this context.

While I was in Japan I often heard people voice the opinion that Suzuki had 'revealed too much'. Criticism of this sort does the late scholar great injustice. It is true that his books were a revelation of the first order for the West, opening up a religious dimension which almost no one there had been aware of before, but they did not disclose anything which could be misused. Suzuki himself was perfectly well aware of the fact that, for the time being at least, Zen would remain an insoluble mystery for the Western mind, for it demands a complete transformation of one's mental approach; and that is not something which can be managed overnight. He made no promises regarding Paradise or a 'Father in Heaven', nor did he say that there would be a 'reward' of any kind for good deeds or hard work. He made it very clear that the way of Zen is the way of purposelessness, and that the disciple of Zen, if he is to be successful, must be free of all intentions and desires. Free, even, of the desire for God and the attainment of union with Him in the One.

The way of Zen takes the seeker through his own individual Void, into the Universal Void. Most people in the West see this path as a path of utter negation, the negation of everything which is, and reject it for this reason. They believe that such an approach must result in a state of total despair, a belief which is as understandable as it is wrong. I hope that both this book and my first book about my experiences on the path of Zen have helped the reader to see that this opinion could not be more mistaken. I have done my best to describe the *practice* of Zen, in terms which everyone can understand, avoiding any speculation or theorizing 'about' Zen. And despite the fact that the ultimate experience itself cannot help but remain mysterious, I have also taken great pains to keep my account as clear as possible. Mystification doesn't help anyone, and it would be unworthy of the great goal of Zen. In any case, enlightenment only seems mysterious until one experiences it oneself. Then it is as clear as day.

In my account I have several times reached points at which it was simply not possible to say any more. My silence does not mean that I wish to conceal anything from the reader – it is simply an expression of the fact that there are some things for which language is inadequate. I think that the reader will agree that I have done my best to express everything which *can* be expressed as clearly and honestly as possible. The vain attempt to describe the indescribable is only made by those who have not experienced it themselves.

On the other hand, I have, hopefully, been able to demonstrate that it very definitely is possible to experience 'It' for oneself, and that this experience results in a total transformation of the seeker.

In the moment of illumination the seeker's 'I', his ego, dissolves into nothingness. Thus, in a sense, he becomes utterly, totally poor. But in the same instant this nothingness is filled by the endless bliss of the One, and from that moment onwards the One is able to express itself through the nothingness which the seeker has become. The process of illumination transforms the seeker into a tool of Heaven. 'It' expresses itself through him and works through him, and the seeker who is now no more accepts the tasks which he is set in the knowledge that the great 'It' within him is both taskmaster and servant. 'It' decides what is to be done.

'It' makes use of all of the knowledge and experience of its 'vessel', no matter whether it is spiritual or all too human, taking possession of everything which the seeker has ever learned, without exception, and putting it to use. With a feeling of overwhelming bliss and gratitude the seeker suddenly realises that nothing of that which he has surrendered has been lost. It has simply become a part of the Whole, and from now on it is used in the service of the Whole. It belongs to the seeker, as before, and yet it does not belong to him, for it is in the hands of the One.

However, the fact that nothing is lost does not mean that nothing has changed. The experience of illumination transforms the seeker totally. For example, suppose that the seeker is someone who has always been completely devoted to music, never missing a single important concert. At first he will probably not even notice that he no longer feels the need to attend concerts which he wouldn't have missed for the world before. But when he does notice it he will suddenly realise, with a sense of shock, that he no longer needs any of the 'essential' things which had previously gone to make up his life.

This freedom from attachment is something which cannot be lost. Once one has experienced 'It' one can no longer be attached to anything, even if one tries. Objectively speaking it is a state of total poverty, for one does not 'have' anything, but experientially it is a state of total freedom. Something else which one learns in the course of the great experience is that there is no such thing as partial freedom. One is either free, or one is not. I should also like to stress that the realisation that one no longer 'has' anything, that one is no longer attached to anything, is not in any way a source of loss or regret. That too is not possible, for as I have already pointed out, nothing has really been lost, and everything has been gained.

Ever since the publication of my first book I have received a seemingly never-ending stream of deeply moving letters from my readers. All of these letters have been a source of great joy to me. A few days ago, however, I received a letter from a woman in Switzerland which I should like to mention here, for it is the only negative comment which I have ever received. After a friendly greeting she went on to say that she felt that the driving force behind everything I had done had been boundless egotism. 'You have achieved the ultimate,' she wrote, 'but only for yourself, and yourself alone. What good does that do for the whole?'

Unfortunately I was unable to show this lady the piles of letters which demonstrate what 'good' my own experience has already done. Nor did I feel that it would be worth while to try to explain to her just how totally I have placed myself at the service of 'the whole'. However, in my reply I did point out that she must have misunderstood my book – if she had not it would not have been possible for her to arrive at this conclusion.

I have already made it very clear in my first book, and I repeat it now, that all Zen monks who seek enlightenment must vow (this is the so-called 'Bodhisattva Vow') that they will not enter into ultimate Nirvana until all beings, past, present and future, have been liberated. I doubt whether the author of the letter which I mentioned above is capable of comprehending the full implications of such a vow, for they are beyond human comprehension.

But when does one become capable of contributing something to the liberation of other beings? Only when one has ceased to exist as a being made up of desire and personality oneself, and not before. This is something which cannot be repeated often enough: no one who has not completely erased themselves as an ego can do anything to help liberate anyone else, and the attainment of this goal is not easy. The journey is very long, and the sacrifices and efforts which must be made on the way are immense. I do not deny that all of these efforts are directed towards the attainment of one's own liberation, not the liberation of others, but it cannot be otherwise. Until one is liberated oneself one is simply not capable of helping anyone else.

Before the first barriers can fall (the 'barriers' referred to by the Zen Master Mumon Ekai in his commentary on 'Jōshū's Mu'[1]) the seeker must first free himself of all faults, must become a *tabula rasa*. And that too is only the beginning. Many many more barriers must fall before he is self-less and empty enough for the One to begin to work through him.

When someone who is enlightened is approached by a seeker asking for help and advice he does not consider what would be 'best' for the seeker (even though his experienced opinion might admittedly be valuable, but that is not the point); it is the One which uses him as a channel and works through him, it is the One which speaks through his mouth. He himself is a zero, a mere tool in the hands of the will to which he has surrendered himself. And, miraculously, the seeker sitting before him believes what he says. Those who are sent to the enlightened being always trust – no matter what their social class or worldly station – for in their hearts they know that selfless Truth itself is speaking to him.

How do they know this, one may ask? They know because a great 'yes' wells up in their hearts, because their own divine spark suddenly bursts into flame, and because the overwhelming light of Truth radiating from the enlightened being is so self-evident that it is impossible to deny it, no matter whether he is a great scholar or a modest farmer.

It is not possible for such a tool of Heaven to do his work with more than a few people. Large-scale organisations may make a lot of money, but real help on the path can only be given on an individual, one-to-one basis. In the same way the 'call' to embark on the journey is also an individual matter, and has been for thousands of years.

After attaining enlightenment the individual no longer pursues any goals, for no goal, however lofty it may be, is wholly pure. The enlightened being must be completely free from all desires and all attachments, including the attachment to any particular creed or religion. Attachment precludes freedom, and where there is no freedom 'goals' arise. The following are a few of the famous Zen Masters' statements on this subject.

> The authority of Zen consists in Non-Duality (Hisamatsu[2]).

> No dependency upon anything during all the twelve divisions of the day (Huang-Po, 850).

Lin-Chi (known as Rinzai in Japan, the founder of the Zen sect which was named after him, died 867) describes the awakened being as 'The Tao man of Non-Dependency'. 'Tao man' can be loosely translated to mean, 'he who walks the way of Heaven'.

Lin-Chi is also recorded to have said the following shattering words:

> 'If you meet Buddha on the way, kill Buddha.
> If you meet a Patriarch on the way, kill the Patriarch.
> If you meet an Arhat on the way, kill the Arhat.
> If you meet your father and your mother on the way, kill your father and your mother.
> If you meet your relatives on the way, kill your relatives.
> Thus you will become free, self-sufficient and unattached.
> Your essential nature is illumination and freedom.'

The ancient Masters always stressed that the 'true man of Zen' (i.e. one who has become enlightened) is free of everything, 'even of the Buddhas and the Patriarchs' (Hisamatsu). The primary objective of Zen is the attainment of freedom from all attachments, no matter what they may be.

Rōshi Hisamatsu adds:

> If one is attached to something unimportant it is easy to become aware of it. However, if one is attached to something important and noble one tends to be blind to this fact and to be totally unaware that this too is an attachment.

In Zen terms even the attachment to a religion or one of its sects is a source of non-freedom. This non-freedom arises as soon as the attachment results in compulsions, even if they are of a noble and lofty nature.

In Zen the statements of Lin-Chi's which I have cited above are regarded as pure expression of the doctrine of Buddha Gautama, and of the doctrine of all the Buddhas before him. I have occasionally been asked how it is possible to square these statements with Buddha's 'noble eightfold path'. The answer to this question is simple: The eightfold path is for the seeker, and unless one adheres to its requirements strictly no progress is possible. Lin-Chi's statements, on the other hand, are for those who have arrived. One should not confuse the beginning of the journey with its end.

When Lin-Chi says that one should 'kill Buddha' and 'kill the Patriarch', what he means is that the seeker who has attained enlightenment should destroy every distraction, no matter what it is. The attainment of the state of unity is made possible by the teachings and discipline of Buddha and the Patriarchs, in combination with the seeker's own ceaseless, superhuman efforts. Once it has been attained, however, the seeker must throw his schoolbooks away, for at this point on the path even the teachings of Buddha and the Patriarchs are a distraction from the Truth. He no longer needs them. He no longer needs anything. And until the disciple attains to the state of total and perfect enlightenment, a state which gets deeper and deeper of its own accord, his Master will continue to hammer away at all his attachments, never tiring in his insistence that they are barriers to self-realisation.

The unbelievably strict path of the true Zen Master is not for everyone, and it is hardly surprising that only a very few extremely advanced disciples are ever successful. But when they *are* successful the freedom to which they attain is absolute and unbounded. They become free from everything, free even from their own beloved teachers and Masters.

The actual moment of final liberation comes unexpectedly, like a bolt of lightning from Heaven, and it is not the result of any action on the disciple's part. It simply happens. This phenomenon is the reason why Zen Masters often speak of 'sudden enlightenment'. It happens when the seeker has freed himself from himself, when not a single barrier, no matter how fine and gossamer-like, is left, when the enlightened one and enlightenment have become one. Then the divine bolt of lightning can strike.

I can see now that the hidden purpose of my own personal journey has been the production of a first-hand account of this process of liberation. This is the work for which Existence, in its eternal wisdom, has used my life. Enough has been written about the 'theory' of Zen; my work has been to describe its practice. If I have succeeded in my aim, which was to demonstrate that enlightenment is something attainable, and not an illusion or a far-away dream, then I am deeply grateful. Then my life, filled as it has been with hardships, disappointments and joys, has not been lived in vain. What I have given I have given as a servant of the One, as a modest link in a chain which has no beginning. Other links will follow.

Those readers who are familiar with the *Ten Bulls of Zen*, compiled by the Chinese Zen Master Kakuan in the twelfth century, will immediately understand the significance of the final stage on the path of liberation:[3] When the 'enlightened one' returns to what we refer to as 'normal life' there is no difference whatsoever between him and his surroundings. He has no halo, nor is there even the slightest odour of sanctity about him. His utter ordinariness is the outward sign by which his equals recognise him, and it is also the reason why others do not recognise him. For him there is no difference between the sacred and the profane, there is no such thing as higher or lower. He can converse with anyone about anything, for he is one with everything with which he comes into contact. There is, perhaps, a certain nobility and remoteness about him, but one accepts these qualities without question, in the same way that one accepts the perfume of a flower: they are not mere play-acting, they are a natural, integral part of his being. Bodhidharma expressed this criterion for the true enlightenment in two succinct words: 'Nothing holy.'

I would be the first to admit that the path which must be travelled to attain this state is both long and stony. Anyone who thinks that a little bit of *zazen* here and there is enough to do the trick is in for a great disappointment. But at the same time I can attest to the fact that it is a path upon which anyone can travel, without any exceptions whatsoever.

Seekers after enlightenment have been seeking, and finding, ever since Man started to think. The chain has never been broken, and it is only the names of the very great Masters which have been passed down to us. The vast majority of those who have attained to enlightenment are nameless.

Man has been searching for God ever since the dawn of his history: in the caves of the stone age, in ancient North America long before the arrival of the white man, in the cult of the 'Great Mother' in Europe, in the cult of Isis and Osiris in Egypt, and later in the so-called World Religions. And no matter where Man searched, no matter what conditions he searched under, when he searched for God he always found him. Even before he had built a single temple to the Divine or its attributes, the Gods, there is not a single place on this earth where Man was not praying, searching and meditating. On our earth, wherever one sets one's foot one is treading on holy ground.

There is no denying the miraculous truth of it: Man has always carried the divine spark within him, since time immemorial, and he has always been able to realise his divine potential. The outward expression of this realisation may have been different at different times and in different cultures, but it was always there. Man is in reality immortal.

Our task, and God's desire, is to awaken this inner spark and, if possible, to fan it into a great flame. The eternal question is, how? The best way to begin is by having an objective look at your situation, taking great care not to allow any emotions to distort your observations.

Then, no matter whether your situation is good or bad, satisfying or unsatisfying, your next task is to accept it. This is the first great obstacle which must be overcome, and it can only be overcome if you understand the nature of karma.

The situation into which one is born, one's parents, one's surroundings and one's profession, is determined by one's karma – that is to say, it is the fruits of one's actions in previous incarnations. Once you really understand this you will begin to see that you are, in fact, exactly where you need to be, and that there is no place on earth which could possibly be more right for you at this stage of your evolution, even if you don't find it particularly pleasant at the moment. This understanding is the beginning of acceptance.

The next point which must be stressed is that your acceptance of your karma must be absolutely unconditional, without any ifs or buts. It must come from the heart. Don't make the mistake of simply gritting your teeth together and hoping that things are going to get better if you force yourself to 'accept'; that will not do any good at all. You must really understand, and really accept, totally. Once you have managed it, however, you can rest assured that you have overcome the first great hurdle on the path. I admit that it is not easy – it takes a great deal of insight and inner strength – but the rewards are tremendous.

D. T. Suzuki, whose unerring, sober and lucid insights make him one of the greatest modern teachers of Zen, also expounds on the subject of karma at great length. In his book, *The Essence of Buddhism*, he confirms that all human suffering is a result of our karma, and that we all bring a heavy burden of karma from the past with us when we are born. This is simply a fact, a part of our existence.

Even though the doctrine of karma originated in ancient India I have chosen to cite Suzuki as an authority of this subject, and not one of the ancient Indian sages. I have a number of reasons for making this choice: first of all, of course, he is a man of Zen, and Zen is my subject. But in addition to that he is also a modern man who speaks in modern terms for a modern audience. For instance, in the series of lectures which he delivered in the Imperial Palace in Tokyo he discussed the role of karma in the lives and work of Zen Masters. The more tradition-bound authorities on Zen would not deign to discuss such 'beginners' questions', but Suzuki understands their importance for the modern mind. Finally, he is a man who speaks with authority. He is not merely a scholar, he has himself experienced what he writes about.

After becoming aware of your situation and accepting it the third step on the path is to set about working off the karma which you have brought with you from your past lives. No matter whether the karma of your situation is pleasant or frightful, everyone involved in the drama of your life is there in order to balance out what has gone before, each of the actors has something to learn.

The karmic relationships in families, between parents and their children or brothers and sisters, are often negative in the extreme. So much so, unfortunately, that people involved in relationships of this kind are, at first, either unwilling or unable to have a closer look at their karma.

If you are in a situation like this you are going to have to understand that it must be faced, there are simply no two ways about it. The path towards God which you long to travel on will remain blocked until you clear away the karma which you have brought with you. It is, quite literally, an obstacle on the path, and it is not possible to jump over it or walk around it. One must face it and deal with it, otherwise one cannot continue. Even so, it is not really as difficult as it sounds at first. It is simply a question of perseverance and patience.

The daily practice of *zazen* is also a great help. (I have already described the 'how' of *zazen* at great length elsewhere, and so there is no need for me to go into it again here.) The first objective of *zazen* is the attainment of a state of inner peace, and at the beginning of your practice your attention in your 'sittings' should be concentrated on silence and emptiness. The length of time needed to reach this state varies from person to person.

At the same time you should also work on eliminating negative thoughts about other people, especially about people you regard as your enemies. You will probably find that such thoughts arise very often and with great force at first, for deeply ingrained habits and emotions have a powerful resistance to change. Paradoxical though it may seem, however, this is a very good sign. It is an indication, albeit a negative one, that something has started moving in your inner world. The next question is, how to deal with negative thoughts of this kind? The first tendency of the beginner, which should be avoided at all costs, is to suppress them. As soon you become aware that you are thinking ill of someone simply allow yourself to wish them well, without trying to imagine what form this positive turn of events should take. Concentrate on creating a positive thought, not on fighting the negative thought. For instance, you could say something like, 'I wish him well,' or, 'I wish her well.'

Negative thoughts arise on a regular basis, and each time one arises you should balance it with a positive thought. If you persist in this practice for several months you will begin to notice that the negative thoughts are becoming less frequent. Later still, to your great astonishment, you will find that the entire problem with the person in question has simply dissolved into thin air, and that the feelings of annoyance and anger which had weighed you down have been transformed into relaxed equanimity. This discovery is always accompanied by a feeling of overwhelming, indescribable bliss, for it means that the first small burden of karma has been eliminated. I doubt whether most people understand just how significant this step really is, for its true implications are beyond human comprehension. That isn't important at this point, however. All you really need to know is that you are now free to tackle your next task.

Something which should be resisted at all costs, however, both while you are practising these exercises and afterwards, is the emotional temptation to confront your 'enemies' with sentimental demonstrations of your love. Such actions are a great hindrance to progress, for they are motivated by human desires and wishes, and as such they can only produce negative results. One silent, spiritual exercise is much more effective than a hundred thousand good deeds. The reason for this is that every physical action produces an equal reaction, thus creating more karma. Only spiritual 'action' dissolves karma rather than creating it.

If you wish to come closer to the divine you must first free yourself of your burden of karma, beginning with the karma you can see and recognise. The rest will then reveal itself of its own accord.

'But what about my enemy?' you may ask. 'His responsibility for the situation is just as great as mine. Why doesn't he do anything? Why should I do all the work?' The answer to this question is that the 'work' of spiritual transformation must always be carried out by the knower. If you have been graced with the ability to see and understand then you are also responsible for effecting the necessary change.

One of the miraculous aspects of this process of transformation, quite apart from one's own liberation, is the fact that one's enemy is also released from the burden of karma, at least as far as the situation in question is concerned. When one is successful in dissolving one's own feelings of hatred and one's desire to avenge oneself for imagined wrongs a portion of one's enemy's karma is dissolved at the same time.

I say 'imagined wrongs' for a very good reason, for in reality there is no such thing as a wrong. Injustice is an illusion which disappears as soon as one understands the law of karma. If injustice were possible, if even a single person were to suffer a genuine injustice, then this universe would not be divine, it would be an arbitrary chaos.

However, the fact that the universe *is* indeed divine has been proved again and again by all those who have ever sought and found God, ever since the beginning of human history. And that is not the only proof: The simple fact that the human race is still here, still seeking and searching and questioning despite the terrible misery and despair in which most people live, demonstrates that there is a tiny spark of Eternal Truth within each and every one of us. It is there, we are all born with it, and no matter what hells one passes through it cannot be destroyed. If it could, mankind would have died out long ago. It is only this spark of the Divine, connecting everything and everyone, which has given the sons and daughters of Man the strength to survive and go on in the midst of the despair which surrounds them. Seen in this context, Man's despair is not simply despair, it is also part of a process of purification.

If you proceed as I have described above you will find that you can achieve a great deal on your own, so long as you persevere patiently. Once you have succeeded in freeing your heart of the greatest obstacles to progress (the grosser forms of karma, involving your relationship with your environment, or other serious obstacles which you may discover in the course of your meditation) you can then set to work on your own weaknesses and faults. Start with your grossest and most obvious faults, and work on them slowly and patiently, one at a time, either dissolving them completely or transforming them into positive qualities.

It is possible to carry out all of this 'preparatory work' without the help of Master. If you are strict and honest with yourself, then the divine spark within you will come to your aid, enabling you both to find the obstacles in your path and to dissolve them. Every single successful step on this journey to God is worth the efforts of an entire lifetime. This self-discipline is difficult, but it is possible. Anyone can do it. I can confirm this from my own experience, for I did it myself.

When I reach this point people often look at me accusingly and protest that the fact that I managed to do this doesn't mean that it is possible for them, as though I were some kind of special, unique case. This is a misconception which I should like to get rid of once and for all. I have no intention of denying that, looked at objectively, my life looks like an endless series of miracles. From the very beginning I devoted all my energy to the search for God, I struggled ceaselessly and never gave up, getting up and entering into the fray again and again every time my delicate body collapsed beneath me. In addition to this I have been blessed with many great gifts from the beyond which have helped me on my way. But none of this means that I am in any way special. All it means is that I am, perhaps, older, that I have been through more incarnations than the majority of my fellows, incarnations in which I have searched and suffered and made endless mistakes. In these past incarnations I also forged the eternal, spiritual bonds which have now been manifested once again in my present life.

The spiritual journey which I have described, both in this book and my first book, is not something special and exalted which others are incapable of attaining. It is simply the logical culmination of many lives in which I suffered and searched and died again and again in my efforts to transcend my own limitations.

Everyone is capable of travelling this path, and everyone will reach the goal when their time comes. Nor is it necessary to enter a monastery, all one needs is the willingness to grow. If we understand them properly our lives, with all their difficulties, problems and joys, are our kōans, kōans given to us to solve by our karma, which is the sum total of everything which we have ever done and experienced.

That is also the ultimate meaning of Zen: nothing more or

less than life itself. All the Zen Masters, past and present, have always taught that life, and living life totally, is the only truth. The following story about the Chinese Zen Master Nansen (748-834), after whom the Nansen-ji temple in Kyoto is named, illustrates what they mean by this.

> One day, Nansen was working in the fields together with his monks. He was dressed exactly as they were, and nothing about him betrayed the fact that he was in fact the Master. An itinerant monk came walking by, and he stopped to ask the way. As luck would have it, it was Nansen that he asked.
>
> MONK Excuse me, can you tell me the way to the monastery of the Master Nansen?
> NANSEN (*Holding up his sickle*) I paid thirty coins for this.
> MONK I did not ask you the price of your sickle, I asked you to tell me the way to Nansen.
> NANSEN This sickle is wonderfully sharp.

Now, what is the meaning of this seemingly absurd dialogue? There was nothing unusual about the itinerant monk's question, and if he had asked one of the other monks he would have received a perfectly normal answer. As it happened, however, he asked the Master and not one of his disciples. Nansen's absurd answer was designed to test him. It is reasonable to assume that this monk who was on his way to see the greatest Zen Master of the time was no beginner on the path of Zen; this is why his next answer was so provocative. Nansen's only response, however, was to show him the sickle once again, praising its sharpness.

For someone unfamiliar with the ways of Zen Masters Nansen's replies look like the ravings of a madman or an idiot. What do they really mean? Nansen was demonstrating something of great importance to the novice who had come to see him. The message of his answers to the monk was this: 'If you have come here looking for abstract knowledge or discussions about philosophical systems of thought then you are wasting your time. The only thing which matters here is life itself, each moment in its unique totality. That is what you have to realise, and live.'

The quintessence of the teachings of all the enlightened ones is that truth can only be found and realised in the experience of the harmony of heaven and earth.

There are times when one must work in the fields with a sickle in one's hand, there are times when one must sleep, and there are times, of course, when one must sit and meditate.

People who try to storm the gates of Heaven in a rush usually fall back to earth again with a bump. If you are absolutely determined to scale these heights and to practise the way of the Void, which leads to the realisation that everything which is, is nothingness, then you would be well advised to begin at the beginning. The first step is to set about the Herculean task of purifying yourself of all of your desires and passions, even the most subtle ones, so that you yourself are transformed into a living emptiness in which Heaven can express itself.

If you search and delve within yourself sincerely nothing which is will be hidden from you. Your journey into your own being will reveal to you the nature of all beings. In finding nothingness you will find everything.

A great deal of time and effort is required, of course, but then, even the greatest pianists had to begin their training by practising simple scales and learning how to read music. One has to start with the basics and build firm, deep foundations, then understanding is bound to come of its own accord. How long the journey ultimately takes is irrelevant.

I simply get up and start walking. I know the direction I must take, I know my destination. It is at the end of the world, it is at the beginning of the world, it is in the eternal omnipresent centre of time and space between the two. Some time, somewhere, we, beginning and end, shall meet in the centre. We shall recognise one another and melt into one another. My pilgrimage has begun.

That is the way it should be. That is the way it can be.

Notes

1. Mumon Ekai, 1183–1260; Jōshū Jūshin, 778–879.
2. Professor Hisamatsu is a living Zen Master, mentioned by Gerta Ital several times in *The Master, The Monks, and I* (*Translator*).
3. *Translator's note*: In the 10th Bull, the last, entitled 'In the World', Kakuan writes:

> 'Barefooted and naked of breast, I mingle with the people of the world.
> My clothes are ragged and dust-laden and I am ever blissful.
> I use no magic to extend my life:
> Now, before me, the trees become alive.'

English translation taken from Paul Reps, *Zen Flesh, Zen Bones* (Pelican, 1986).

4. Here Ms Ital cites the English title of Suzuki's work (*Translator*).

Postscript to the German Paperback Edition

What has happened since I wrote the last words of this book, apart from the fact that the book itself has gone out of print? Amazing, unbelievable things have happened, and yet – nothing has happened. Let me begin with the latter, and explain what I mean when I say that nothing has happened.

I am sitting in my room in Berlin, my notebook in my lap, working on a postscript for a new edition of this book. It is the same room in which I wrote my first book, *The Master, the Monks, and I*,[1] when I returned from my first visit to Japan in 1963. (The *Frankfurter Allgemeine Zeitung* described this book as 'the almost unbelievable story of the first Western woman who has ever been admitted to a Zen Buddhist monastery and accepted as the disciple of one of the most famous living Zen Masters.'[2]) It is the same room in which, five years later, I wrote my account of what I experienced during my second visit to Japan, the book which you have just read.

And now I am back here again. I have been living in Munich for the last several years, for my pupils' sake, but I happened to be here in Berlin when the time came to write this postscript. I find this deeply touching. It is as though this room and my own spiritual journey are, in some way, intimately connected with one another. In all my years in Berlin this was the place where I worked and meditated, it was my ascetic retreat. The room and I have become one. It seems that the time has come for us to take up again where we had left off.

What has changed in the course of the last seventeen years?

Objectively speaking, nothing at all. It is true that my body and my spirit have travelled far and wide in the meantime, but now I am sitting in exactly the same place where I sat before setting off on my great adventure, breathing in the delightful perfume of the huge linden tree in front of my balcony, and writing. Everything is just as it was then. From a spiritual point of view, however, nothing is the same, for these years have been years of ceaseless spiritual transformation.

In Zen Buddhism one must pass through the Void, or 'nothingness', before one can experience the light of enlightenment (satori), and to reach this point one must practise hard for many, many years. Nor is the journey over after one has passed through this nothingness: if one continues diligently with the process of one's own dissolution in meditation one finds that the nothingness continues to unfold and reveal itself in ever different ways, everywhere. And one finds, to one's astonishment, that one can move around in the realm of nothingness just as easily and lightly as other people in the so-called 'real world'.

What has taken place is not an outward change, it is a change in one's state of consciousness. For people who haven't experienced it themselves this state sounds alien and frightening, but in actual fact it is nothing of the sort. I say this because I know that many seekers who are interested in Eastern teachings in general, and Zen Buddhism in particular, are alarmed by what seems at first to be something terribly strange and unknown. There is no need to be afraid. 'Life' doesn't change when one enters into this realm. In fact, nothing changes – all that happens is that one's eyes are opened. The seeker discovers that that which all the great Masters all down the ages have taught about the Void is not only true in a theoretical sense, it is something which can actually be *experienced*.

Even after attaining to this great experience, however, the man of Zen cannot afford to allow himself to develop an attitude of *laissez-aller*, assuming that he has 'got it', and that he no longer needs to concern himself about anything. If he makes this mistake he will, in time, lose everything which he has gained. On the contrary, every single moment of his life must be lived totally, as an expression of the highest peak of awareness and artistry. Accepting everything and rejecting nothing, he must be even more responsible and alert in his daily life than his more materially-oriented fellows.

Everything is in a constant state of change, and everything comes to an end sooner or later. The man of Zen understands this with his very being, not just with his intellect. Accepting this reality totally he is always at peace, no matter where he is and no matter what the situation, and he lives in harmony with the One, his heart completely empty of all desires and 'character traits'. In this state of total emptiness and unity things become possible which seem absolutely incredible for people of normal consciousness. For the man of Zen, however these things are as undramatic as eating, drinking and sleeping.

It is a common mistake to think that the Void, the nothingness of Zen, is a negative, nihilistic vacuum. The Masters have always taken great pains to stress that this is not the case. In fact, it is precisely *because* the Void is empty that it can contain the unbounded abundance of the infinite.

Rōshi Mumon once gave me a fan on which he had drawn the following saying in Chinese characters: 'In the heart all things are contained.' In Zen the heart is a symbol for the One (also referred to as Buddha Nature), for the human heart contains inexhaustible, endless secrets of which we are usually unaware in our daily life. It is the doorway to the Divine, to the One. If one only takes the trouble to look within one discovers one's true nature, in all its awesome vastness.

After I had passed through the experience of 'Mu' (nothing) several times, by dint of long, gruelling, unremitting meditative practice, the Rōshi's next command for me in *sanzen* was, 'Be oneness with the One,' a command which he repeated again and again, ceaselessly. And then, after a dark, seemingly endless journey, came the breakthrough into the breathtaking, brilliant light of the One. Its light, and the joy and bliss of that light, were so intense that my heart simply broke apart and dissolved into nothing, for only nothing can contain such endless abundance. From that moment on my heart, as an isolated phenomenon, was no more. My entire being had become a heart.

In the following years, in which I continued with my daily meditation as a matter of course, that which I had attained became yet more concentrated and profound, it became a permanent, irrefutable truth: I had become one with the One. When I experienced, it was the One which experienced through me, when I answered questions, it was the One which answered through me, when I acted, it was the One which acted through me. And when a true seeker on the path stood before me, it was the One which gave him directions and guided his steps on the path. Here again I must stress that such guidance can only be individual, and that it can only be given on a one-to-one basis; the very nature of the process makes working with large numbers of people impossible.

It is now twelve years since I left the temple in Japan for the second time. I felt no sense of pain or loss when I left. My repeated experiences of satori had filled me with the euphoria of liberation, dissolving each and every one of my attachments, small and large. It was the beginning of a new life for me. In time the euphoria disappeared, and was replaced by a quiet, serene equanimity. From then on my life was devoted to my work with my own pupils. I did not go out in search of them, they came looking for me, and for a spiritual home, led to me by my books.

My heart-to-heart connection with Rōshi Mumon, and with his wonderful temple and the monks there not only continued, it became even deeper as time went on. We exchanged regular presents, symbols of the unique bond between us.

In February 1978 I received a letter from Rōshi Mumon's most senior disciple, who had by this time become a Master himself.

'I have good news for you,' he wrote, 'Rōshi sama has been elected to the position of Head Priest of the Rinzai sect which, as you know, has its headquarters in Myōshin-ji in Kyoto. Please write him a letter.'

Rōshi Mumon Yamada had always been revered as a 'saint' by all of the most illumined Zen Masters. Now, finally, he had been given a position of authority within the hierarchy of the Rinzai sect which matched his spiritual standing. My joy, and that of my pupils, was indescribable. In his next letter the monk informed us that the great inauguration ceremony was to be held on 21 May, and that 3,000 guests were expected. Accommodating such huge numbers of people in Myōshin-ji is no problem at all. The temple buildings are located in very spacious grounds, and the entire temple complex is as large as a medium-sized village. Rōshi Mumon sometimes took me with him to attend ceremonies there, and whenever I tried to find my way around on my own I almost invariably got lost.

A year later my friend the monk sent me an even more exciting piece of news: 'Rōshi sama is planning to visit Germany.' There are no words which can describe the joy which I felt at the prospect of seeing my deeply beloved Master once again. As it turned out, however, my patience was to be put to the test for months on end, as the plans for this visit were overturned and changed again and again.

Before describing our reunion I should like to discuss another subject, that of the Second Vatican Council, and the amazing and revolutionary new attitude of the Church to non-Christian religions which became evident at this Council, initiated by the Vatican itself. Since the Second Vatican Council the discriminatory word 'heathen' in reference to non-Christian religions has been all but eliminated from the language of the Church.

Although the person who informed me of this fact was very reliable, and I had no reason to doubt his words, I nonetheless wished to receive confirmation of this amazing change of course from an authorised representative of the Church itself. In October 1980 I thus paid a visit on Emmanuel von Severus, the prior of the famous Benedictine abbey of Maria Laach, in order to ask him for more information on the subject. The prior and I were already well-acquainted with one another from my visit to the abbey the previous year (more of that later), and he received me in his office immediately. We had a delightful conversation about religious experience, lasting several hours.

He was very understanding when I told him how important it was for me to see written proof of the fact that the discriminatory term 'heathen' really had been purged from the language of the Church. He allowed me to read the text compiled by the Second Vatican Council regarding the relationship of the Church to non-Christian religions, which confirmed their standpoint.

The results of this change of attitude are already becoming apparent, in ways which would have been unthinkable just a few years ago. Christian monks have been allowed to study in Zen Buddhist monasteries in Japan, Zen Buddhist monks in monasteries here in the West. In 1979, to mark the occasion of the admission of a group of around thirty Zen Buddhist monks to a number of selected Benedictine monasteries, in particular the Benedictine abbey of Maria Laach, the Ostasian Institut of Bonn organised a conference entitled *A Christian–Buddhist Dialogue – A Search for Openings.*[3] The conference began on 26 March, lasting four days, and was held in the town of St Augustin. I was not present myself (it was only open for carefully selected Catholic guests), but later on I chanced to come into the possession of a copy of the transcripts of the opening address and the lectures.

There were nine speakers. The following quote is taken from the marvellous opening address of Dr Jan van Bragt, the director of the Nanzan Institute for Religion and Culture in Nagoya.

> The main purpose of this conference is to lay the groundwork for the meeting which is to take place between Christian and Buddhist monks. The discussion of the significance of this meeting is bound to be one of the central themes of our speakers in the course of the next few days.
>
> If I may, I should like to say a few opening words about the significance of this meeting myself. The first important point to be borne in mind is the fact that this programme has been organised primarily for the benefit of the Japanese monks, in order to give them the opportunity to familiarise themselves with Christian monastic life, and thus with Christianity. The task of the Catholic monks, for their part, is to show their Japanese visitors how they live, and to share their spirituality with them.
>
> It has been becoming increasingly clear to those taking part in the Buddhist–Christian dialogue in Japan that this dialogue will never be able to go very deep so long as it remains restricted to the discussion of dogmas and doctrines. Expressed positively, what this means is that the dialogue must be extended to include the dimension of religious experience. This exchange programme has been organised in order to achieve precisely that. Today, as in the past, it is still the monastic life which is most conducive to the experience of God. Thus, if we wish to comply with the injunctions of the Second Vatican Council, it is imperative that as many monks as possible should be involved in this dialogue, in order to include the dimension of religious experience. While I am on the subject it is also worth mentioning the fact that religious experience is absolutely central to monastic life in Buddhism, much more so than here in the West.

Monastic life has always played a much more seminal role in Buddhism – even in Japan – than it ever has in Christianity. Donald Swearer, an American specialist in comparative religion, discussed this subject in his lecture:

> Nowadays monastic life plays a very secondary role in the life of the Church. The influence and status of the monastic calling in modern Buddhism is immense in comparison, and it is only in the Middle Ages that we can find anything even remotely like it in the context of Christianity. Increasingly, the monastic tradition in the West is being pushed away from the center of church life and

> towards its periphery. I feel that the time has come for us to rediscover and reinterpret our own monastic tradition in the light of the religious needs and spiritual chaos of our modern age, and it is my firm belief that this can best be done with the help of the monastic tradition of Buddhism.

In his exhaustive talk Mr Swearer then went on to describe the various schools of Japanese Mahayana Buddhism, their ideas and objectives.

The next lecture was delivered by Dr Horst Rzepowski, from the St. Augustin Institute for Missionary Studies.[4] He described the beginnings of the first Buddhist communities in Germany (the first was founded by Seidenstücker in 1903) in great detail and with admirable objectivity, following their development all the way up to the consolidation of all the various groups (including the Old Buddhist Community[5] in Utting, which had resisted all attempts at consolidation right up to 1955) in the German Buddhist Union[6] on the 21 September 1958.

The following is one of the more interesting passages from his very sober and factual account.

> Something which is very apparent in all these groups is their emphatic rejection of any kind of 'missionary intentions' [. . .]
>
> Their rejection of the concept of missionary work is, to a great extent, influenced by their misunderstanding of the intentions of Christian missionaries. Even so, we nonetheless find evidence of missionary tendencies in the Buddhist communities themselves.
>
> For instance, in the Buddhist Catechism we find the question, 'Did Buddha also delegate other people to spread his message?' The answer which is then given to this question is a simple yes, followed by a brief explanation: 'His teaching is timeless, eternal Truth, and it was thus independent of him. And so his teaching was preached by many different people of all social standings.' [. . .]
>
> He [Buddha] also insisted that everyone should learn his teaching in their own native language. In another place Buddha makes the following proclamation: 'He who works not only for his own liberation but also for that of others is the greatest, the best and the most worthy.'
>
> In the process of finding their own identity the German Buddhists' two main interests appear to have been the interpretation and adaptation of the teachings of Buddhism.
>
> The publications and letters give us little insight into the more external, sociological structures of the groups. One thing which is striking, however, is the large number of strong personalities and individualists to be found among the relatively small number of

Buddhists in Germany. It seems that there are a whole series of talents and scientific disciplines which have a close affinity with Buddhism. These include artistic talents, philosophy, psychotherapy and psychiatry, and also medicine in general.

The majority of the followers of Buddhism in the West feel that Christianity has failed them. When it comes to dealing with their personal problems and conflicts it offers them insufficient help and no solutions. These are the kind of people Buddhism is looking for.

Among the other speakers were Dr Shimisu Matsui, of the Japanese Congregation of Sisters in Misono, and Dr Wilhelm K. Müller of the Monumenta Serica in St. Augustin. Dr Matsui spoke on 'Zen Buddhism', Dr Müller on 'The Historical Background of Buddhist Spirituality'. Much as I would like to cite passages from these admirable lectures I have decided to resist the temptation, as it would simply take up too much space. The time has come to deal with the revealing lecture in which the 'Yes, but . . . ' which was to be expected in such an eminently Catholic conference was finally presented.

The lecture was delivered by Dr Joseph Zapf, Professor of Religious Philosophy at the University of Philosophy and Theology in St. Augustin.[7] Nine years before the conference Dr Zapf had attended a *sesshin* (a course in *zazen* meditation) which I had conducted in St. Augustin – the first *sesshin* which had ever been held in this town, which is a centre of German Catholicism. He visited me in my room several times a day, whenever he had a free hour, and we had many wonderful discussions about religion and religious experience. I remember him as delightful man, and at the time I was particularly impressed by his sincere, heartfelt enthusiasm for the mystery of enlightenment (or satori) in Zen.

Dr Zapf's lecture was entitled, *The Anthropological and Spiritual Prerequisites for Successful Interreligious Dialogue.* The following passages illustrate the main thrust of his argumentation.

An interreligious dialogue is seldom a genuine dialogue, in the ideal sense of the word. There are too many obstacles. The cultures, religious doctrines, cosmologies and views of Man of the participants tend to separate them from one another rather than bringing them together. In addition to this, the participants in an interreligious dialogue lack a common language with which they can really communicate with one another. It is thus hardly surprising that most attempts to conduct such a dialogue deteriorate into mere discussions, which strengthen divisions and barriers rather than dissolving them. The dialogue then breaks down into two monologues. Again, this is hardly surprising.

Even though interreligious dialogue is very difficult it is more important today than it has ever been before. In the past religions co-existed without any contact; sometimes they actively opposed and fought one another. Now, however, it is becoming increasingly obvious that they are going to have to cooperate with one another, despite their differences. There are many reasons for this: the collapse of our old value systems, the existential fear created by a secularised society, and the search for meaning in a world where man is alienated and the new theology has declared God to be dead, to name but a few examples.

None of the religions is going to be able to avoid facing this challenge. Cooperation is the order of the day. Their opposition to one another has always reduced the credibility of their teachings, for all of them preach doctrines of love, and say that love is more important than anything else. Despite this fact, however, the members of 'other' religions are still seen as unbelievers or heathens, and the belief that the grace of God, the one true doctrine and salvation are to be found in one's own religion or creed and there alone is still predominant. Dialogue is not possible in such a situation, it is replaced by mere apologetics. In this situation the universal tendency to regard other people's faiths as untruth rather than as truth is strengthened rather than weakened. But how is one to decide what is truth and what is untruth? Judaism, Christianity and Islam all claim to be the one and only true religion.

Hinduism and Buddhism see themselves as the universal religions of the future, capable of absorbing all other religions. Their claims are in fact just as absolutist as those of Judaism, Christianity and Islam, they are simply phrased in a different way.

Such absolutist claims create barriers, making dialogue impossible. Dialogue is openness and a willingness to encounter the other. And that is not all. Dialogue also involves understanding, an understanding which arises out of empathy with the situation of the other.

What, then, are the prerequisites for successful interreligious dialogue? Specifically, what are the anthropological prerequisites and what are the spiritual prerequisites? These are the questions to which we shall now turn our attention.[. . .]

The Spiritual Prerequisites

The central religious experience is the experience of the Divine. Each of the participants in the dialogue must find this central experience in his own religion, at least to begin with. The Jew shares with the other members of his race the experience of the covenant made with Yahweh on Mount Sinai. The Christian experiences the new life in Christ proclaimed in the New Testament as the fulfilment and culmination of the covenant made in the Old Testament. The Moslem sees Allah in the divine revelations of the Koran and seeks to attain unity with the Divine by acting in accordance with the Divine Will. In Hinduism there are a variety of different experiences of the Divine. The most profound is the *vedanta* experience: *Tat twam asi*, Thou art That, you yourself are the Divine. In the case of modern Hindu saints such as Ramakrishna (died 1886) or Ramana Maharshi (died 1950) the experience of *advaita* (non-duality) is combined with that of devotion (*bhakti*) to their personal Lord (*Ishvara*). Buddha's religious intuition illumines the hopelessness of human life. In his 'eightfold path' he teaches the way of liberation. One becomes liberated when one is enlightened. Enlightenment dissolves all desire to exist. The wheel of reincarnation stops moving. In the experience of Nirvana the emptiness which is free of everything relative is filled by the transcendental bliss of the Absolute.

If we attempt to compare these experiences from without they are nothing more than empty words, without any power to transform. We are like the blind man who is unable to say anything meaningful about colour. Despite their endless variety all colours are contained within one and the same light. The Divine Light can only be seen with the inner, spiritual eye. Christian philosophy and theology describe a relationship between man and God, a paradoxical relationship in which they are connected with one another without mingling. The Human and the Divine are similar to one another. The more similar (or analogous) they become to one another, however, the more dissimilar they are. As Absolute Being God is more aware of all the aspects of created being than created being can be aware of itself. That which disappears into mystery when one attempts to grasp it with the rational mind appears again in the form of Jesus Christ, Man and God in one. His words, deeds and life reveal God to be the Father. The Resurrection of Christ and the descent of the Holy Ghost at Pentecost form the basis of the Church, the Mystical Body of Christ.

The Christian spiritual experience involves living participation in the wholly divine, wholly human life of the crucified and resurrected Christ. It is a multi-layered experience. It includes the experience of listening to the words of the New Testament with the heart of a believer just as it includes the experiences of the baptisms of water and fire and of the profound, sacramental surrender on the cross. It is nourished by prayer and the Eucharist, and strengthened by direct mystical experience of the Divine. Thus, the Christian mystical experience too is an experience of revelation, a revelation cloaked in the robes of faith. In the Christian context, however, this experience takes place in the very centre of one's own individual being. The divine grace which one receives in the sacrament of baptism is at one and the same time a gift of grace and the realisation of Triune

Life in the soul of the baptised. In its ultimate intensity this process of divine transformation makes man more God than man, without suspending the ontological difference between the two.

At this ultimate peak the Christian spiritual experience is very clearly distinct from that of other religions. This is not to say that genuine spiritual experiences of a profound nature are not possible in other religions as well; their existence cannot be denied.

In the context of our theme the question of the relationship between the human and the divine as expressed in spiritual experience is also of interest. Can this relationship be communicated in a dialogue? The problem here is a problem of expression, of language in its broadest sense. The language of spiritual experience is moulded and formed by many different factors: history, poetry, philosophy, ideology, theology. Within a single culture it is possible to interpret the differences between religious experiences, because the individuals concerned speak the same cultural language. But what about individuals from different cultures? Or from different religions? What language, what context of communication should we use to interpret religious experience there, without distorting it? It is frequently impossible to express one's own religious experience adequately in another language, and any attempts to do so usually change and distort our meaning.

Is it at all possible to translate experientially the religious experience of one religion into the context of another without distorting it? There is still a great deal of disagreement on this subject among the authorities in this field. The discussion on the possibility or impossibility of 'Christian Zen' is a case in point. Some people believe that the meditation techniques of Zen can be separated from their Buddhist context, others say that this is not possible. The latter group bases its arguments on the findings of depth psychologists like C. G. Jung.

Jung draws attention to the problems involved when the conscious mind and, more importantly, the unconscious mind, are faced with two widely contrasting cultural inputs. The roots of our culture are to be found in the depths of our unconscious minds. Every religious tradition comprises the heritage of many thousands of years, and this heritage is an integral, living part of the unconscious mind of the believer. And the unconscious mind plays a very important role in spiritual experience, and in the nature of spiritual experience. In the secularised culture of the West a process of alienation from these unconscious roots has been in progress for the last two hundred years. It is only now, however, that we are beginning to become aware of this process. Asian meditation techniques are a source of genuine help for people suffering from the one-sided rationalism of Western theology and the atrophy of religious experience. However, if these techniques are practised haphazardly and without the proper control there is a danger that the individual who practises them may alienate himself from his own tradition. In another context Jung warns that this alienation from one's own cultural base can create neurosis and, if it becomes widespread, can lay the groundwork for collective hysteria.

Despite this, however, in exceptional cases it may be possible to travel the inner spiritual path within the context of a religion which is not one's own. There are two reasons for this. Firstly, even though the influence of the tradition in which one grows up is, of course, particularly strong, the unconscious nonetheless contains the entire history of mankind. And secondly, one should not forget that Divine Being is the source and foundation of consciousness as such. However, although consciousness participates in Divine Being, Divine Being itself is neither divided nor reduced; it remains whole and complete, in absolute simplicity. In the mystical experience Divine Being comes into direct, experiential contact with the individual. The absolute enters into the relative, dissolving the limitations of consciousness. In Buddhist enlightenment this leads to an experience of unity of cosmic dimensions, which cannot be expressed in mere words. It is an experience which transforms the consciousness of the experiencer radically, a fact which is indicated by the kind of terminology which is usually used to describe it, terms like 'returning to the source', 'awakening' or 'rebirth'.

Buddha made a point of remaining silent on the subject of the transcendental, insisting that it was ineffable. The spiritual experience of Hinduism is richer here, recognising as it does both personal and impersonal expressions of the Divine. In the teachings of the Vedanta, however, Hinduism describes the personal as being subordinate to the impersonal.

[. . .]

The Christian mystic draws no dividing line between the personal and the impersonal aspects of the Divine, which are revealed in the form of Father, Son *and* Holy Ghost. This is the revelation which has been given to us through the life of Jesus, which is the manifestation of the Father in the form of the Son. Jesus forgives sins, just as the Father does, and He is in all things one with the Father. Then, after being awakened from death by the power of the Spirit He sends His presence to His disciples in the form of the Spirit, to be with them always. If it were not for this revelation in Jesus Christ we would have no knowledge of the mystery of the Trinity. The Hindu doctrine of trinity, in which the three elements are described as Being, Consciousness and Bliss (*Sat-Chit-Ananda*), comes astonishingly close to the Christian mystery of the Trinity. *Nonetheless, it is only in Christianity that this mystery is revealed in its entirety.*

What, then, are the spiritual prerequisites for successful inter-religious dialogue within the context of these three specific religious experiences, the experience of the Absolute in Buddhism, the Divine in Hinduism and the Trinity in Christianity? Communication on an intuitive level is certainly possible in the presence of spiritually experienced individuals. The effects of the transformation which has taken place within them are felt by others, and the experience is thus transmitted directly. People who have experienced the Divine recognise one another. However, this does not neutralise the discrepancy between the different experiences. The initial reaction to this discrepancy on the part of the individuals involved is usually an attempt to subordinate the alien experience to their own. The alien experience is thus qualified and relativised within the context of the known experience. The known experience is taken as the yardstick by which the alien experience is measured.

There are also subjective reasons for the fact that Buddhism and Hinduism subordinate the personal aspect of the Divine to its impersonal aspect, regarding the personal as relative and the impersonal as absolute. Both these religions see the personal in man as an illusion, which they contrast to the absolute reality of his Self, and they translate their interpretation of human nature to the divine context, assuming that the Divine Being is the same as man. In Christianity the opposite is the case: the Christian cosmology and the Christian view of man have been formed, in part, by Divine Revelation.

Which of these two viewpoints is correct? Is the personal subordinate to the impersonal, or is the impersonal subordinate to the personal? In order to pass a definitive judgement on this question we would have to be able to judge from a standpoint of utter objectivity, something which is not humanly possible. Only voluntary self-disclosure on the part of the Divine can demonstrate the truth of this matter. However, this divine self-disclosure is beyond human reason. It can only be comprehended through the vehicle of faith. And this faith, in its turn, moulds the interpretation of the Christian spiritual experience, in the same way that the holy scriptures of the Hindus mould their experience. How, then, is one to conduct a dialogue?

The future of all religions is going to be a future of cooperation. It is no longer possible for them to continue on their separate ways, like parallel roads which do not meet.

The diversity of religions is a historical fact. The question is, what is the true religious significance of this diversity in the context of human history, a history which can be seen as the continuing revelation of God the Father, the One God, who created all men as his children? This is a crucial theological and spiritual question, and it must be answered before the dialogue begins.

From the Christian point of view the selection of the Israelites as the chosen people of God marks the beginning of a very significant dialogue between God and man. God has kept the promise which He made to man in his covenant with the Israelites, sending Jesus Christ as the fulfilment of that promise. In the mystery of the death and resurrection of Christ this fulfilment marks yet another new beginning, the beginning of a new creation and a new life in the Holy Spirit, which will, in its turn, be fulfilled by the Second Coming of Christ at the end of time. *The historicity of this revelation as expressed in both the Old Testament and the New Testament and fulfilled in the person of Jesus Christ is unique and unparalleled, and as such it is unrepeatable.* Christ is a beginning, and the future of this beginning is open. It is not possible for this future to exclude the spiritual revelations and insights of other religions, for the nature of the Spirit is such that it creates unity within diversity. The very abundance of the diversity of creation is a demonstration of the endless, inexhaustible nature of the Divine out of which it is born. *The Truth of Christianity is that Jesus Christ has been sent by God as the universal Saviour of all men everywhere. Christ's Church is the vehicle of His work of salvation, and thus it is now necessary for this Church to expand its boundaries and become a universal body into which the other religions can incorporate the spiritual fruits of their own individual traditions. In order for this to be possible the Christian Church must be transformed into a universal, ecumenical and catholic World Church.* [Author's italics]

The implications of this last passage are shameful. The conference in which these statements were made, a conference whose title included the promising phrase 'A Search for Openings', was only open to carefully selected Catholic participants. It appears that this lecture was designed to provide those people who were to conduct the coming dialogue with the Buddhist monks with a leitmotif, so to speak, to tell them which direction their work should take.

I find this deeply shocking. The overwhelming joy which I felt at Article 2 of the declaration on non-Christian religions made in the Second Vatican Council has been completely destroyed.

The transcripts of the lectures delivered at this conference were only intended for the participants. It must have been Providence which allowed a copy of them to fall into my hands a little more than a year ago, for I myself had made no attempts to obtain them. There is always a hidden reason for significant events of this type, they are never coincidental.

I had been looking forward to reading Dr Zapf's lecture enormously, and for this reason I had saved it until last. And now this monstrous text. It made the seemingly wonderful declaration of the Second Vatican Council appear in a totally different light. At first I was speechless with shock at being confronted with the evidence of these unholy machinations on the part of one world religion against another, and I had to spend a long period in solitary meditation before I could even begin to find words to express what I felt. But I must speak out, for to remain silent would be to betray Buddhism and the great Zen Buddhist Masters who have helped me to attain to the light of enlightenment, and whose willingness to engage in a dialogue is not tainted by any ulterior motives.

Those Zen Masters I have had the honour of knowing personally are beings of such total purity that they are incapable of imagining that the attempts of another religion to approach them could be anything other than an expression of absolute Truth. Dr Zapf's lecture makes it very clear that the high-handed purpose behind the creation of *'a universal body into which the other religions can incorporate the spiritual fruits of their own individual traditions'* (the word 'can' here has a suspicious, patronising ring to it) is the total absorption of the other religions by the Church. The Zen Masters' way of thinking is so unpolitical, however, and so totally devoted to the Truth, that something like this would simply seem incredible to them.

Of course, I realise that the primary objective of the decretals of the Second Vatican Council was to help deal with the situation of internal and external crisis in the Church, which was falling apart at the seams. Even so, the insights which these decretals contain brought a welcome ray of light into the darkness of the Church's previous policies. Unfortunately, it seems that this light was no more than an illusion, and that this situation is unlikely to change for some time to come. The Church still insists upon retaining a position of absolute supremacy. Its arrogance towards other religions is absolutely intolerable.

It would be wonderful if Christians could find it in their hearts to be a little more humble. They have always claimed that theirs is the religion of love, the religion which teaches one to love one's neighbour as oneself. Where was this love of theirs when they were exterminating the inhabitants of the West Indies? Where was it during the genocide of the highly cultured peoples of North and South America? The monstrosities which have been committed in the name of this love are simply unbelievable. Take the accounts of the Dominican friar Las Casas, for instance, who describes Christian atrocities in South America in great detail. And where was this famous Christian love during the Spanish Inquisition, with all its unspeakable, inhuman tortures?

These are just a few of the more blatant examples of the way in which this so-called love has expressed itself, the love of a religion which has the audacity to claim the title of superiority and the right to rule.

In the case in point, for instance, we see Christianity claiming to be superior to Buddhism, the most peaceful of all the world's religions. No crusade, not one single war has ever been fought in the name of Buddhism. Even the confrontation between Buddhism and the imperial Japanese religion of Shintoism, which took place in AD 522, was utterly peaceful and characterised by mutual respect, a respect which continues to this day.

The respect which Zen Buddhism shows other religions is unique. When Rōshi Mumon Yamada accepted me as his disciple (and remember, I was the first Western woman who had ever been admitted to a Zen monastery) he didn't even ask me what faith I belonged to, let alone demand that I should abandon it. All that he expected of me was that I should work diligently on the task he had set me and live in accordance with the rules and discipline of the monastery. Our relationship was based upon profound mutual trust. My first book, *The Master, the Monks, and I*, is the story of my shattering spiritual journey under his loving tutelage. It seems to me that there is no better, more noble way of serving the eternal One and learning the way of humility than by showing tolerance and respect for expressions of religion and spirituality which are different from our own. Zen is the best possible example of this spirit.

The seminar in St. Augustin took place in March of 1979. At the beginning of September the thirty Zen Buddhist monks, representing all the different schools of Zen in Japan, arrived in Germany to begin their sojourn in the Benedictine monasteries where they were to be introduced to the Christian monastic life.

'They were unbelievably disciplined,' replied Dr von Severus in response to my question about the monks' visit, 'they attended every single service, even though they didn't understand a single word of what was said.' And that is the problem. Dialogue is simply not possible unless both parties speak a common language. Even with the help of the very best interpreters one can hardly expect to do more than gain a smattering of the theoretical basics. Interpreters communicate the mundane essentials and nothing more. Any attempts to even begin to communicate the true essence of a life devoted to God within the context of a foreign religion through the agency of an interpreter are almost certainly doomed to failure. The only people who might be capable of managing this feat are the few European missionaries who have spent their entire lives in eastern countries such as Japan.

Even in one's own language, expressing the most profound inner experiences is virtually impossible. At the very best one can talk around the experience, one can never really put it into words. As far as the complex and subtle languages of the East are concerned conversations, dialogues and debates are only possible between people who are absolute masters of the language being used, and even then there is no guarantee that they will really understand one another on the spiritual level. A man can be a great theological scholar without having had any of the experiences of a true seeker. Those who have experienced the Divine know that only others who have had the same experience are capable of understanding them, and between such people no words need to be exchanged.

I promised that I would return to the subject of Rōshi Mumon's visit to Germany, and I shall now do so. As I mentioned earlier, I received a letter from the Myōshin-ji temple in Kyoto saying that he was coming soon. The letter arrived in the early summer of 1978, but as it turned out it was to be many weeks before the final decision that the Rōshi really was going to come was to be made. If he had been an ordinary monk there would have been no problem, but as it was he was the official head of the Rinzai sect, and a number of political considerations had to be taken into account. On 28 August I received a message from Kyoto saying that everything was still uncertain. But then, on 10 September, confirmation that Rōshi sama really was going to make the journey after all finally came. I was overjoyed.

I called the abbey of Maria Laach and asked to speak to the prior, Dr von Severus, who was kind enough to come to the telephone at once. He informed me that the Rōshi was due to arrive on 20 September, and said that he would arrange a meeting for me, promising me with great warmth that he would do everything he could to help. He also said that he would ask his most senior monk to take care of everything personally. I arrived at the abbey early in the morning of the 20th and gave the gatekeeper some presents for the Rōshi and his attendant monk, who were expected to arrive late that afternoon, after an almost non-stop flight from Tokyo to Cologne via Paris, followed by a long drive from Cologne to the abbey. No plans had been made for the next day, as it was expected that the Rōshi would need a good rest after this gruelling journey.

On the morning of the 22nd I returned to the abbey, dressed in my very best clothes in honour of the occasion. I arrived in the visitors' room a quarter of an hour before the appointed time. An interpreter and two Japanese photographers were already waiting there. The photographers didn't speak a word of German or English, and they bombarded the interpreter with questions. They were astonished that I was being granted a private audience with the head of the Rinzai sect, and they were determined to find out everything they could about me and my relationship with the Rōshi.

I was filled with a profound silence. Not so much as a single thought about what the meeting with my beloved Rōshi was going to be like, after being away from him for so many years, arose within me. Nothing. Only my heart was awake and watchful. When the door finally opened and I saw his familiar figure standing there quietly (he was dressed in a white robe beneath a kind of transparent, golden-brown over-robe, as always), his eyes gazing into mine, all the years which had passed simply disappeared. With a joyful cry of 'Rōshi!' I bowed down to the ground and made the ritual prostrations prescribed by the ancient tradition of Zen. When I was finished the Rōshi sat down. I kneeled on the floor in front of him, and he stroked my head, long and lovingly. A few moments later I started in surprise at the clicking of the cameras.

'Yes,' said the Rōshi, looking up at the photographers with a gentle sigh, 'they follow me everywhere.' We were suddenly back in the real world.

We gazed into one another's eyes. There was no need to say anything. We were one. The communion between us was beyond words, and couldn't have been expressed in words even if we had wanted to.

What is happiness? A moment of eternity, a moment like this one. It was only when I finally stood up, a little shakily, that I realised that the Rōshi's attendant monk, Nan san, was standing behind him. He too was now a Master in his own right. I rushed over to him to greet him, and he spontaneously flung his arms around me and hugged me warmly. The machine-gun clattering of the camera shutters started up all over again.

I am sure that the photographers were completely flummoxed

by the Rōshi's and Nan san's totally un-Japanese behaviour. In Japan it simply isn't done to touch people physically when one greets them. One simply bows, with one's hands clasped together respectfully. And for the head of a religious order to do more than incline his head slightly in response to a visitor's bow is virtually unheard-of.

Today, however, all of these rules had ceased to apply. After he had finished hugging me Nan san spread out a number of presents which he and the Rōshi had brought me. Of all of them the one which delighted me most was an exquisite calligraphic rendering of the Chinese character for the Universal One, made for me by the Rōshi himself.

We spoke in English. I suggested to the Rōshi that I should come to Japan in the near future to pay a visit on him in Myōshin-ji in Kyoto. He was delighted at the idea. I asked after some of the monks who had been my friends, and he informed me that some of them were now in other monasteries. (It is quite common for advanced Zen monks to be sent elsewhere to teach or to learn, or for monks who are not up to the rigours of a particularly strict monastery to be sent to another where the discipline is less severe.)

'But all of them will return to the temple to greet you when you come,' he said jubilantly.

The half hour we had been given for our talk was over in a trice; almost before it had begun, it seemed, a bell rang indicating that our time was up. We got up to leave. Then, for a few blissful, eternal seconds, both the Rōshi and I stopped in the doorway and faced one another motionlessly, silently. There are no words for what passed between us in that moment. One could say, perhaps, that it was a communion of transcendental spiritual love, but that too comes nowhere near describing it.

That afternoon I accompanied the Rōshi and Nan san on their guided tour around the abbey, which was a little tiring. The young German interpreter whose services the prior had engaged was very impressive. His Japanese was so fluent and perfect that he didn't even need to stop to think when it came to translating our guide's endless and extremely boring descriptions of all the embroideries and other treasures in the crypt. I felt rather impatient at all this, for it seemed to me that it was a waste of the Rōshi's valuable time. After all, he had not come to Germany as a tourist, he had come to help establish a spiritual rapport between two religions.

The next day I attended High Mass in the abbey together with the Rōshi and Nan san, who were given seats of honour in the very front row before the altar. I couldn't help comparing the Mass to the services in the temple in Japan, and for the first time I became consciously aware of the enormous difference between these two worlds, worlds which were now seeking to communicate and cooperate with one another. On the one hand the sublime emptiness and exquisitely artistic simplicity of the *hōndō* in the Zen temple, an emptiness which is filled with the Eternal for the simple reason that there is nothing there to distract the seeker's attention, and on the other the overwhelming pomp and ceremony of the Church, a place where one must search in order to find God. The services of these two religions are a perfect expression of how deeply divergent their paths really are. Of course, this makes no difference to the inner experience of the true seeker after God, but for the majority of people from both Zen and the Church I can imagine that the extreme contrast is a little hard to stomach at first.

The Rōshi was due to leave Maria Laach on 23 September, after spending two days and three nights in the abbey. I received a phone call from one of the monks from the abbey, who informed me that the Rōshi's taxi would be coming by to pick me up. And so the next morning the Rōshi, Nan san and I drove to the railway station in Koblenz together to catch the Augsburg–Munich Intercity. It was a lovely autumn day.

The entourage of photographers and reporters were waiting on the platform when we arrived. The Rōshi, Nan san and I had a reserved compartment. The interpreter took care of getting all the press people seated. The Rōshi sat next to the window. He was terribly tired, and he fell asleep as soon as the train pulled out of the station. We soon woke him, however, as we couldn't bear letting him miss the sight of the sunlit landscape along the banks of the Rhine. 'Wonderful, wonderful,' he murmured quietly again and again. And it really was wonderful: the gentle autumn sun bathed the river and the castled hills along its banks in a golden glow, giving them the aura of fairy-tale magic for which this part of Germany is so famous. A little later the Rōshi went to sleep again, and Nan san didn't wake him until a few minutes before the train was due to arrive in Augsburg, where our ways were to part. The Rōshi was expected at the Benedictine abbey of St Ottilien, which is near

Augsburg. After spending a day there he was then going to fly on to Rome for a meeting with the Pope.

The Rōshi's slight physical body seemed almost transparent, a mere breath of matter illumined by the inner radiance of the Spirit, so brilliant that even I could see it. This light, the light of the Eternal, is the source of his seemingly superhuman strength. It fills him and carries him, enabling him to remain always calm, alert and relaxed despite the extreme demands which his calling makes upon him.

Nan san withdrew tactfully to the other side of the compartment so that the Rōshi and I could spend our last few minutes together alone. I knelt down before him, and he took both of my hands in his.

'We must go on. You know it,' he said softly, his voice serious. He paused for a moment, and then his wonderful sense of humour suddenly bubbled up again, wreathing his face in smiles and dissolving the pain of parting as though it had never been there. He pointed a finger at his own breast. 'I shall live to be ninety-nine!' he said with a laugh. Then he placed his hand on my head. 'But you, you shall live to be a hundred!' We both laughed and gazed gently into one another's eyes, and for a few moments I was in Eternity.

The train pulled into the station. Nan san hugged me again, then he helped the Rōshi out of the carriage and on to the platform. The train jerked, getting ready to pull out of the station. I shall never forget the sight as long as I live. The slight, small, luminous figure of the Rōshi and beside him Nan san, tall and strongly built and dressed in his dark monastic robe. They both lifted their hands and waved gently until the train was out of sight. I sat down in my seat again. All that remained was silence.

It was only several months later that I realised that I hadn't asked the Rōshi a single question about his impressions of the Catholic abbey of Maria Laach, even though our train journey together had lasted for several hours. This too is Zen. One must act in harmony with each and every situation. It was not the time to ask irrelevant questions, it was time for the Rōshi to rest. And even if I had asked him, his only reply would have been a gentle shake of the head, and silence.

A Zen Master's answer to such questions can be neither yes nor no, for they know that only the One exists. This has nothing to do with the so-called 'tolerance' with which we are familiar in the West. It is something much more profound, born of the experience of the satori: choiceless awareness, the ability to see and accept everything as it is, without judging it one way or the other.

Why then, one may ask, did Rōshi Mumon come to Europe at all? Why was he interested in engaging in the proffered 'spiritual dialogue'? After all, just as most Christian priests have some understanding of the basic principles and practices of Buddhism, Buddhist priests are conversant with the doctrines of Christianity. It was not as though he needed to travel to Europe to learn anything. His journey was simply a gesture of respect towards the spirit of our times. It was also an expression of the pure nobility of his spirit. He travelled in utter spartan simplicity, with a single monk to accompany him, without pomp or ceremony or red carpets, exactly as he did when he visited the Buddhist countries of Asia.

What a contrast to the Catholic Church! The preparations for the Pope's visit to Germany in 1980 cost millions upon millions of marks, and one can only assume that he felt that this was an appropriate way of greeting him, otherwise he wouldn't have permitted it. The conscious simplicity of Zen, chosen as an expression of the Truth of the Void in the world, is infinitely distant from the extravagant attention-seeking of Christianity. Even though there is much which I would like to say on this subject, I know that it is better to heed the wisdom of Zen and remain silent.

Nonetheless, it would be foolish to ignore the fact that the doors which Pope Paul VI opened wide during the Second Vatican Council, inviting an open dialogue with other religions, are now being slowly and carefully closed again. The new papal dictatorship is not willing to tolerate such openness. I should thus like to take this opportunity to remind my readers of the words spoken by Dr Zapf in the lecture which he delivered at the conference in St. Augustin, a conference which was supposed to pave the way for a dialogue between Christian and Buddhist monks:

> *The Truth of Christianity is that Jesus Christ has been sent by God as the universal Saviour of all men everywhere. Christ's Church is the vehicle of His work of salvation, and thus it is now necessary for this Church to expand its boundaries and become a universal body into which the other religions can incorporate the spiritual fruits of their own individual traditions.*

In order for this to be possible the Christian Church must be transformed into a universal, ecumenical and catholic World Church.

This is nothing more, or less, than the will to power, the bane of humanity all down the ages. Whether the conquest which Zapf refers to here is achieved with the sword or by 'incorporation', the ultimate aim of the Church, as expressed here, is obviously to devour the other religions completely.

It is not yet too late, thank God. We still have time to come to our senses and learn to love and understand one another, despite all our many differences, and to save our sad world from the sorry mess which Man has made of it. After all, our differences are nothing more than yet another expression of the God-given variety of existence, an abundance which is there so that we may learn to know and love Him in all His abundance.

If we learn to look deep within our own beings with the eyes of the seeker and meditator, then we will come to realise that only God exists, within and without. He is everything which is, and there is nowhere in this world where he is not. We don't even need to go in search of Him. *He is already here.* Always, and everywhere. Let us put our swords aside, and learn to know Him, for through knowing Him we shall finally learn to know ourselves.

Then we shall be at peace.

Gerta Ital
December 1980

Notes

1. English edition published by The Aquarian Press (Thorsons Ltd) in June 1987.
2. *F.A.Z.*, 31 October 1967.
3. *Auf der Suche nach Ansatzpunkten für einen christlichen Dialog mit Buddhisten.*
4. Missionswissenschaftliches Institut St Augustin.
5. Die Altbuddistische Gemeinde.
6. Die Deutsche Buddistische Union.
7. Philosophisch–Theologische Hochschule St Augustin.